DIRT WORK

Christine Byl

DIRT
WORK

An Education
in the Woods

Beacon Press • Boston

BEACON PRESS
25 Beacon Street
Boston, Massachusetts 02108-2892
www.beacon.org

Beacon Press books
are published under the auspices of
the Unitarian Universalist Association of Congregations.

Grateful thanks to the editors of the publications listed below, where
earlier versions of material from this book first appeared: "Hunkered at
the Gateway" in *Permanent Vacation: 20 Writers on Work and Life in Our
National Parks* (Tahoe Paradise, CA: Bona Fide Books, May 2011);
"Hunkered at the Gateway" (excerpted from above) in *National Parks:
Magazine of the National Parks Conservation Association* (Winter 2012);
"Xtra Tuf" and "Soul Food" in *Cold Flashes: Literary Snapshots of Alaska*
(Fairbanks: University of Alaska Press, 2010); "Dirt" in *A Mile in Her
Boots: Women Who Work in the Wild* (Antioch, CA: Solas Press, 2006).

All events and characters herein are based on real people and situations,
with no intentional composites. Names have been changed, except with
express permission otherwise.

16 15 14 13   8 7 6 5 4 3 2 1

This book is printed on acid-free paper that meets the uncoated paper
ANSI/NISO specifications for permanence as revised in 1992.

Text design by Wilsted & Taylor Publishing Services

Library of Congress Cataloging-in-Publication Data
Byl, Christine.
Dirt work : an education in the woods / Christine Byl.
   pages cm
ISBN 978-0-8070-0100-4 (hardcover : alk. paper)
ISBN 978-0-8070-0101-1 (electronic)
1. Byl, Christine 2. United States. National Park Service—Officials
and employees—Biography. 3. Foresters—United States—Biography.
4. Nature trails—Alaska—Design and construction. 5. Nature trails—
Montana—Design and construction. 6. Park facilities—Alaska—Design
and construction. 7. Park facilities—Montana—Design and construction.
8. Denali National Park and Preserve (Alaska) I. Title.
QH31.B95A3 2012
363.6'8097986—dc23   2012034479

For traildogs everywhere.

For Gabe,
the original workingman's thinker.

If your feet aren't in the mud of a place,
you'd better watch where your mouth is.

—GRACE PALEY

Place is one kind of place. Another
field is the work we do, our calling,
our path in life.

—GARY SNYDER

It's a good life if you don't weaken.

—TRAILS APHORISM

CONTENTS

Introduction   xi

What We Carry   xxiii

Axe   1

CHAPTER 1: NORTH FORK: RIVER   3

Rock Bar   35

CHAPTER 2: SPERRY: ALPINE   37

Chainsaw   75

CHAPTER 3: MIDDLE FORK: FOREST   77

Boat   111

CHAPTER 4: CORDOVA: COAST   113

Skid Steer   150

CHAPTER 5: DENALI: PARK   152

Shovel   185

CHAPTER 6: DENALI: HOME   187

Afterword   223

Traildogs' Index   226

Acknowledgments   228

Works Consulted   230

INTRODUCTION

On the front porch of Frida's, we sit feet-up on the railing. If you walk by, glance at the clapboard bar, you'll see us there—four men and one woman; dirty pants, boot soles mud-caked. Eyebrows black. In West Glacier, Montana, on the front porch of Frida's, it's beer-thirty on the last day of a hitch and we've forgiven each other everything: the annoying way one guy chomps his cereal, how so-and-so always leaves the tool cache a mess. On the porch on day eight, crew leaders and laborers, fast hikers and slow, we're just company. We rib each other and toast a job well done. We narrate the week, ushering it into our oral tradition: *Can you believe the packer lost a load on the Ole Creek ford? How big you think that tree you logged out was? What was the best dinner? The worst weather? Are your boots dry yet? Are yours?*

A woman in river sandals and a visor stops on the stairs. "Are you trail crew?" "Yup," Justin nods. Her boyfriend works on the east side crew, she says. She's a raft guide, but she might put in for trails next year.

"How do you keep up with them?" she asks me, a girl-to-girl aside.

Justin answers before I can: "She can't keep up. We carry her everywhere." He pauses for effect and grins. "No, no, for real, she kicks my ass." All I do is shrug.

"That's so cool," says the rafter. "You're so lucky."

She's right. I am lucky. I'm lucky my job smashes me face-first against my limits. Lucky I get paid to sleep in a tent and piss in the brush. I'm lucky to be one of these guys, yet also not: lover to one, leader to some, daffy kid sister to the rest. I'm lucky that I like my eyebrows matted, my knees a little stiff, my heart rate low and steady. Who knows how any of us ends up where we're meant to be? I'm lucky that I stumbled into this life and got to stay.

We finish our beers, swigging the last warm inch of Miller Genuine Draft from plastic cups, and clump down the stairs. Some of us will meet to climb a peak on our days off. Others go home to families, houses in town, and won't see anyone from work until we gather at the barn for the next hitch. We slap grimy palms, grab fingers, and punch fists in the routine crew farewell. Peace out. See you next week, fuckers. So long.

The National Park Service was formally established by Woodrow Wilson in 1916, and in 1983, writer Wallace Stegner called it "the best idea we ever had. Absolutely American, absolutely democratic, [parks] reflect us at our best." Today, the Park Service is one of the United States' most widely emulated federal innovations; over one hundred countries have comparable agencies for protecting public lands. In the United States, the Park Service manages 84 million acres in 393 areas, places where more than 285 million visitors—American, Swiss, Korean—go each year in search of leisure, education, wilderness, or respite. Parks vary in focus—from Philadelphia's Liberty Bell to Florida's Everglades to Wrangell-St.-Elias in Alaska, the largest of all parks (nearly double the size of Vermont)—but they are united around the intent, as written in the Park Service Organic Act of 1916, to "conserve the scenery and the natural and historic objects and the wildlife therein and to provide for the enjoyment of the same in such manner and by such means as will leave them unimpaired for the enjoyment of future generations."

I first visited national parks on family vacations, after long road trips complete with car sickness. When I was twenty-two, the Park Service became an employer, the job a summer diversion. And then, over years, a park became a home, the way any home gets made: through work. As in employment, and as in effort. Each with its own set of tools.

I've now been a "traildog" for sixteen years, a laborer who works in the woods maintaining, repairing, building, and designing trails. The Park Service runs on the backs of my cohorts and me— seasonals, we're called—and we perform every manual task. Most people recognize the seasonal NPS poster children, rangers in flat hats giving campfire talks, but few see behind the curtain, where mechanics keep the fleet running and maintenance guys empty rest-stop outhouses. Carpenters, firefighters. The road crew, repainting traffic stripes, steaming ice out of culverts. And the traildogs.

Our numbers may be invisible, but our tasks are concrete. We're the ones who hike a trail first in the spring to log out fallen trees that cross it. My crew has built the rock steps climbing a mountain pass, and the gravel path that connects parking lot to visitor's center. We clear rocks from drainage ditches, fill muddy spots. We build bridges, sink signposts, grub reroutes, blast snowdrifts. To get to every job, we hike.

If it sounds like simple work, in many ways it is. Once you learn the tools and develop the eye, once you discern your limits and strengths, trailwork can be brute simple. Dig trench. Move log. Roll rock. Swing axe. Yet, like any craft, it's as complex as you ask it to be: how to sand a tool handle so it fits your grip, tuning a carburetor by ear, what width a bridge stringer can span. And the dawning understanding of *why:* the way trail grade relates to the angle of the slope it traverses, that aged wood is better than green. If you're curious, any task can offer something new.

There are almost as many reasons to turn hands to physical work as there are tasks that require it. Some people fall into labor because of lineage—a father's lumberyard, a trade union membership generations long. Others choose labor because it suits them—they're good with their hands, they see how things work. Sometimes, it's necessity: an immigrant takes an hourly job when she was a doctor back home. A recession hits, and we do any work we can find. In many cases, labor happens when you can't afford to pay someone else to do it. We learn a task because the timing was right and an opportunity came along. Or the work just needed to be done. One way or another, there is always work to do, and someone who has to—gets to—wants to—do it.

I was not born to labor, not led to it by heritage or expectation. In the age-old dichotomy made too much of, I was headed away from physical work, toward the education meant to save me from it. This is a familiar polarity to many of us, used as we are to lives based on split realities: mind over body, now or later, men against women, work then pleasure, culture versus nature, blue collars and white. In my case, despite a diverse family (teachers and tradesmen) and the climate of 1980s feminism, I inherited a common unspoken baseline. Boys took shop. Smart kids went to college. Think about your future! Sharpen your mind. Sports after homework is done.

We all encounter these assumptions and more, and it might surprise us to notice how many of our choices are circumscribed by them. Exercise must fit into the workday. Nature is where we go to escape our ordinary lives. Women in certain arenas are token, if welcome at all. Such schisms may seem purely theoretical until we start to wonder, *Who would I be if I chose the opposite?* Or, perhaps even more revolutionary, *What if they aren't really opposites at all?* Can't our work bring us pleasure? Culture be based on nature, not carved out? What if manual tasks are mentally rewarding? What if a woman in a man's world makes it anyone's world? The problem with my old dichotomy—education, not labor—was the problem with all of them: it entirely missed the point. It turns out, reality is more interwoven—more interesting—than dichotomies allow; it turns out I had a lot to learn.

Sixteen years have passed since I went from school to the woods. The details of my life and job are no longer novel. Trailwork is not fetish, hiatus, or a meander off a truer path. Through two decades of changes, years of both drudgery and stimulation, trailwork has been an unexpected constant, the magnetic pull that swings my inner needle true, the thing that has taught me, in a way, how to live. When spring comes, fieldwork calls, and I migrate—back north, back outside, back to "trails," as we call it from within. Back to a world so tangible to me now I can taste and smell it as I write—chainsaw mix and spruce pitch, diesel fumes and sweat.

Henry David Thoreau famously wrote, "I went to the woods in order to live deliberately," and with this statement, the godfather of American nature writing entrusted to the genre its lasting foundational question: what does the natural world have to do with an authentic life? When I first read Thoreau in high school English, I lived in urban Michigan and had no experience with subsistence tasks. My tomboy youth spent playing in the mud was as close as I'd been to wild, but I'd traded dirt for college prep trimmings: Greek myths and Ivy League catalogs. I had not hoed a row of beans, split firewood, or learned the birds in my backyard by name. Yet I loved Thoreau from the first page. Something about what centered him made sense to me—life connected to the place where you lived, and what you did there. I liked how he was humble yet sure of himself. I liked that he admired squirrels.

Despite my attraction to Thoreau, it took me years more to go to the woods, and when I did, I went haphazardly. If you had told me when I was a sophomore intent on grad school in philosophy that I would one day bring home a paycheck by hauling brush and then spend it on the porch of a ratty bar, I would have laughed. I thought of myself as a thinker. My mind was the muscle I'd trained, and as Plato and Augustine taught me, it was the place where my elegant soul dwelt. I didn't think much about what the body could do.

By the time I finished college, I was more tired of school than Socrates had hinted possible. I moved out West after I graduated, broke and ready for a different life, and ended up in Missoula, Montana, a town where writers and laborers, professors and loggers not only drank at the same bars, they were sometimes the same people. In this place, I had to earn money, and goaded by new friends who worked seasonal jobs, I went to the woods in order to get a paycheck. I wanted to get to know the Rockies, which I had admired mostly from a distance, and I had thought a lot about Wilderness, which I was ready to experience firsthand. But mostly, I wanted to make a living, and to make it learning something new. My boyfriend, Gabe, and I went to work on a Park Service trail crew. As it turns out, dirt was calling me back.

I was hired on by flat luck, since my résumé didn't assure that I'd know which end of a hammer to hold. That first season, I studied everyone—the lifers, the newbies, the cranky mule packers, and the tough-ass women kind enough not to laugh in my face—and I absorbed enough to do my job. My effort was worth money. For the first time in my life, my salary was connected to palpable, not intangible, work. My inner dirtball began to reawaken, and novelty aside, I found I loved trailwork, and a lot of the people who did it. Over seasons, as my expertise increased, I saw that the skills I was honing had uses beyond the work site—log notches for bridge sills could be used to build a cabin. I could fell, limb, and buck trees for firewood the same way I cleared a trail. The endurance and strength and confidence I'd built up from long days of work outside would do me good living in any wild place. The skills I was learning were old ones that had served working people for a long time, and in that sense, I was apprenticed not just to mastery, but to history.

Here's a puzzle: our culture is at once almost totally disconnected from the rhythms and limits of nature, yet obsessed with what is "natural." Some of the thinking about this is deep and critical: what should we eat? Where should it come from? What are things made of? Who makes them? How do our actions affect this planet? How should the planet affect our actions? Other riffs on the nature theme are purely commercial: lanky magazine models loll in grassy fields with wicker picnic baskets. Log homes are status symbols, the "rustic look" perfectly orchestrated by an interior designer. "Mama grizzlies" are leashed for political fund-raising.

Yet, a hunch persists in many of us that a life connected to nature has little to do with commerce, and less still with image. "I want to get back to the land," we say earnestly. But arriving at the doorstep of our own Waldens, we have to ask, *What do I do now?* This is where "going to the woods" gets difficult, because *what to do* is not among the skills twenty-first-century Americans know best: which stuff to get from which catalog, what message to cultivate, how to broadcast it widely. "What to do" is tasks and tools and the experience—or the openness—to put them together. The truth is, no one can live on the land without touching the land. And touching land requires old, unglamorous, sometimes artful, sometimes boring, dirty *work*.

Which brings me back to Thoreau's question. What exactly does it mean to live deliberately, to have an authentic life? I asked a handful of people this question—from an urban freelance writer to an off-the-grid homesteader —and here's what I heard: *living within your means, having a sense of purpose. Feeling grounded, being responsible for the necessities of living. Being happy, but in a deep way, more like content. Existing with a sense of natural limits, where progress isn't everything. Knowing how to do real stuff. Something's a little wild, everything's not figured out. Living the way we evolved to, where our surroundings matter.*

By these definitions, which echo my own instinct, an authentic life will not be built on what we think ("I've escaped the city") or of what we buy (a pine bench for the entryway, the perfect work pants). Not of what we say ("buy local" and "live in the moment") or even what we find (feathers, shells). An authentic life will be built, at least in part, of ordinary verbs: wake, plant, dig, mend, walk, lift, listen, season, note, bake, chop, store, stack, harvest, give, stretch, measure, wash, help, haul, sleep. And verbs bring nouns, what doing requires: shovel, needle, basket, axe, seed, pencil, boots, match, handle, bucket, knife, ear, saw, tape, bowl, barrow, boat, level, soil, wedge, hand.

Perusal of this list quickly reveals that life attached to a location does not require forty acres and a herd of heirloom goats, or a kayak and four months without human contact. The questions that nature triggers are persistent and subtle, and they arise in any place: when does the sun rise? When does it set? Which birds come in spring, and leave in fall? How much does it rain in July? November? Which plants are edible? Is it cold for this time of year? Will a tomato grow in the windowsill? Is the pond frozen enough to cross, or should we walk around? Through questions and tasks and endless figuring, authenticity sneaks up on you, and perhaps by unnoticed accrual is the only way it can, because authenticity comes not from trying, but from being. Witness my first months of trailwork: I longed to be a "real traildog," but mostly, I felt like a poser. Once I had become a real traildog, I didn't think about it anymore.

Of course, only someone who's never done any would say that grunt work alone is path to a fulfilled existence. Days made up solely of hard labor or mindless chores create a different kind of deadness, even as they invite another kind of meaning. We need our minds to organize our actions, to set up scaffolding for our choices, even as we need our bodies to enact them. In my experience, this is why a deep education is one of both head and hands. Over the past twenty years of my life, books have taught me some things, people have taught me many things, and tools have taught me everything else. I mean this as neither romantic nor prescriptive. It just means that *touch* and *work* are part of what I had to learn.

Back on the porch of Frida's, the guys are shaking their heads. "You talk too much," Max might say. "Have another beer." I flip him the bird, Socrates quick to my tongue: *Dude, the unexamined life is not worth living.* But Max is right. The over-examined one isn't, either, and every road has its potholes. A life on the land sometimes sucks. You get soaked, your feet hurt. What you have to carry is too heavy, where you need to go is too far. Moose eat the garden. It rains for a month straight. The corners aren't square. Exhausted, you lose your temper. There's no one to fix it but you.

An authentic life is often held out as utopia, but I hope I am clear: I don't believe in idylls, not iconic men and women made better by proximity to "nature." Life in the woods has its charms and its burdens, like any life; a rural, even wild existence holds no redemption inherent. If dirt does not damn us, it doesn't save us, either. Wherever we end up, we are human once we get there, as vulnerable to unease and envy on talus slopes as on Broadway corners. And yet. I have a bias, because my life in the woods changed me. Work changed my trajectory, my days, changed the shape of my hands.

Take my friends on the porch. If Max and Justin and Gabe held out their hands for your scrutiny (which they won't), you'd see labor's imprint: knobby joints, chapped knuckles. A purple thumbnail, taut tendons in the wrists, the tan that extends to midbicep and stops where a filthy T-shirt begins. Despite the common wilderness maxim, passage on land cannot possibly *leave no trace*, because just as we mark the world when we live in it, so the world marks us. A place—a certain sky, the feel of walking on one type of ground, the unfurl of seasons—stakes its claim, makes itself familiar, which is sometimes to say, known. And work always marks a body. Mine has small muscles on skinny limbs, two broken fingers permanently crooked, callous-shod feet, legs that can eat up the miles. Carpal tunnel syndrome in both wrists, two hernia surgeries, joints that feel older than I am. Also, work marks the spirit. Foresight and patience not innate in me have taken root, fixed by impermanence—erosion, aging. I look for new clouds in an old sky.

———

To paraphrase another beloved American nature writer, two roads diverged, and I, I left school for work in Montana and Alaska and got myself an education anyway. I learned from men and from women, jobs botched and jobs done right. I learned to move fast sometimes and slow others, to watch closely, to measure twice, cut once. I saw how place becomes as much part of you as idea or experience; how inner shifts happen knee-deep in a hole. And inner shifts predict outer ones. A strong body can usher in mental clarity. Noticing how the world works keeps you open to it. When working side by side with someone, trust can arise; tasks cultivate community.

Community means admitting straight up that this book is my story of a certain kind of work, but the story of this work does not belong to me. I share it with people and plants; the tools, animals, ridges, and rivers I've come to know; the details, both sensory and intangible, that this life enfolds. Most of all, with the people, who would not speak like this themselves. I'm breaking ranks with the gang here, writing about work instead of doing it. I worry about this; no story can move from barstool to bookstore without some essence lost.

I have to try, though, in part because of some arrogance in me, a writer's insistent urge to explain what's significant, a storyteller's itch for the oral tradition, preserved. I want to honor this world, show you its value. The mule packers coiling ropes in the barn, the shop mechanic, lip thick with chew—they much prefer their status below the radar, I know. I'm spurning an unwritten rule, a cherished code of laborers. Our work speaks for us. We don't draw attention to ourselves, and most of all, we don't draw attention to each other. I mean it as a love song, not a secret told. I hope they'll forgive me. The tools, I know, won't hold a grudge. They don't scorn or withhold approval, just as they do not praise, or extend it. They neither crave recognition nor shun it. A shovel, an axe, teaches its usefulness by its use.

———

This book is built of six chapters that trace my education by way of trailwork, my passage, by way of place, from onlooker to participant in a very specific world. Each chapter begins with a profile of a tool associated with the trailwork in that chapter's region. I've structured the book around these tools for several reasons, not least because their histories, their quirks, and their uses are worth knowing about. Also, tools have taught me plenty, free of judgment, and I mean to pay them due by hanging the book's framework on their pegs. If my experience is the lens through which this story is told, tools are the artifacts that ground it, and its most central characters—my curriculum, my classmates, and my teachers, all.

It's easy to see a tool as a prop used to enact intent, an object subordinate to intellect. In many ways, this pragmatic view is part of a tool's appeal—elegance and worth stem from its material purpose; metaphor is unnecessary. But there's depth in our relationship, too, which deserves notice. Because we invent, finesse, and tinker with them, feel pride—or chagrin—at what we do with them, tools are also receptacles for self. As extensions of our limbs, tools are like pieces of our bodies that we can lay down.

From my first day on the job, tools have met me as a student and made me into a learner. Axes, saws, rock bars, and sledges taught my body how to swing and sharpen and carry and stow, and they taught my mind that over time, in a place you open yourself to, competence will come. There are always things to do, to get better at, to keep learning, and to teach. For any of us, freedom arises from education. For me, that freedom is in transcending dichotomies of *body* and *mind, think* and *do,* watching apprenticeship and expertise braid between my own two hands.

This book is not meant to be a memoir or a how-to manual, not a wilderness treatise or a polemic on how anyone should live. It's meant to be the story of a few wild places, people who work in them, and how I came to be at home there. No matter which porch we rest on at the end of a day, I believe that the surprising turns our lives take can bring us to our unexpected selves. I believe in a wildness imbedded in the places and the habits of our days, which needs investing in. And I trust the shedful of tools we can use to this end: axe and query, saw and open hand. Some tools are dirty, the edges dull, but I want to choose one anyway. This is where work begins, after all, with the task, the tool, and the doing: pick it up, swing it, breathe, swing again. First, learning motions. Strength will come.

WHAT WE CARRY

Backpack: 25–40 cubic liters

Water: 2 quarts minimum, up to 1 gallon

Layers: 2 more than you wear to stay warm standing still

Gloves: 2 pairs (1 leather, 1 fleece)

Lunch: 3,000–4,000 calories, plus a morning and afternoon snack

Miscellany: Matches, knife, cord, duct tape, flagging, bandana

First Aid: Ibuprofen, Band-Aids, ibuprofen, moleskin, tweezers, ibuprofen

Tools: Axe, pulaski, shovel, chainsaw, clinometer

Fuel: 1 gallon gas, 1 quart bar oil per saw

Hats: 1 baseball, 1 toque

Attitude: Don't quit, complain, lag, or brag. Pretend nothing hurts.

Expectations: Fix it; bust ass; do it fast; know it all, or learn it quick.

AXE

History One of the oldest tools for shaping life in the woods, an axe is a
metal head mounted to a handle. This blend of simple machines—
lever, wedge—traces as far back as 6000 BCE. Its predecessors
include an edged horn or antler (Mesolithic period), a stone shaped for
cutting (Neolithic period), and a honed metal blade (Iron Age). Axes
migrated with people: up the Silk Road, over the Bering Strait. By the
turn of the twentieth century, Oakland, Maine, billed itself as "the axe
capital of the world."

Warning A sharp blade (or bit) reflects its user, indicating a careful steward
who knows that a tool is only as useful as its condition is good. A
sheath (or scabbard) prevents the bit from snagging nylon pack
cloth, slicing leather gloves or the hide of a pack mule, or laying open
uncalloused skin. A sharp blade is an asset and a liability. On a fire
crew, a woman put an axe through her kneecap, slicing to bone. A
friend splitting kindling with a hatchet severed his thumb above the
knuckle. An axe can leave a mark.

Etymology Ax, or axe—lucky for Scrabble players, both are correct. The
word "axe" may originate from Latin, *ascia*, or Greek, *axine*, or from
Old English, *eax* or *aex,* all meaning "cutting tool." (The Dutch word
for axe is *bijl*— Americanized to "byl," it's my last name. Perhaps my
ancestors were woodsmen?)

History The handle of an axe (also the haft, or helve) was seen as an
extension of the user's hand, the cutting edge called the fingernail.
Metalsmiths forged axe heads and the swinger crafted an ash or
hickory handle to suit his grip. Families retained handle patterns over
decades, like a cattle brand, connecting tool to user. The handle's

distinction enabled the easy return of a borrowed or lost tool to
the proper owner; counterfeiting a clan's handle pattern showed
serious disrespect. Artistic fancy was not uncommon, even to ascetic
Puritans—scrolled lines, decorative details. Bible texts have been
found engraved on antique tools, a nod to the spiritual realm. A
relationship to a tool often resulted in a pet name—an axe called
Jack, a hoe called Tom.

Varieties A felling axe has a fine blade that cuts across wood grain, the
double bit with two blades, a single bit with one; the butt (or poll) is
used for pounding in wedges. A splitting axe's thicker blade cuts with
the grain—imagine chopping firewood rounds. Other relatives: hatchet,
maul, broad axe, adze, pulaski, tomahawk.

Mythology In Greece, Sweden, Japan, and Brazil, the axe symbolizes a
thunderbolt. When buried in the ground, it wards off lightning. Want
to prevent a hailstorm? Throw an axe. Protect your crops against
inclement weather? Hide an axe in the field. If you meet Hermes and
tell him the truth, he'll reward you with a golden axe. Little Red Riding
Hood's woodcutter used one on the wolf, as did Jack on his beanstalk.
To keep away witches, bury an axe upright under your house. If it's a
male heir you're after, keep an axe under the bed.

Scenario Say there's a large tree to cut, miles from a road. An axe is the
simplest tool that will do the job. Lighter than a midsize chainsaw by
a good twelve pounds, an axe cannot run out of gas, throw its chain,
or kick back. An axe is slower, and when efficiency is required, or
volume, you'll wish for the fumy grace of a chainsaw. But as a backup
for the saw, or if you have miles to walk and might not need to cut at
all, an axe is the most stowable choice. Anyone who thinks an axe
is quiet has never had to chop through an old-growth larch. Work is
noisy, with or without gas.

CHAPTER 1

North Fork: River

(Where I went in search of wildness)

Reba and I arrive at the barn by 6:50 a.m. It's my first month as a laborer on a Glacier National Park trail crew, and my leader and I are headed into a ten-day hitch on the north shore of Logging Lake. To get there, we'll need the packers. I'm green as spring, but I sense to stay out of the way. A cowboy in a black hat busts out of the barn door and I press my back and palms flat into the side of the truck.

Yer late, where's yer rig, pull up over here, it's blockin' the truck, gaddam it, ain't even 8 an' we're fucked six ways from Sunday! What is she new, stay outta the way, Reba grab me them ropes, start mannyin' up, I wanna be outta here in twenny. His boot steps scuff up dust, just like in a western. My eyes track his body: across the lot, in the barn door, out to the paddock, through the fence gate, up the ramp of the stock truck. Somehow he's loose and cricked up at the same time. *How in the name a hell should I know, ask Sheldon. Where's her hair? Looks like a gaddam guy. Hire all these wimmen, don't make no sense.* I'd hoped for invisibility, but my buzz cut caught his eye, so Reba tries to introduce us. *Give a shit what her name is, get outta the way, I want yer help I'll tell ya. Don't pet them critters, kick the hell outta ya, damn well should.*

Leaving the barn forty-five minutes later is pure relief. Reba sees my stricken face. She grins and guns the F-350 out of the lot, a rooster tail of gravel splayed behind. "Don't worry about it. He's always like that," she says, drumming her fingers on the wheel. We drive north. At the trailhead, we'll hike six miles in, joining another crew at a cabin on Logging Lake to work for ten days on trails projects. I don't exactly know what it means to "build turnpike."

"That's okay," says Reba. She's spunky and freckled, bounces more than walks. "You'll have ten days to figure it out."

Day one, I figured out that I didn't pack enough food. (Reba said this was a common rookie mistake and I could eat canned goods from the cabin stash if necessary.) Day two, I figured out that white gas for the Coleman stove was different than chainsaw mix. By day three, I figured out that it was better to stand back and watch than ask a lot of questions; I'd get answers eventually, and was much less annoying. Day four, I figured out that a whole hitch of good weather is unlikely. Day five, I figured out that traildogs don't like to be mistaken for rangers. By day six, I figured out that Abby, the project leader, was a chocoholic whose mood improved drastically after she ate sweets. On day seven, I figured out that every person on the crew knew more than someone about something, and less than someone about something else. Day eight, I figured out that no matter how I stuffed myself at dinner, I was always starving by breakfast. By day nine, I figured out that I wouldn't be run out of the woods with a scarlet "I" on my back (idiot, incompetent, imbecile, or inept, take your pick).

And sure enough, ten days in, when the packers showed up to haul us out, I had figured out what "build turnpike" meant. We dropped trees and peeled off the bark (to prevent rot), dragged logs out of the woods with the impressive tool called the Swede hook. While the sawyer did log joinery, the crew dug massive lateral ditches to drain the water alongside the trail, and shoveled out troughs for the logs. Building, we notched and spiked the logs together and filled the box with large rocks, smaller rocks, then gravel dug from upended root wads or hauled from the creek bed in metal buckets and canvas miner's bags. The result was a humped turnpike, the logs, so carefully measured and joined, now buried, and previously muddy tread elevated into a swath of navigable trail. An eyesore the day we finished, all hacked roots and dead plants and displaced dirt, by the next season the turnpike would blend in so completely that only a trained eye would notice the site as altered. By the end of ten days, I learned that "turnpike" is one of many words on trails at once noun and verb, the functional meaning "to fix."

On the last day's work, I was impressed by the bulk of the finished project. Standing at one end and looking down hundreds of feet of trail, I thought, oddly, of the carpeted aisle that movie stars travel when they mince toward the stage to accept their Oscars. I imagined myself clumping the length of it in my no-longer-shiny leather work boots to receive the "Traildog of the Hitch" award.

A laughable fantasy, as I had done little skilled labor on the project. Too timid and lurching to be trusted with the chainsaw, too unpracticed for carpentry, I was by far the skinniest, least-muscled of the bunch. I learned fast that in lieu of skills, you become useful by taking initiative and staying busy, which thanks in part to my father's lifelong injunctions, came easy to me. To become one of the gang, I'd step up to the shittiest jobs. For eight days, I carried fill from creek and borrow pit—tripping across sidehills through alder and devil's club, metal buckets passed to the next gloved hand, fire-line style. Other folks switched out, took turns felling a tree, prepping sills, spiking logs, but I—content to labor where I couldn't screw up—I dug, lifted, and carried yards of fill, so many loads that the outside of my legs from midthigh to midcalf were purpled with bruises from the buckets, and my new government-issue gloves had a permanent groove bisecting the palm from the metal handle.

I have probably built miles of turnpike since then. By watching closely and asking questions, I learned what to do, and in time could tell someone else how to do it. The parts I love best are choosing a tree for stringers and dropping it from sky to ground, the first twenty minutes of peeling off bark, and marking and notching the joints. Still, my proudest turnpike is that first one, when, invisible and naïve, I devoted myself to the least-skilled, most-backbreaking labor, and at the end of the week, staring down that length of corridor, I could not name a better thing I'd ever done.

The North Fork of the Flathead is a greenish river, swift in some places and slow in others, forming the western boundary of Glacier National Park. It flows south out of Canada's Kootenai Mountains into northwest Montana, running the international border as if a blinking yellow light, and then farther south through airy meadows and scorched forest, the craggy silhouette of the Northern Rockies' Livingston Range often just in view. The North Fork converges with the Middle Fork of the Flathead about forty miles south of the Canadian border, just upstream of the Blankenship Bridge. West Glacier sits a mile away, the town that houses the park's headquarters.

The North Fork originates in hundreds of feeder creeks that tear down the slopes of the Rockies, creeks flowing from the Forest Service land to the west (Fish, Hay, Camas) and the Park to the east (Kintla, Bowman, Kishenehn, Quartz, Logging, Akokala, Dutch). Topography knows no park boundaries, and on whichever land they began, the creeks end in the North Fork. It's a formidable river and a friendly one at the same time, so cold and clear in some spots you're swimming in tinted air; in others fast and muddy, kicking up silt and stones, jamming logs in narrow canyons until they resemble structures joisted from the force of water.

The North Fork is also the district in Glacier National Park whose trails and bridges and travelers must contend with one or another of the river's tributaries. It's an area of a couple hundred thousand acres—one-hundred-plus miles of trail; a few tire-puncturing roads; scattered cabins and fire lookouts—a wide sweep bordered by the river to the west, the Continental Divide to the east. The North

Fork district is dominated and defined by the North Fork River, so when someone says, "I was up the North Fork today," you can only guess whether they mean the region or the river by proximity to a truck or canoe.

Besides the river and its creeks, the North Fork is home to twentysome lakes, a couple of wolf packs, shaggy grizzlies, osprey, fireweed, marmots, old-growth larch groves, snowy passes, and the occasional *Calypso bulbosa*, the fairy slipper orchid. The fairy slipper is purplish-pink and lilylike, a weighty blossom on a bowed stem that looks like a tiny, fancy shoe. *Calypso* is Greek for "concealed," and true to name, the lily grows low to the ground, often obscured by larger undergrowth or fallen needles; a special orchid, it's not exactly rare, but a sighting feels precious. Like many inhabitants of the North Fork, it's often looked for, and easy to miss. It seems that only in the absence of seeking do senses clear enough to see: lily, wolf, falling star.

Behind the North Fork ranger station sits the trail maintenance shop, a small room in a nondescript outbuilding. It's tidy, mostly because there's not much in it to make a mess—just enough essentials to be sure you won't run stuck, but no excess, no rusted coffee cans full of odd-size bolts, no broken axe handles, hanks of twine too small to use, too big to throw away. It's nothing like the main shop near headquarters, with a work bench and drill press; extra gloves and earplugs and six kinds of tape; a shed full of tents, coolers, tarps; ten Stihl power brushers hanging from a plywood ceiling rack like a fleet of orange-and-white Storm Troopers. Because this auxiliary shop is thirty miles from the main trails headquarters, everything here gets used up, repaired on site, or taken down to headquarters if it needs fixed. This shop supports the North Fork trail crew, four or five people instead of the entire west-side crew, and it has that kind of intimacy, the way a room feels different than a house. Gas stains on the floor, wet sawyer's chaps clipped on nails to dry, five pulaskis hanging by their heads in the rack where they belong. It smells like wood chips and bar oil, someone's drying T-shirt, and the thick perfume of mules.

I learned to swing an axe at the age of twenty-three. In my first weeks on trails, I learned lots of new things. How to run a chainsaw, eyes glued to the tip of the bar, alert for dreaded kickback. How to approach a mule without getting booted. Which tools you could grab anytime, which were kept under lock and key. By the time I'd been working for a week, it was hard to recall if I'd ever known how to do anything. Except hike. I could do that, walk miles carrying a daypack without complaint. So, hiking behind Reba one afternoon, I felt mildly adept. Our day's task finished and a couple hours before quitting time, we were going to chop out two downed trees near the Park Creek trailhead, skipping the chainsaw, which was back at the shop, in favor of the double-bit axe in the truck bed.

We came to the first downed tree a few hundred yards in, a spruce, its branches jutting out, barring passage. Reba unlashed the axe from her pack and unbuckled the leather sheath from the head. I stood back as she swung at the bases of limbs, hacking off enough of them to clear a section of trunk for chopping, a few feet off the trail. She turned to me. "Wanna try?" she asked, extending the axe by the head so the handle pointed at me.

I took it. It didn't occur to me to think, "I don't know how to chop." I had split firewood rounds before (with a maul, I know now, though back then all the handled chopping tools looked the same), and compared with the specific and easy-to-confuse logistics required to start the chainsaw—*brake on, choke on, pull, pull, fire, off choke, pull, pull, fire, off brake, throttle*—the axe seemed too simple to require much instruction. (If you know how to swing an axe, you know that I am about to make a fool of myself.)

I stepped up to the trunk. I can't recall each motion, but I've since watched many people who don't know how to swing an axe

try to swing an axe, and I know what I looked like. Axe head up next to my ear, arms awkwardly cocked with hands spread wide on the handle. Then, the downward motion we picture when we hear the word *chop,* a vertical blow akin to the board-breaking karate move. The blade hit the trunk straight on, bounced off lamely, just missing my shin. I tried this a few times, putting more muscle into it, until the pure ineffectuality of the whole thing stopped me short. I looked to Reba. She was laughing, not unkindly, the guffaw I'd hear many times over the next months. "Any tips?" I asked her.

"Watch." She took the axe from me, squared her body to the tree, and, swinging the axe over her head, hands moving up, down the handle with each blow, she dispatched the tree in less than ten minutes. Karate-style, it would have taken me all day. Reba didn't explain the mechanics—she wasn't given to clear verbal instructions, instead gesturing, *like this,* and lighting into the task like a storm— but watching her, I could see that what she was doing made sense. Her swings had constant rhythm, the motion of the axe while not in contact with the tree as important as the chopping. The blade hit the wood at an angle, chiseling out pieces the way you'd whittle with a knife, and making clear the origin of the word "woodchips." Reba swiveled the handle in her palms in midair so she used both bits of the head to chop on alternate sides, the width of the cut twice the diameter of the tree, leaving plenty of room for the angling cuts to meet in the middle and sever the trunk. My technique, I could see, was at best bludgeoning, more suited to driving a spike with a sledge-hammer (the twelve-pound version of which would later make a different, equal fool of me). When Reba swung, it looked not exactly effortless, since her T-shirt was soaked with sweat and she stopped to catch her breath, but at least graceful. It seemed clear why you'd use that tool to do this job.

I watched Reba chop and tried to picture her somewhere else— at an office job, in front of a fourth-grade classroom—and I couldn't really do it. In clothes that filthy, with all those freckles and so much energy to burn, she belonged where she was, before that tree. She'd barely turned thirty. She'd just gotten married, and Rob, her husband, was a packer for the Forest Service. Tan and quick and light on her feet, she was at ease in the woods in a way I didn't even know how to describe. Before I started my trails job, back in Missoula spreading out maps and counting new pairs of socks, I wondered what my co-workers would be like. I guessed, as I usually do when joining a gang late, that they were much different than me. And they were, stronger, confident, knowledgeable. But Reba didn't fit my worries. She was a chatterbox, easy and open, and she told me stuff. The names of flowers, which truck couldn't go in reverse, don't ask the foreman questions until after morning briefing, how much she missed her husband when they were apart for a month. I was starting to know her. The axe was the bigger stranger.

Reba finished the first cut and I began the next one, swinging as she had shown me, the head at an angle, my hands loose on the shaft. The axe still glanced off here and there and I had to rest often. I started the cut too narrow, and at the bottom of the V, the wood pinched the blade of the axe tight. The last swings to chop it free were the most difficult and awkward of the half-an-hour's production, and taught me a critical thing: even a simple task relied on precision, and was easier if you planned ahead. The six-foot section finally dropped free of the trunk. Reba and I rolled it off to the side of the trail, then tipped it onto its angled butt and toppled it forward in a move I'd soon learn to call an "end-o." Its bulk surprised me. So recently alive, the log was full of sap and water. It would take a year on the ground before it dried out enough to mimic the lighter-than-expected heft of well-seasoned firewood.

I couldn't linger over my success. Reba had already shouldered her pack and moved up trail. The second tree was smaller and I chopped the whole thing myself, planning the cuts, their width, how far apart. It took me twice as long as the larger tree had taken her to chop, so it was almost quitting time when we left the site. But I'd done it. Every

step. Reba gave me a jubilant high five and we slammed a quart of
water each and jogged to the truck, stomachs sloshing. On the ride
back to headquarters, my shoulders were hunched high and already
sore to the touch. I stretched my wrists, holding the fingers bent back
from the palm the way I'd seen Reba do. We pulled in to the shop at
6:30 p.m., long after the other crews had left for the day. That night,
getting ready for bed, I could hardly lift my toothbrush.

Hitch: *n*—An extended stint in which a trail crew lives and works
    in the backcountry, typically eight or ten days long. Most of the
    summer is spent "on hitch." Also called "the woods," as in "when
    did you get out of the woods?"
Hitched out: *adj*—The state of participating in a hitch. *Usage:* "How
    long were you hitched out at Quartz?"
Spike camp: *n*—Our home while on hitch—a cabin, or a cluster of
    tents around a kitchen tarp. Also called a "gypsy camp."
Note: It's important to get these phrases right. You don't say "camp-
    ing out" if you mean "hitched out." Camping out is fun. Hitched
    out is work. And you wouldn't say "backcountry camp": too
    many syllables. You'd call it spike. Language isn't all it takes, but
    getting words right is how you start to belong.

Who belongs more than the critters? In the North Fork, as in all of
the Northern Rockies, there are animals everywhere. Wolf, mountain goat, bighorn sheep, black bear and grizzly, coyote, moose—the
superstars. And smaller creatures, too: snowshoe hare half-turned
white, marten on a tree branch, dippers nesting beneath a bridge,
pika lifting the lid of my Tupperware lunch box, star-nosed mole
burrowing in the duff. Animals stay far clear of the chainsaw's roar,
but when we lived and worked ten days in the same place, we'd see
the fawn sleeping in the stamped-down bear grass, hear the swoop of
an owl's wings over the tent in the night.

    There are humans out there, too, us working, and hikers, kids with their parents and their pockets full of stones, college students on a long-planned backpack trip, newlyweds from a big city with brand-new gear. They're eager to chat, full of questions, often thankful for our work. But when people grow quiet, or crowds scatter, animals appear. One early morning at the job site, a wolverine ran off a switchback in front of us and we watched it scramble up three tiers of waterfall pouring over sloped rock. Hiking out of a hitch, fast, heading for the truck six miles downhill, we saw a quick snake cross the trail and my crewmate jumped, pack and all, into my arms.

When animals appear, clichés sidle up close. Watch out. Soon there will be "electricity" between a bear and me, "dignity" in a lone wolf's eyes. Trite as it is, such telescoping from the experience of an animal to a philosophizing about it is not such a base instinct. I want to make sense of creatures, at once exotic and kin, and as I try to interpret their presence against the backdrop of my own existence, it's a very short leap to the owl as talisman, elk a stately messenger from a wilder world. I am more eager to see what an animal means to me than what it means to itself.

Why do we do this? (Don't you do it too?) I have some hunches, about power and connection and disappointment, about the margins of ego, and the urge to idolize. Short heroes of our own kind, it's no wonder we build pedestals for bears. But if I push past the initial urge to codify, or else, to *ooh* and *aah*, if I force myself to watch without judgment, philosophy soon falls away, the meaning of the animal quashed by the actual animal, moving, through the same world as me. Wait. The same world? Well, that's frightening, isn't it? Me and a grizzly bear, in the same exact world?

Which brings us to danger. Part of what fascinates me about wild animals is the element of threat, not because they are bloodthirsty or even necessarily predators, but because their actions are not about me. My wolf-faced dogs share the social contract of domesticity—I trust they will not hurt me, and they look to me for food, exercise, companionship. With animals I do not feed or sleep beside, there is not trust. I am curious about them, I can guess how they will behave based on other experiences, or what I've read, but I do not know, despite my field guides, what their priorities are, what they aim to do, and when. A grizzly could maul me if I stepped between it and a carcass. A moose might charge if I skied past its calf in the alders. A fisher could bite my leg if I sat too long in the outhouse it has made its winter home.

The specter of danger mingled with curiosity results in an otherness that both beckons and warns. This potent blend leaves me off-balance, invigorated, and by necessity, returns me to watching. To feel as safe as possible in situations I cannot predict among company I don't control, I have to trust my senses and read signs. A congress of ravens circled and hollering might indicate a fresh kill nearby. A calf prompts a look for its mother. On a brushy creek, I scan for fresh bear prints in sand. Evolutionary lessons ring true: keep eyes open, nose pointed into the wind. Notice everything.

There's a funny thing about connection, though. I say it's the animals I'm drawn toward, but these sightings usually bring me closer to humans, whether the crew mate in my arms or the hiker we tell later on the trail, *Watch close for you'll never guess what we how cool was that.* The bond over animals is one of the strongest I have with particular friends; stories about the fox that stood for minutes on a creek bed watching fish, and how the Sandhill cranes seem early this year. We ask questions: This feather frozen in ice, do you know what kind? We point and wonder: How'd that get there, a Dall sheep skull on a gravel bar, half-filled with sand?

The Polish poet Czeslaw Milosz wrote, "We're separated from nature as if by a glass wall. . . . We are akin to it and yet we are alienated by our consciousness—our curse and our blessing." But, Milosz, we *are* nature. Don't you see? Still, he's on to something, the egocentric positioning that lets us fool ourselves. Sharing space with wild creatures stirs me (blessing), and as soon as I've said "stirs me," I cringe (curse). Sheepish or not, proximity to wild things makes me feel feral—incautious and frisky and willing to gamble on what I cannot prove. And proximity to wild things makes me feel tame—glad I don't have to hunt for every meal, eager to hunker next to a fire on a cold night. Wherever I am, banging against the glass.

Some mornings when I crawl out of my tent to a bright sky and stretch the kinks out of my back by lifting my arms and twisting left and right with a muted howl and when I walk across spruce needles in my socks to the food prep area for my cereal and banana while sitting on top of a pile of pungent duck-cloth mannies and when I hear the red squirrels *sssk*-ing in the branches above me and the violet-green swallow sing as the sun starts to heat the dirt, and as I think about the day to come, the lifting and laughing and tinkering and eating and hiking and figuring and eating and cussing and hauling and eating that will mark the next ten hours, and when I lace up my boots over the last three hooks in that familiar rhythm and strap tools to my pack and fall in line with the group, I feel something I almost can't describe. A contentedness located down near my kidneys, a radiant center, like a full bladder or a deep breath held in to bursting. Purposeful and competent, almost embarrassed that the rituals of work can make me feel so *happy.*

If most laborers have strong opinions about work boots, traildogs are fanatics. Since we spend ten-hour days on our feet, many of them hiking, a good boot is critical. I've never met anyone who did backcountry trailwork for more than a season in cheap boots. Loggers' boots are popular, high-laced leather with a swayed back and stacked heel, ubiquitous in fire camps. White's are the Cadillac boot, made to order for every foot, but several off-the-shelf brands do the trick for less. Logging boots lend stability and protection for saw work and are bomber in mud, but hard for hiking long miles, as they pitch your calf into a forward position—good for side-hilling, awkward on flats. Full-grain leather hiking boots are a solid choice, especially for long miles; with a coat of Huberd's boot grease, they're far more watertight than sweaty and expensive Gore-Tex. Some boots split the difference, with the shin-tight fit of a logging boot and the flat lug sole of a work boot, like Danner's popular "Rainforest" (my favorite).

A durable boot is critical, because in addition to pounding trail, boot sheaths foot, a trailworker's ace-in-the-hole tool. Use feet for dragging fill, kicking roots, prodding rocks, freeing bucked log rounds, testing structural soundness, sampling soil, digging a hole for an unexpected crap, leveling grade, and finishing touches. You can wear out a boot in a couple seasons. Nothing's worse than a boot with holes. Rain and rocks get in, stink gets out. Boots indicate character, competency measured on the break-in scale. New boots scream "novice" (though everyone needs them sometimes), but hammered boots carry the same shameful whiff as a poorly maintained tool. Want a clue about a person's work? Look at her boots.

Also, look at her hands. I trust dirty fingernails. I am drawn to people with that half moon, the sliver of filth that indicates kinetic expertise. Perhaps they do fieldwork—ratty truck, weathered tools. Are they teachers, the ones who kneel next to kids examining earthworms in mud? Potters, naturalists, firefighters, farmers: dirt is a secret code, dusty knuckles the special knock of a fraternal order. I trust this small sign because it implies a tangible relationship. To get dirt under your fingernails, you have to touch the world.

Randy is a ranger in the North Fork. He lives at the station just inside the boundary, on the Park Service compound near the river, complete with brown buildings and green-and-gray uniforms. The town site of Polebridge is two miles south on the road, made up of an old mercantile, a saloon, a few cabins for travelers, and a bunch of rusty trucks and roaming dogs and horses. People who live in Polebridge can be a little odd, and people who work for the Park

Service are also often odd, so people who work for the Park Service in Polebridge are, on the whole, wonderfully odd.

Randy's from Jersey (or Queens?), but he's been working seasonally in the North Fork for so long he qualifies as a Polebridge local. He hikes trails, checks cabins, monitors permits, mans the station, tinkers with vehicles. He's isolated and chatty, a wicked combination, and when the right truck passes through, he'll lean on the driver's rearview mirror. Randy likes to talk shit, to tease and bluff. "I just heard on the radio that Charley's looking for you," he'll say. "He sounded pissed!" When the leader reaches for his radio to call the foreman, Randy slaps the side of the truck and cackles. It's hard not to fall for Randy's jokes. It's almost an agreement: when you talk to Randy, you are buying tickets to a certain kind of show, and you can't ask for different once it's started. If you aren't in the mood to talk, or be ribbed, keep driving, lift two fingers from the steering wheel in the standard rural-road greeting.

You might be sorry you didn't stop. Randy's helpful, and he knows the district. Maybe he needed to tell you that the road is flooded at Kintla Creek, or there are six trees down in the Bowman campground. In that case, when you come back through, Randy will let you hear it, laughing: *You shoulda asked!* And suddenly, you're the joker, not him.

The prized pulaski is a hand tool with adze and axe on either end of a midsize head, named for the Polish American firefighter who invented it, his moniker as stout as the tool itself. Tools and equipment used for trailwork have names that tickle anyone who likes words. Listen: hazel hoe, Swede hook, come-along, pulaski, McLeod, manty, donkey dick, sandvik, misery whip, pigtail. Picture it: some old immigrant, the bend of his saw blade moving through wood. A whole narrative in a single word.

———

I practiced swinging the axe when no one was watching. Limbing a tree felled for a log project, bucking up small deadfall in the woods off trail, each cut a lesson. I knew that, swung right, the axe should begin in an arc high above my head and end with a wrist snap, grip loosened just before the controlled slam that vibrated up into my elbow. I knew that, after extended chopping, my back and neck muscles would feel sorer than forearms or biceps, the stereotypical bulges of a strongman. I knew that a well-swung axe relied on the proper use of gravity, a good aim, and persistence more than pure muscle (thank God). I knew there were no tighter shoulders than the ones you got from swinging an axe.

Still, I dreaded having to chop something in front of Max, the brawny West Lakes crew leader whose physical strength and grace gave him mythic status, or the Middle Fork guys, twentysomethings from ranches or farms who seemed to have been born with tools in their hands. I was grateful that only Reba saw my early efforts. It was for me then, and remained for years, easier to take lessons from women. The majority of us were not raised to perform the skills we were being paid for, some even shielded from labor by college prep classes (not shop!) and brothers mowing the lawn. Perhaps some women in manual-labor trades bond because of an inherent sorority among men, but I think what deeply unites us is the fact that most of us have so recently been beginners. In the labor world, women more often remember what it felt like to not know, to be expected not to know, to be taught, and then later, to teach. The expertise we have feels earned, not inherited. We are grateful for the times someone chose not to make us feel foolish.

I eventually got very good at swinging an axe, often chopping out a tree just for the satisfaction. In Missoula, where Gabe and I spent winters, I volunteered on a playground project at a city park. A large tree root impeded a posthole and I offered to whack the thing loose. The axe was sharp, and in three clean and perfect swings, the root came free. "Wow," said one middle-aged volunteer to his friend.

"She can chop." He could not have known what a long, tortured pageant his tiny comment gestured toward. My turned face concealed what would have been the sure blush of pride.

I'm ashamed to admit, however, that for me, prowess doesn't always go hand in hand with the easy and generous humility I admire in others. I've often been in Reba's position since my first day with the axe, standing by while someone young or inexperienced or just not very strong whaled, fruitless, at a tree. I hate to admit that I laughed at them, but sometimes, I did. Especially the men. With women I was quicker to demonstrate the right technique first, or to step in and help before they sunk the axe into a kneecap. With girls, I'd confide, "You should have seen the first time I tried to chop a tree," rolling my eyes, subverting present competence. But the cocky first-year laborer who could pick me up with one arm and toss me off the trail if he chose, who wanted to put him at ease? I let those boys flail. I smirked on the sidelines before asking if they wanted a hand. (They usually didn't.) One know-it-all Sierra Club volunteer "chopped" at a tree for five minutes, causing only a dent in the bark before throwing down the tool with a withering "This axe is too dull." Nothing subtle about the way I picked it up, inspected the sharp edge of the blade with my finger, and chopped the tree through in ten neat swings. I could see John Henry's demise in my single-minded vigor to show that man up. "Not that dull," I said as I handed the axe back to him.

I've seen those I work with negotiate the same tension, women and men. Some are insufferable, quick to lecture and correct, covering insecurities with the chest-thumping bravado that hopes to keep the reek of unknowing at a distance. Others are so self-effacing you have to twist their arms to get them to teach you anything, its own kind of arrogance. Most, like me, are somewhere in between. I like to think I've gotten better at the dance of the old hand, the delicate riff between modesty and expertise, the ability to give what I know as an offering, not a weapon, and to keep learning, eager for the many tasks I haven't mastered. I like it far better when I can be the gracious mentor, not the know-it-all. Too bad there's still that occasional thrill of seeing someone else stumbling along and thinking, relieved, *This time, it's me who knows.*

My pitfalls this obvious, you'd think they'd be easier to avoid.

The North Fork in July explodes with flowers: arrowleaf balsamroot, fireweed, trillium, arnica, columbine, lupine, gentian, Indian paintbrush, clematis, larkspur. Spoken, they bloom again.

Polebridge, Montana: town site established in 1911 by a loner from back east who built a homestead cabin on the edge of nowhere, and in the yard planted the first known beech tree west of the Continental Divide. Now, the cabin is a saloon, the only watering hole in the North Fork's only human enclave, where long wooden picnic tables rest in the shade of the beech. The Northern Lights Saloon is more than twenty miles from the nearest town, and in rock-tossing distance of wilderness, you can get most drinks, except a slushy margarita—no blender. But local beer on tap, a shot of Jack, an elk burger? Put it on the tab.

After four o'clock, dusty trucks line the dirt strip out front. The vista from the porch spans a twenty-five-year-old burn, dead trees in front of the mountains beyond, and the foreground props include two ancient gas pumps whose numbers scroll by like a slot machine, a rusty fire engine, two dogs, and a horse foraging the sand pits behind the Mercantile. A hand-lettered sign nailed to a utility pole reads, "SLOW DOWN, People Breathing." Even years after the 1988 fire, char tints the air, mingled with the smell of burnt sugar, from the Mercantile Bakery's daily special. A cardboard sign nailed to the saloon's porch warns, "Unleashed Dogs Will Be Eaten." Under the sign sleeps Sasha, a three-legged Karelian bear dog. She is black, with a dirty-white fur apron. She lies unleashed with her head on outstretched paws, ready to enforce the local rules.

———

Dirt is an old word, an earthy word. It inhabits its meaning as it sits on your tongue when you speak it, onomatopoeia made flesh. "Dirt" never came out of Caesar's mouth; it can't be declined in a lyrical list. There is nothing fancy or trilling about the sound of dirt. It's not dressed up like "excrement" or "detritus," unlike "organic matter" or even "humus." From Old Norse, it made its way into Middle English as *drit*—the filth that collected on the soles of Chaucer's travelers' shoes. Dirt stands alone, underneath everything, hidden in the creases of our skin, blowing in the air. It's solid and unglamorous. *Old.*

Perhaps because of its permanence, dirt is a comfort. It comes from the purest elements: rain, rock, ice, wind. Glaciers form and move slowly, carving rock and mineral thrust up from Earth's core; ice melts into rivers, coursing through the path of least resistance, forcing incremental change. When rivers and air meet, condensation forms. Weather results, and weather makes dirt. Water from the sky—snow, sleet, downpours, sprinkles—impacts the surface of the Earth in small drops and wide puddles and rushing currents. Wind blows across it all, urging dirt and water onward, to drift and finally come to rest in a distant place. There are molecules of dirt on Boulder Pass that blew in from Egypt's pyramids; the mud caked in my boot treads may have once cradled the bones of some delicate, gossamer wing.

The North Fork is the only place in the Lower 48 I've seen a wolf. Driving south down the road, back to West Glacier, long past dark on an October night. We'd had a few beers, a big dinner at the saloon, and I leaned my head back against the seat in the drowse between wake and sleep, listening to soft pedal-steel on the radio, washboard ruts vibrating my thighs. The truck lurched as Gabe tapped his foot on the brake and stuck his arm out in front of me, an instinctive gesture. "Look," he whispered, "wolf." I opened my eyes. Gabe turned the wheel slightly, casting headlights toward the shoulder. Twenty feet ahead, it stood just off the road in profile, as still as if zapped in midstride.

If you've ever seen a coyote and wondered, *Could that be a wolf?* it wasn't. I've seen a coyote and wondered the same thing. Seeing a wolf, I did not wonder. Even if I hadn't known anything about how large wolves are, how long their snouts, their legs, I think I would have known. The world seemed to close in around the edges of my perception until *it was only me and the wolf, our eyes locked, some ancient knowledge passing*—stop. Did I think this? Please. That wolf cared nothing for ancient knowledge, and in any case, I had little of it to give. To the wolf, I was neither augur nor soul mate, only an obstacle in the terrain, an odd creature that inched close. Its eyes were distinct, its gaze forward. We sat that way for a minute, probably less. The wolf walked slow, out of the beam of our lights and along the length of the passenger side of the truck, five, eight feet away. Gabe switched off the lights. My window was rolled down a third. It was too dark to see well but I could hear it outside the window. The night's noise went on around us, I'm sure, the squeak of a far-off rusted fence gate, a wind chime clattering in the eaves of an abandoned barn, but I remember those moments as if the world were muted, as if the wolf and I were the only things passing before a set stage. No Gabe. No truck. When it reached the tailgate, the wolf cut across the road and trotted down into the ditch line and up again, vanished into the woods between the river and us. Gabe and I sat in the truck in the dark. No talk. No touch. For a minute, just dark.

Of all the animals I've seen over the years, all the brief glimpses and long stares, I remember the wolf more clearly than many. Not so much the motions of it, not where the wolf walked and how long it took and what I thought when it disappeared. But I remember its eyes reflecting light, how the shoulder muscles undulated beneath the thick beginnings of its winter coat. I remember that it didn't run. It never seemed wary, or curious. Not canny, smart, devious, or fierce. We crossed its path and it regarded us briefly before making its way toward pups in a den, a deer kill buried in a hole, or miles more hungry walking under the slim moon. That night, whether because of culture or nature, my wishful tilt toward wildness or an evolutionary hunch, I felt the borders of physicality and transcendence shift until one allowed the other in, and when the wolf slipped into the woods, I wanted to follow it. I wanted to dip my face to the river to drink, tear flesh with my teeth, flatten myself a bed of needles with a circling pace before sleeping. Never mind the blood on my face. Never mind the cold.

When it's clear in the North Fork and you're having a beer at a picnic table outside the saloon, you can see east across the river valley to the mountains, twenty miles away. Long Knife, Kintla, Rainbow, Bowman, Vulture, Nashukin. Beyond those, more, and beyond those, still more, over the divide to the east side of the park, the rain shadow where red talus slopes run into prairie's edge. Gunsight, Bearhat, Two Medicine, Sentinel, Apikuni, Rain Shadow, Bad Marriage. Animal names, Native names, white men's names—mountain names. Rainbow Peak's name nods to three snowy couloirs on the south face that mimic, in monochrome, the spooned arcs of refracted sun. *Kintla* is the Kootenai word for sack: the drainage that leads up to that peak is like a loose bag, wide at the bottom, drawn tight at the top where the creek rockets down off the cliffs through a tapered gap. The summit ridge of Gunsight looks like the notch on the muzzle of a shotgun, from such height the world a target below.

Most peaks have other names, too, names that aren't on the map, the ones chosen by those who have slept and played and traveled and worked in them. *Cabin mountain; the peak where the snow stays year round. Thirsty Pass. The blond bear's mountain, the ridge I climbed in a hailstorm, the one where you left a shovel lying in the thimbleberries, the summit where two old friends died.* Names are our most condensed narrative, the one-, two-, three-word stories we tell ourselves about places we know, or wish to.

The mountains in the North Fork, as in all of the park, were formed by the creative force of tectonic upheaval and glacial revisions. Near a large body of water, an open meadow, or above tree line where the view is unobstructed, geology's alchemy is evident. Eras ago, through compression and uplift and carving, dirt and rock, water and ice turned into mountains. And since then, over centuries, the process reverses. A hard rain, hot summer sun, the freeze and thaw of the darkest days. A forest fire, the warming Arctic's winds. Mountains revert again to dirt and rock, water and ice.

From the high peaks, or the passes below them, you can see glaciers hanging shiny gray in the sun, scant remnants of the ones that shaped this land. Some of them are named, too: Agassiz, Weasel-Collar, Harris, Thunderbird, Two-Oceans. They look impressive, but not vast; small, really, in the context of the world's great ice fields. It's hard to believe these little patches of ice could have once dominated the faces that tower above them. Earth's constant scientific lesson: size is never the whole story. A new reality has emerged in the years since I first discovered Glacier. If I have children, and if they do, those kids won't see a glacier in the park. Like the grizzly bear on California's state flag, the story in Glacier's name will be a nod to something gone, the fact of language no longer matched to the truth of place. How startling, that a world I knew so well could vanish. And that despite my loving it, *in* my loving it, I helped it disappear.

What is *wild?* To Henry David Thoreau, it's "the thrill of savage delight" at a woodchuck in his path, and the urge to sink his teeth in; it's "the preservation of the world." Gary Snyder says the wild is the process and essence of nature, an ordering of impermanence. Annie Dillard gives a lyric: a cat's bloody paws on a pillowcase, things whole and things broken. To Edward Abbey, wild is the one true place, and there are many of them. Wallace Stegner says wilderness is "the geography of hope."

In margins, bedrooms, maps, and minds, wild hovers, lingers, skulks.

Morel mushrooms are hard to cultivate. Once domesticated, certain wild plants—huckleberries, too—do not thrive absent the indigenous chemistry of the places where they grow on their own. Musky and sweet, morel caps look like tiny cone-shaped brains, rutted with grooves and wrinkles. They grow all over the Northwest, dotting especially the understory of a forest recently burned. The first growing season after a fire, the woods burst with both the mushrooms and the camo-clad foragers who crawl on the ground after them. Morels are the North Fork's midsummer currency, bringing in fifteen bucks a pound in the height of the season, and pickers come from all over to fill buckets, pockets, trucks. Picking mushrooms is illegal within the boundaries of the national park except for immediate consumption, so commercial traffic clusters on the dirt road leading north to Polebridge, with limitless access to national forest land on both sides. Mushroom buyers' camps sprout up in response to the supply, huge tents in fields off the dirt road, and the atmosphere is all backwoods Wall Street, people throwing elbows and eyeing the competition, trying to unload their crop before the word comes from buyers' headquarters in Portland that the price has dropped. By late summer the frenzy dies down as pickers migrate to the next seasonal hot spot; locals are left with morels overlooked, the ones hoarded, dried, or stashed in a brown bag under the basement stairs to keep them cool. In late October, when even Indian summer's long gone and the fall rains have begun, morel gravy on mashed potatoes tastes nothing like the distant commerce, only like a chewy mouthful of summer dirt sweetened by fire.

———

Some mornings when I crawl out of my tent and my neck hurts and one sock's gone missing in the bottom of my sleeping bag and my knees pop when I stand up and my breakfast is the crumbs from the bottom of a damp paper bag and a banged-up banana, when the weather's turning and the first huge drops start to fall like they'll go all day and when the saw's carburetor won't stay in tune and the axe handle's busted and I can't stand the sound of my crewmates chewing and my knife isn't in the pocket where I thought I left it and I'm itchy from cow parsnip and old mosquito bites, when I'm out of peanut M&Ms and I want to sleep next to Gabe in a bed where our feet can touch without feeling a zipper and when $13 an hour seems like working for free, I feel crabby and sore. I'd rather have any other job, one without physical misery, or better yet, no job at all. There's a deep rottenness in me: no one's going to please me and the only words I can think of are crass and ugly—*fucking shit job, crappy bastard crewmates.* Where most people go for vacation, I go to dig another boring hole, and how long after I quit will it take for me to associate being in the woods with something other than this goddamn *job*?

In the North Fork, the bugs can be bad, one of the worst places in the park, everyone agrees. By midsummer in a year of normal precipitation, mosquitoes run the place, trailing warm-blooded critters like the cloud of grub that follows Pigpen. They swarm anything that stands still—elk, mules, bears, people—burrowing in ears and nostrils, inserted into any crevice. Which is worse, the raw itch of a bite on sweaty skin, or the whine of a single bug circling the cabin at 2 a.m. when everyone is asleep but you? (Both are worse.)

You can't work for long in the woods without gloves. Some tasks—sharpening chain, clearing a culvert—are better done with bare hands, for dexterity or quick cleanup. But most jobs are eased by gloves. Swinging an axe, dragging brush—without the thick leather palms of gloves to protect them, hands will be blistered, wet, embedded with splinters and the prickly sting of devil's club.

Government-issue gloves, with size stenciled on the gauntlet in black and a little strap to tighten them around the wrist, are ubiquitous. Anyone who's worked for the feds in the woods knows them. Just issued, they're bright white and inflexible (just like the higher-ups, we joke). We use the pliers of multi-tools to turn the gloves inside out so the rigid seams along fingers and palm face outward and the hand slides into smooth, cowhide lining. They're undeniably more comfortable this way, but the exposed seams abrade quickly. By the middle of a ten-day hitch, the thumb yawns like an envelope, the tip of the middle finger worn away. You bring a spare pair of gloves on a hitch, but still keep wearing the old ones, duct-taped, jury-rigged, until after pinching a fingertip through the hole. Like most standardized benefits, government gloves are a mixed blessing. They're free (leather gloves at the Army-Navy store cost upward of $12), but clumsy, inelegant, and cheap.

There's no consensus on favorite gloves; preference varies. Goatskin is tough, deerskin buttery soft. Cotton gloves are cool in summer, but awful in rain, and wear out fast. Neoprene is good for working in wet fall or with submerged hands, but leaves your fingers damp and white, the skin easy to tear. Lined gloves delight on cold autumn mornings, or in unexpected snow, but after ten minutes, they'll be too hot, and do you really want to carry more than one pair for day work?

No glove is a good glove when wet. Wet gloves are slippery inside and out, hot and clammy when you're sweating and icy as soon as you stop moving. And heavy. Wet gloves are worse than a wet hat, but not as bad as wet socks. When you stop for a short lunch in 40-degree rain under the dry tent of a low-branched spruce, is it better to take the wet gloves off, or leave them on? Eating lunch with wet gloves is horrible, and it's hard to mine trail mix with a gloved hand. But taking the gloves off is bad, too, because your hands get cold (unless you keep them in your pockets, which you can't do and still eat), and by the time everyone is shivering badly enough to prefer an extra fifteen minutes of heat-generating work over the rest of the entitled lunch break, the gloves will be soggy and freezing. Sliding a cold hand into a colder glove is like ripping off a Band-Aid; you know it'll be over soon, but it still makes you cringe. You grit your teeth, tense up your stomach muscles, and hope no one notices your whining. But no one is watching. Their gloves are wet and cold, too, unless they've brought a spare pair. In that case, they pull them on and quietly gloat. Comfortable, yes, but then, their gloves will be soaked in ten minutes, and they forfeit the tortured satisfaction that comes from the tolerable, temporary suffering the rest of us share. Who comes out ahead?

Should you have an unexpected shit-in-the-woods scenario, look for "toilet paper plants": false hellebore, thimbleberry, mountain maple. A clump of anything soft works in a pinch—ferns, moss, fireweed leaves rolled tight. Do not use tempting cow parsnip, especially if the sun's out. Its oils are photo-reactive and contact with skin brings an itchy rash that's bad enough on hands.

Forest fires shape the North Fork, as commanding a force as glaciers in eras past. Decades of misguided suppression tactics and climate change's heavy hand have resulted in tinderbox groves throughout the West, and the North Fork's dog-hair lodgepole and spruce forests are easy fodder for conflagration. Late-summer heat, a dry year, a lightning strike, and the skies grow apocalyptic with ash and plume, a dirty glow visible from miles away. Some fires burn out fast and others are nipped in the bud, spotted by the fire lookout, extinguished by initial-attack teams or the glamorous smoke-jumpers who leap from the sky like superheroes. But every few years, Glacier sees a big one, often in the North Fork.

Trail crews are backup Type II firefighters; when the need for people power trumps expertise, we get called in. Sometimes we do day work, washing hoses and cleaning saws, or, if lucky, fly in a helo to a remote cabin for structure protection. Other times, the stint is longer, a detail in fire camp, a little boomtown with canvas tents and trailers, IT systems for payroll, and two catered meals a day, more meat than even a cowboy can stomach. No steaks if you're spiked at a backcountry site or unexpectedly out overnight—then it's MREs with microscopic bottles of Tabasco sauce and space-age meatloaf salty enough to sap out of you whatever moisture hasn't already gone by way of smoke or sweat. Our yellow shirts and green pants, made of fire-resistant Nomex, chafe the skin, and by the end of a two-week tour, they smell like a laboratory that went up in flames.

The world of fire evokes ambivalence in me. Fighting fire can be fun, a welcome late-season break from the monotony of trailwork, a chance to envision ourselves heroes. There's adrenaline and camaraderie, doing good work and bacon every morning, and, of course, overtime pay plus occasional hazard premiums. (Fire seasonals in the West like to sniff smoky air and say, "Smells like money!") But there's also the militarized mentality, the "hurry up and wait," macho smoke-jocks strutting like hopped-up Marines, and the almost-too-hot-to-bear weather that nurtures fire, underwear soaked with sweat. Eventually the sneaky pleasure at getting paid premium wages to play Hacky Sack while "standing by" gives way to demoralizing sluggishness. Weeks of inefficiency and the rumbling machinations of bureaucracy grind all but the staunchest work ethic to a pulp.

Nationwide fire policy has improved dramatically in the past thirty years, with an increasing emphasis on fire ecology and the role it plays in forest health. Some of my best friends work in fire, mapping fuels, plotting burn patterns, and prescribing where to manage a burn and when to let the flames do their work. On the ground, though, a crisis-response outlook still eclipses the long view, and the tone of fire camp lingo is all battle and charge. Epic blazes predicated on prior mismanagement don't do much to help the ordinary citizen see the benefits of fire (for example, certain plants need fire to propagate the way other plants need water), and the media fuel the problem with their drama-hungry emphasis on *homes lost! acres devastated!* In mainstream rhetoric, there's little critique of a continuing trend—multimillion-dollar home construction in fire's version of a flood plain, which increases the human-fire interface and the likelihood of displacement. No one, it seems, can look a guy who's lost his house in the eye and ask him, *Why the hell'd you build it there?* So fire remains nature's whipping boy; a century of bad press is hard to undo in a decade or two, and for many, fire will always be the enemy to be vanquished, not a necessary part of ecosystem health. Smoky the Bear can't be part of the problem, right?

In spite of the media and politics fanning the flames, the smoke eventually goes out. Enough crews on the ground, a rainy spell that raises relative humidity and dampens fuels, or the inevitable September frost puts an end to the burning season. After fire camps pull up stakes and the fat paycheck's been spent on a new truck or a plane ticket or last year's bills, the ash begins to work its way into the soil. Charred stumps smoke and underground roots cradle fire's warmth. Lodgepole pines incorporate the chemistry of ignition into their reproductive ritual, some cones opening to spread seeds only under extreme temperatures. By the following summer, morels will peek out of the ground. Fireweed leads the flower brigade, and in two years, a burn is laced with green plants that draw ungulates to forage.

The talking heads call the blackened landscape of a very hot fire a "holocaust," a "ruin," and people watching TV say, *What a shame.* Which it is, and it isn't. On one hand, this landscape has burned and bloomed for centuries without spokespersons or contingency plans, and really, what lies ruined? Our fragile illusion of control, mostly, which needs a good drubbing. On the other hand, forests are different than they were even ten years ago. Climate change has had documented effects on tree mortality, temperatures, increased lightning strikes, snowpack depth, and snowmelt timing, all of which create imbalance. Fires burn longer and hotter and more frequently than ever. Because of us. There is the shame.

Forest fires strike a chord in part because they force us to confront a fierce Mother Nature, with everything at stake that matters: work, shelter, money, ruin, ego, remorse, power. And also, somewhere in there, love. Love for forests, and for the creatures that live in them, and love for trees, especially the green-needled Christmas-y kind, strung with glittering symbols we don't even realize we've asked them to bear.

How many forms of dirt are there? Loam, clay, muck, dust, grime, loess, fill, mud, silt, grit, soil. Language seems most perfect this elemental. When beneath the single syllable, there is bedrock.

Larch trees grow all over western Montana, from Yellowstone to the Canadian border, bristling the west side of the divide like a five o'clock shadow. They are dense in the North Fork, growing small on the mountains in twisted subalpine form, or in forested valleys, clumped in old-growth groves. The western larch, cousin to the eastern tamarack, is a deciduous conifer, a tree in the pine family that sheds its needles every year and grows new ones the following. In summer, to the unknowing eye, it looks like any evergreen, its brushy branches and elliptical cones blending in amid the Engelmann spruce and Douglas-fir. But closer inspection reveals the larch's distinctive needles clustered on twigs, a vibrant, almost neon-green compared with the duller needles of other trees. Larch feels most singular in autumn, when it shucks its evergreen guise and the needles turn yellow-orange over the course of September and October. A hillside of larch in late fall is a spectacle, trees lighting hills in wavy colored swaths like the aurora borealis gone to ground.

The larch is a well-loved tree in the North Fork. Aside from its autumnal beauty and the brilliant green it lends the summer canopy, it thrives in cold climates, burns hotter in the woodstove than many conifers, makes decent timber for building, and better survives the frequent fires that clear out junk pine and brush from the understory. Also, larch has personality. Its slender branches ringing a one-hundred-foot trunk look, I swear, joyful, silhouetted against sky. The needles bristle, standing at attention like they've been shocked and the tree's aura is at once stately and gleeful, bringing to mind an old man with a joke or a dizzy child balancing.

Up Kintla Lake, the snowstorm dumped a foot and a half in twelve hours. It was May, and assigned to an alpine crew for the rest of summer, this would likely be my only hitch in the North Fork for the year. The foreman sent me and Gabe and our housemate, Kent, an old friend from Missoula days, the one who'd gotten us into this world in the first place. *I work trails*, he'd said when Gabe first met him in the apartment they'd shared on Front Street. *Park Service, up in Glacier. You guys would love it.* In six years, we'd never been on a hitch just the three of us before. Old friends, chainsaws, the North Fork, beer and brats coming in on the mules. Nothing to add.

The first day we'd hiked in seven miles to the cabin at the head of Kintla Lake, clearing light deadfall, maybe two trees per mile, hardly enough work for three. The next day we planned to hike to Upper Kintla Lake, clearing as far as we could get. It was usually a long day, but with such sparse downfall, it looked doable. We woke at dawn and peeked out the cabin window to things changed: blowsy snowflakes, a winter sky over spring ground.

Gabe went to the outhouse first and came back urgent: *Come look, quick!* The new snow was thick and unmarred, a sea of white on which bear tracks stood out like flares: prints as big as pie pans emerging from the woods, past the cabin, disappearing at the shore of the lake. Where did it go? For a swim? We investigated, followed the tracks backward from the beach into the woods. Under the cabin window near the bunks, the four-paw gait pattern shifted to two where the bear must have risen up on its back legs, paws to the pane above Kent's bunk, and peered in while we slept, nose pressed against cool glass. *Them again. Winter's over. The cabin creatures are here.*

Inside, we ate a quick breakfast. Steeped hot drinks, packed our backpacks, topped off the saw and filed the chain, fitted the scabbard around the edge of the felling axe. Bears, snow, whatever. Trail crews work no matter what, something we're proud of.

An hour into morning, a quarter mile from the cabin, we realized the futility of it. The snow was heavy and wet, burying fallen trees so that sinking the saw in where the tree should have been was like slicing through the frosting on a cake, the bar invisible beneath snow. Through safety goggles and thick snow, we could hardly see. As Kent bucked one tree, two fell around us. The late snow, accumulating on branches with roots in thawing ground, was too heavy for the trees to bear and they dropped hard, the way tired kids who've been up too long finally collapse.

In a wet, dark forest with saws running and trees falling, the three of us called it a day. This was nearly unprecedented—in five seasons, I had had perhaps half a day where inclement weather was stiff enough to warrant truancy (then, it was lightning at a high alpine work site, our hair fuzzed out, metal tools tossed aside in the brush.) This day off wasn't hard to justify. Visibility was shit, sawing sketchy. At this rate, we'd have to clear the trail again anyway, and there was no other task to do instead, the drains all covered in snow, the tool cache organized, the cabin clean from last season's closing-up hitch. Reasons aside, why turn down a free day in such a strange and quiet world? We stashed our tools and hard hats, opening senses to the unexpected snow. We hiked a while together before Kent, with wet feet and a sore Achilles, headed back to the cabin, promising hot drinks for us when we returned. After two miles, I turned around, my mind on the book I'd left beneath my sleeping bag that morning, and the hot chocolate Kent would have waiting. Gabe said he wanted to get to the clearing ahead, and he'd catch up. We parted, disappearing into opposite ends of the whiteout.

On the hike back, my noisy mind shut up. Walking in the woods alone, in the snow, in May, was lovely and weird—snow on green ferns, inches of melting white beneath my boots, the sway of quiet through branches. I forgot, as I often do, to call out, to yell, *"Hey bear!"* as is prudent when hiking alone. I forgot myself. Halfway back to the cabin, I saw a bear. Off the trail to my left, lumbering through the trees, snapping branches beneath its feet, a huge male grizzly moved, also alone, parting the snow in the air before it. Unaware of me. Had this one peeked through our cabin window? A stripe of white mapped its spine, flanks falling away like slopes off a high ridge, corniced along the top. I stopped, blood rackety in my veins. I watched the bear move in steady snow with an ambling poise, rolling to one side and the other like a graceful fat man in no particular hurry. Thirty yards away? I saw my hand stretched out in the air, separate from me, palm out, inviting in, warding off. Noticed, it fell to my side.

I didn't want to surprise the bear. It was too late to yell out without alarming it, and I didn't want to jar the stillness. I wanted to watch the bear, keep it in sight for the rest of the day in the snow. But really. I couldn't hike along parallel, risk surprising it suddenly. It would charge me if startled. It was so close.

I kept walking. So did the bear. A minute later it turned toward me, swung its square head, and paused. It wasn't a stop, exactly, just a longer moment between strides. Had it noticed me, or known I was there all along? The bear loped into the woods, disappearing from my view as if it had been erased. I saw its rump peppered with white, then nothing. Snow kept falling. "Hey bear," I sang out when I started walking again. *Hey bear, hey, I saw you, brown bear in a white world, so big how can you be so graceful, so close to me, so far away?*

The next day, the snow had mostly melted and left trees down everywhere. We hiked to our stashed gear and cleared as far as we could, two on saws, one hauling brush, busting ass to absolve ourselves of the previous day's secret. We barely made it to the foot of

Upper Kintla Lake, slowed by heavy steps in the last inches of muddy snow and tangled piles of trees to cut, one after another with barely any hiking between. We followed more bear tracks in the trail, half brown, half white, one set bigger than my hand, a second set much smaller. They preceded our path all day, sometimes veering off trail for a few yards, then joining us again, until, crossing a snow-covered meadow, we lost them for good. The tracks were fresh, from that morning, still crisp around the edges. Two bears together, probably a mother and a subadult cub. Not the curious lake bear, nor the lone male of the day before, his paws like snowshoes. We never saw the mother and cub that day, but they were there, watching for us as we watched for them.

A well-used wooden axe handle is smooth, almost soft, having absorbed the oil of hands. To properly care for a wooden handle over its life, use sandpaper on cracks that may cause splinters or blisters. Rub the handle with linseed or neatsfoot oil when it feels dry. Treated as such, with the care you'd give a friend, an axe becomes a thing you can also rely on. The axes I've used for work have been communal tools, belonging not to an individual, but to the trails shop, to a certain crew, over many years. When I oil the handle of one of these tools, or feel it rotate midswing in my damp palm, I imagine all the people who held this axe before me, men and women who strapped it to their packs, hefted it over shoulders, felt its weight arc out from their arms. They are both teachers and witnesses, and the axe is what they pass on to me, wiping their sweat from its handle, placing it in my hands.

ROCK BAR

Usage A rock bar, sometimes called a pry bar, is an essential tool for
trailwork, especially in high alpine areas where most trail structures—
steps, retainers, culverts, walls—are made of rock, not metal, not
wood. (Above treeline, the tiny gnarled alpine larch and Krumholtz
spruce hold little architectural potential.) A rock bar is typically five
feet long, weighing sixteen to eighteen pounds with a beveled tip.

Simple Machine A rock bar works because of leverage. Slide the beveled
end under a rock, the curve facing the ground. With fulcrum in place,
push down slightly on the handle and the rock will lift, your effort
magnified. If the curve faces the rock, not the ground, the fulcrum is
misplaced and any advantage will slip away. As with all hand tools, the
rock bar asks for wise use. (A tool, like a word, can be used badly, its
beauty rendered moot by carelessness.) Physics ignored, the rock bar
is just a heavy stick.

Safety A fulcrum operates on the pinching principle, so careful monitoring
of hands (in gloves) and toes (in leather boots) is a must. A rock bar is
often used with more than one person, so teamwork becomes critical.
Make sure everyone involved understands the big picture, each step
in the move before it begins. If you don't know what's happening, or if
you enter the scene late, please stay out of the way.

Weight A rock bar is made of tempered steel, with almost no flex even
under great pressure. Its weight, though loathsome when hiking it on
your shoulder, has a clearly apparent advantage when compared with
a shovel, which, if used to pry, almost always snaps at the handle or
bends at the head. A rock bar's weight is also handy when the tool is
used as a drop hammer to widen cracks in rock or drive in a stubborn
chock.

Comparison Things you carry over your shoulder that are heavier than a
rock bar: the powerhead of a rock drill, a gassed-up 036 chainsaw, an
axe with a full five-gallon Dolmar hung off the handle, a power brusher,
a cluster of zip-tied rebar, a burlap sack of log spikes, a Griphoist.
What's lighter than a rock bar: an empty 026 chainsaw, a rock rake, a
shovel, a pair of skis, tent poles, an eight-foot two-by-six, a fishing rod.

Relatives Don't mistake the digging bar (or spud bar) for a rock bar—a
digging bar is five or six feet long with a paddle blade on one end and
a disk handle on the other, and unsupervised, a green laborer may
grab it from the tool cache. The blade handily digs postholes, and the
disk tamps down dirt, but the bar is too long and flexible for prying,
and if you use it for rockwork, you're courting an iron fist to the teeth.
A crowbar—some versions known as a wonder bar or cat's paw—has a
curved claw for pulling up nails and removing joined beams or spiked
logs, but is too short for rock use. Other steel bars have a squared-off
end and can be used for tamping and battering, but the lack of a bevel
will make them ineffectual tools for moving heavy things.

Common Injuries A bloody lip from a slipped handle or a crewmate who
moves in an unpredictable manner; a strained lower back, when
tempted to dead-lift instead of prying or rowing; split fingers or pinched
toes, when a rock suddenly slips its fulcrum and finds its natural
resting place; tarnished pride, when sometimes, at 125 pounds
soaking wet, even with a rock bar's mechanical advantage, you've
bitten off more than you can chew. Also, watch your crotch when lifting
off a fulcrum. Never straddle the bar's handle. If it slips with you above
it, you'll holler (female) or puke (male).

CHAPTER 2

Sperry: Alpine
(All I ever needed to know I learned above tree line)

The story of the Sperry Trail crew is the story of women. In a field where "boys" outnumber "girls" by roughly the same margin as in childhood sandlot baseball games, the Sperry district—one of the alpine kingdoms on Glacier's west side—was, during my trails tenure, run by women. I stumbled into this lineage my first season, following Reba around the district with a tool in each hand, trying to keep up with her nimble feet and constant stream of chatter. She seemed to me back then as salty as they came, a feisty woman with a dirty mouth who loved to ski and worked her summer job to support her winter habit. She tromped along taut ridgelines strung across sky and she told stories: *Abby built that retaining wall with a broken thumb. The Middle Fork guys climb peaks on the clock every single hitch! If so-and-so sharpens the saw, he still puts the chain on backward damn near every time. Once Danny got lost while he was taking a dump, fucking hilarious! If you tell we got the saw stuck twice on the same tree, I'll deny it!* Sometimes she complained, and when unsure of herself she could lash out mean, but Reba told on herself with at least as much fervor as she told on everyone else, a reflexive cackle that kept her just this side of gossip. She hoisted trails lore like a glass for a toast, and I was thirsty for it.

Other women were more peripheral than my first crew leader,

but no less memorable. Sherri was barely five feet tall and could out-drink men twice her size; plus she could take apart and reassemble a chainsaw without losing a screw or e-clip, a skill I appreciated more once I'd lost a few myself. After law school, Sherri realized she didn't want to be a lawyer, so she started working seasonally to pay off student loans. I wouldn't be surprised if she's doing it still. Annie was smart and lithe with a handful of advanced degrees and a wicked sewing habit. She made costumes for a big-city opera in the winter and patched worn Carhartts with artistic flair. One year, she sewed hiking kilts for her crew, pleated nylon complete with Fastek buckles. Annie was quirky, with crushes on new boys every year, but was most faithful to her mountain bike, which she rode, fearless, leaving her dates in the dust with skinned knees, hearts pounding. Then there was Abby, a legend by the time I arrived. She'd been a crew leader for years, and she left Glacier my second season for a trails job in Alaska. Abby had the kind of upper-body strength most women never attain. She ran ultramarathons before they were hip and baked memorable brownies. She wielded the chainsaw fast, slashing through limbs above her head, putting in face cuts in seconds. People spoke of her respectfully; she was competent, but also a little rash. Who knew what she'd do?

I apprenticed myself to these women. I studied them, envied their tight-veined hands, tanned wrinkles shooting from their eyes, their easy cussing and the way they strode in their logging boots. At first, I felt pale and skinny in contrast, my hands soft from books, bootlaces always untied. I couldn't ski. I hated Miller Lite. Years later, now that I've been the longtimer younger women looked to, I wonder if Reba and Annie and Abby and Sherri felt like role models. Whether they guessed I wanted what they had, even if I didn't know exactly what it was.

Sixteen years after our first season together, Reba is still a friend. She's a nurse now, and lives south of Glacier with two lively girls and her husband, Rob, a timber framer. Their annual Christmas letters boast photos of Reba hiking in the park with her daughters, past rock walls we built. Annie writes me a postcard once in a while. She's been back to school again, had what our mothers call a "real job" in the Midwest, but kept her house in Montana. Abby and Sherri moved on to other parks, and we haven't been in touch. But when I sharpen a hand tool or drop my knee into a telemark turn, when I teach a newbie to place rocks in a wall that will outlast us both, I think of those women in their flannel shirts and tank tops and work pants, marching around in the sun, packs over their shoulders, modeling for me a possibility. I didn't know then about their worries and insecurities, didn't guess about the eating disorder, fights with a new husband, the joints wearing out, wanting to fall in love for real. Later, I'd see their faults—short-tempered, quick to blame—and also the fullness that comes from vulnerability. But first, I saw toughness, that assurance and vigor. I couldn't take my eyes off it.

Few people in this century know the language of mules. It's an almost-lost dialect, like the words of second-generation immigrants or children growing out of their make-believe tongues. Packers speak this language fluently—what you say to talk about loading and riding and caring for stock, and what you say to the animals themselves. To talk about packing mules, you say:

String: *n*—A group of mules linked by ropes joining the bridle of one mule to a saddle ring on the one behind it. Use: "I'll have a string of five today." A packer leads a string on horseback, though in steep terrain, may dismount and lead the string by hand.

Load: *n*—A pair of evenly weighted parcels that ride one to a side of a packsaddle. A load is made up of bear-proofed ammo boxes (for food and supplies), or toolboxes (open crates with a leather strap to lash down contents), or soft bags (for clothes, tents, sleeping bags) called "duffel." A load is made up of two parcels, but is counted as one, corresponding with how many mules it will take to carry it. If asked, "How many loads you got?" you'd answer, "Three." Six parcels for three loads for three head of stock. Don't get this wrong and answer, "Six loads," or the packer will ready twice as many mules as he needs, and when he finds out your mistake, he'll tear you a new one.

Manta: *n/v*—Pronounced "manny," a large square of off-white duck cloth (tan after one season) for wrapping equipment into loads that can be tied easily onto a packsaddle with manta ropes. The verb form is the act of preparing such loads. As in, "We gotta be at the barn to manny up before eight" or "Do you need a hand mannying?"

To talk to mules, you say, *Hey there girl, easy now, tchk-tchk, hush, hey, pshht, get on back, slow up, shhh.* You talk softly to calm, or loudly to command, but never so loud as to startle. (Only a salty packer can cuss at the top of his lungs without eliciting mayhem.) You make what noises seem right, ones that flow out of your mouth easy, a song or a curse, depending on the moment. When you know the animals, it's instinct.

Learn mule-speak as any language: immersion is best. Hang around the barn mouth shut, ears open. Say nothing for a long time, just listen to the packers talk, and when you are ready to try the words you think you've learned, you'll sound funny at first, to you and to them. It's better if you're humble.

Most of the Sperry district is above tree line, in alpine terrain. The patron saint of alpine crews is Archimedes, who stated, "Give me the place to stand and I shall move the Earth"; his lever is our most reached-for tool. I met the rock bar on a steep switchback halfway up the Sperry Trail, where my crew was to build a series of check steps. Reba pointed to the rocks she had in mind and explained the process. We'd bury them perpendicular to the trail, half stair tread, half barrier for fill, to prevent erosion. The rocks she chose were twenty-five yards off-trail, grown over with alpine plants. But big. Clearly big. Reba told me the number one rule of rockwork: if you can move it by yourself, it's not big enough. I couldn't move much by myself, but even so, the point was clear. Mass meant stability and stability meant resilience. Rockwork has to withstand traffic, erosion, and time.

We walked uphill to the rocks, Reba carrying the bar over her shoulder like Paul Bunyan's take on Huck Finn's hobo stick. I kicked at the base of her chosen boulder with the toe of my boot. It didn't budge. Reba dug around the edges with the pick mattock until she exposed a corner enough to ram the tip of the rock bar beneath. She pushed the bar downward and forced the rock up and out of its bed. Though the tool was self-explanatory, its mechanical principles obvious to any dummy, there were little tricks, smarter ways of use. Through trial and error, I learned to reef a rock upward with hardly any effort, jam rocks beneath it to hold it at an apex, and reposition. You could move a rock forward by sliding the bar under the front corner and rowing it along. You could jack a boulder up high so that it would flip over and move itself. You tried to choose a rock uphill of your work site: one flip could start a fast tumble and all you had to do was step out of the way. I grew fond of the rock bar. I was small and it was elegant. Together, we approximated strength, which I coveted more than a milkshake on day six of a hitch.

Of course, the rock bar amplified the potential of people much stronger than I, so their advantage remained. In Max's hands, the rock bar looked like a kitchen utensil. The same tool that I had to heft with two hands he'd curl in his fingers like a stray toothpick. I could not imagine what it would be like to be that powerful. At six-foot-three and a lean 210 pounds, Max never needed help. In his fifteenth season working trails, he knew how to do everything. He intimidated me from afar, his mythic quality buoyed by dogged stoicism. But before long, I realized Max was shy and a little awkward, kinder than he seemed when I first saw him tossing tools into the trucks. He took trailwork very seriously, could lose his temper in an unpredictable flash, but he was also humble, and the slightest teasing would make him blush. I tried to make Max smile with pointed ribbing, or by telling stories full of loony details, my hands like frenzied birds.

We worked for weeks one summer on the Highline Trail, Glacier's crown jewel carved out of bedrock, and Max ran the seventy-pound rock drill, harnessed by ropes perpendicular to the granite walls, his forearms as big around as my thighs. I hammered away at hard-to-reach cracks with the tip of the rock bar and shoveled shards of busted rock off the side of the trail. At lunch break, buoyed by the crew's high spirits and the panoramic view, I planted the rock bar on its end, bent my lips to its handle like a floor mic, and belted out "I Love Rocks and Rolls," tweaking the lyrics for a trails verse, swinging my hips to make Joan Jett proud, and out of the corner of my eye I was pleased to see Max shaking his head, a loose smile on his face. We all have our strengths.

Glacier lilies bloom where snow just left, as allusive as if winter trailed a scent on its exit. Avalanche lilies, as they're called, flood couloirs and runout zones where late snow lingers. Bears churn up the ground in spring, focused on lily roots. Native people prize them in soup or raw. Unlike summer-lingering fireweed or dogged larkspur, these spiky yellow lilies blow through fast, following snowline as it creeps upward, melting. Sometimes they poke through patches of slush. In June down low, in August at high elevation, one week snow, one week blooms, next week gone. Here's to you, glacier lily, you cusp flower, winter's bright shadow.

What tourists say to a traildog: *Digging for gold? Wish I were young again! Who'd you kill? Do you pick up after the horses? Find what you're looking for yet? What a commute! Where's your ranger hat? Well isn't that nice, you're cleaning up the forest. Are you on the chain gang? What did you do to deserve this work? Thank you for your efforts. Nice office! Seen any bears? Doing time?*

A woman on a trail crew is like a dog in a swimming pool. Even if it can swim, when it jumps in, it gets noticed. The simple fact of show-ing up for work female announces itself. First, there's the regular sizing up, the kind women are used to in any setting (*What's she look like? Is she my type?*), an unspoken commentary we might be privy to later, when we're one of the gang: "I've got a hottie on my crew!" or "Have you seen so-and-so in a tank top?" Then there's the extra level that happens in labor jobs (*Does she seem strong? Will she be a whiner? Can she take a dirty joke?*). Such taking stock is not a one-way street, of course; women do it, to men, to each other. But when "the new girl" enters a trails shop, she isn't rating all the guys; maybe later, but right then there are too many, and they're watching too close. There's a pressure to the air. An attentiveness, the animal instincts tuned in.

Sometimes, we're singled out in ways that seem superficially kinder than the meat-market perusal. Men will say they like having women on crews because it keeps them honest, makes for better con-versation, and because women tend to "work smarter, not harder." All of which are often true, and I know the men who say these things mean well. But like any classification that primarily locates some-one in opposition to someone else, such kindly analyses can ring annoying to the one being characterized. Like blacks—great rhythm! And gay men—that eye for color! And redheads—boy are they feisty! Fawning stereotypes are as unwelcome as cruel ones, because they build you a box before you get to make your own.

Some women respond to stereotype by overswinging—trying to be the crassest, filthiest, most macho—a façade that's unappealing, let's face it, in *people*, male or female. I have little use for this labor version of the Madonna/whore dichotomy, where girls may be either the bawdiest of the bunch or the grounded earth mothers who keep the crew clean and modest, but nothing in between. Who among us takes a woods job in order to be the most foul, or worse, a civilizing influence?

We don't need men, though, to be aware of gender, and when it's just women, we jostle each other in sorority, all the while at watch. We brush up against each other's body images every day, all of us raised in an appraising world, taught to scrutinize others and ourselves. One woman constantly tends her physical appearance, lipgloss always fresh; another won't skinny-dip at lunch break; one prefers the end of the hike line so no one can look at her butt. We know where we fit: who eats more, gains least, whose back is injured, who's had knee surgery, some breasts too large for comfortable hiking downhill, some too small to be evident in a baggy T-shirt, the tactful averting of eyes while we peel off sweaty bras at the end of a workday, the rubbing of sunscreen into shoulders and backs. We notice each other's bodies—the beautiful angles and the sweaty reek, the smooth curves and the puckered bulges—and we circle each other in the same dance we know from junior high, from office jobs, from locker rooms, these bodies different only because we are so fully *in* them.

Here's the twist. Those same bodies, so inhabited, provide us the ungendered moments, too, the times when cultural roles and physical parts deconstruct and we become people working side by side. The best times, with men and women, are those when the moment demands every last thing and there's no room in the brain, no will in the muscles, for the extraneous *who's stronger nice ass I'd sleep with.* We aren't checking each other out, and we even forget to evaluate ourselves, free for moments from awareness and appraisal. Self-consciousness dissipates the longer we know each other, when the initial mysteries of pheromone deepen into the mysteries of personhood. Such moments happen when there are miles to cover in pouring rain, a huge project all but done. They happen while we sweat buckets, if a bear's nearby, when dinner hits the spot. You can see it in our movements, that easy grace of a child at home in her body without a glance to the stands. Maybe we can release our assumptions and assessments in those moments when the physical world becomes so primary because our human skin has sloughed away. When sweating, moving, grunting, relaxing after it's done, stuffing stomachs or stretching our arms to the sky, we aren't men or women. We're animal.

Of course, the sniffing we do later, circling each other, pissing on fence posts, jockeying for position, yearning for contact, that's as animal as it gets, isn't it? But that's sex. Sex is simpler. Beneath the constant specter of gender, the best we can do is pardon one another small vanities, the missteps and awkwardness that arise when men and women work hard together, few of us altogether comfortable in our own skins, constantly negotiating our places on the spectrum between *opposite* and *same*.

The historic Sperry chalet is an elegant two-story structure built in 1914, its native-stone foundation and wooden-railed porches perched on a cliff overlooking Sperry Creek. The headwaters of Sperry tumble west of the Continental Divide, through a hanging valley below Comeau Pass, and join McDonald Creek, 2,500 feet below. The chalet's design suggests, as it was meant to in the nationalistic early days of the Park Service, an American Europe, a destination rivaling Switzerland for the well-traveled elite.

There's a new cabin now, but in my day, the Sperry trails cabin sat behind the chalet, anchored to rock slab, rough-hewn and off-kilter, the bastard stepchild of local architecture. Made of painted plywood, absent the chalet's Swiss ethos and void the historical charm of patrol cabins in the Middle Fork, the Sperry cabin was the bare bones it takes to shelter a crew in an alpine area. The Granite Park crew in the alpine district to the northeast has a beautiful log cabin with a loft and a front porch, a hole blasted in the slab out front so that Granite Creek fills a frigid bathtub. No such luck at Sperry: old carpet scraps on the floor, mangy dish towels hanging from the p-cord clothesline, shelves behind the fold-down table housing left-over nonperishables from years of crews, including MREs from the forties and enough cans of Hungry Man to jack up the floor box, should the rotting foundation finally collapse.

In its favor, the cabin's humble profile protected the trail crew from the hordes of guests at the chalet, few of them curious about what appears to be a tool shed or a pump house, so we could maintain privacy in close range of tourism. Out behind the cabin, an unnamed creek flowed over bedrock in all but the driest years, and the view at night was clear and starry. The chalet folk went to bed and the night quieted, the waterfalls in the cirque below Comeau Pass a distant thrum. When I stumbled out at 3 a.m. to pee, the dark mountains seduced me from sleep to stand and listen to the night until my feet got cold. Even compared with the palatial digs at Granite or the rustic funkiness of the Park Creek ranger cabin, there was magic at the Sperry slum, closed in by plywood, capped by a tilting, rusted vent pipe. When you're dead tired and in love with the world, the shabbiest trappings can make for home.

The eight-day hitch song: *Day 1, trails is fun! Day 2, yahoo! Day 3, still some glee. Day 4, what a bore. Day 5, still alive. Day 6, in a fix. Day 7, feels like eleven. Day 8, ready to MATE!*

My first season at Sperry with Reba was short. I was hired late, on a fluke, started in July, and by mid-September laborers were laid off. The next year, budget cuts were deep and I didn't make the list (Gabe did). Dejected, I made plans in Missoula, and by the time a trails job came through after all, it was too late to back out of them. No one can complain about summer in Missoula, but I missed trails like I'd been fired from my life's work. I worried I'd lost my chance at a future spot, labeled that worst of all tags: "short-timer." But the next spring, new money came through, and I was offered reentry into a world I'd tasted just enough of to know I wanted in for good.

Returning, I was not exactly a newcomer, but anyone could see it: I knew very little. Experience teaches, after all, and two months in the woods two years before is not much experience. Reba wasn't back at Sperry, where I'd been hired to return. Instead, I'd be working for Cassie, who'd come from the east side to lead our two-woman crew.

The first things I heard about Cassie were "she's hot" and "her boyfriend died." As little information as that is about the person who is to become your boss, it's enough to make you worry. What does hot have to do with trailwork, and will she make you feel clumsy and second-rate, or worst, what if she's the kind of girl who hates other women, competitive and flirty? Then there was the boyfriend. Tristan had been a traildog, too, a kid Gabe had worked with the summer before, young and strong and quick to laugh. He'd died that year in a climbing accident on a peak in the North Fork. He was Cassie's high school sweetheart. It was a tragedy that the trail crew had processed together then, when I was not around, and I didn't know how to frame it on my own. Would she be paralyzed by sadness? Should I broach it, or pretend I didn't know? The hurdles seemed many. It could have been very awkward, working with a hot and brokenhearted woman. I have to admit, I worried.

But I liked Cassie right from the start. She was tough, with a fragility belied by ripped biceps and a brutal hiking pace. She had only a few trails seasons beneath her belt, and she seemed young, which was saying something, since I myself felt young. (She had just graduated from college, while I had been out for two years.) The older sister in me could imagine looking out for her, even though she'd be teaching me. We bonded early, oddly early, looking back at what I know about us then—me shy and eager, her guarded and sad, both under pressure, often just the two of us working for days on end. I've had similar situations that went poorly, the two-person crew with a barely tolerable mate, personalities mismatched, outside-of-work stresses insurmountable. We were lucky.

From the outside, we were a funny pair. Cassie was almost aggressively feminine—jewelry and lipstick and sports bras for work—while I was a tomboy in baggy T-shirts and a ball cap. (In one picture of us, standing arms around shoulders at a high pass, I could be her brother.) She'd grown up in nearby Whitefish, the park her hometown backyard, while I knew it as a breathless latecomer. She read *Cosmopolitan*, knew about skin creams and Manolos, familiar to me only from furtive grocery-line perusal. Her lost Tristan was a palpable sadness, and dear Gabe, his presence in my life, must have augmented that empty space.

But the differences crumbled before the bricks that helped cobble together a foundation for a trust that would grow deep over four years working together. Both English majors, we read voraciously, British comedies of manners and courtroom thrillers, and we discovered a mutual penchant for word games, which we'd play hiking to and from job sites. I was a goofball, and under the surface, serious. Cassie was serious, and under the surface, a goofball. We were small and fast and tenacious, competitive to a fault, but also good sports. As we grew to trust each other in the field—*she knows her stuff, she'll pull her weight, she's got my back*—so we let each other into the rest of our lives. She talked me through tough spells with Gabe, and on the anniversary of Tristan's death we toasted him and I hugged her hard.

The clincher, though, was our raging appetites, a product of genes and the ramped-up metabolism that accompanies manual labor. Weighing a buck twenty-five a piece (in boots) we packed lunches you could barely carry with one hand, containers overflowing with bloated versions of the school lunch: Dagwood sandwiches, cold pizza, string cheese, animal-shaped gummy snacks, candy bars. On cold days, I ate hoarded restaurant packets of butter and Cassie spread cream cheese so thick it looked like Styrofoam on her bagel. On eight-day hitches at our backcountry cabin, we'd devour an entire smoked trout with a box of crackers after work, crunching tiny bones while we prepared "real dinner." We mounded cheesy casseroles and fat burritos in our big steel bowls, which we called troughs.

One night, after filling out a *Cosmo* quiz that gave us the right caloric needs for our frames, we calculated our intake for the day at around 6,800 calories each, more than three times the highest thinkable allowance (for active pregnant women). To this day, when I hear the phrase "the way to a man's heart is through his stomach," I think of Cassie, how we weaseled our way into each other's hearts over those two-quart Tupperware boxes at lunch time, how our friendship flared over a Coleman stove where rice, ravioli, dumplings boiled in quantities large enough to stun us both.

The Sperry Hill is steep. It winds from the McDonald Lake trailhead through cedar forest, then rears back and pitches six miles up the Sprague Creek drainage, leveling off only a few times before terminating at the chalet. The lower section is the worst, rutted, dusty even after rain; but the middle section has killer switchbacks and the final hill below the chalet is gruesome because it comes after you've already given away everything you had, and tourists who rode up on horseback stand at the top in a chatty gauntlet. The Sperry Trail always gets a groan in the early season—*Y'ain't even roughed-in yet*, the packers would say—but a month in, it's doable, easy, even, nothing like the legendary Trout Lake Trail, uphill both ways and always demoralizing with a saw on your shoulder, or Cut Bank Pass, which could use a handrail to pull against.

Early my first summer, we hiked four miles up Sperry for the annual blast. A permanent snowdrift blocked the trail and melted out slowly; without dynamite, it would impede summer hiking traffic all season. The blast was exciting and novel every year, the drama of explosion, the break from early-season digging drains, a big group of traildogs from different crews all sent up to play in the snow for a day. But first we had to get there, and I wasn't thinking about explosives or snowballs as I sucked wind, throat full of bile, the packers closing in. I could feel horse breath on my neck. I still remember this hike as one of the hardest physical challenges of my life—worse than backpacking up out of the Grand Canyon with a hangover and no water, worse than day five of a three-week winter ski trip with frost-nipped, blistered toes, worse than picking through a crevasse field on an Alaska glacier in a whiteout—because on the Sperry Hill that day, I had no idea what lay ahead but I knew I was flailing. So did everyone else.

I've hiked that trail probably a hundred times since then, with a rock bar, a chainsaw, a brusher, packing a seventy-pound Pionjar that pressed my heart flat, with a wheeled litter carrying a sobbing, heavy hiker thrown from horseback. I've hiked it trying to dust twelve new laborers, and trying to catch Jake Preline, the Sperry Hill record holder. I've hiked it with a migraine, in 90-degree heat, with giardia (shitting every half mile in the bushes), in thunderstorms that shook bedrock. Though Sperry is relentless and steep, it's much less formidable once familiar, once you can hike it in your mind, each section memorized—when to breathe deep and conserve energy, when to bow your head and drop the hammer. When to drink water so you won't belch it up again, which curve hides a straightaway where you can make up some time, or a series of short pitches that'll burn your quads.

The day of the blast, the packers finally passed me with their load of ANFO in Ziploc bags. At the time I didn't realize that the string passes everyone now and then, whether because you're having a slow day or Slim's spurring hard to stay on your ass. Narcissist that I was, seeking distinction even in humiliation, I thought I was surely the weakest link in the entire history of traildogs. Later, Reba told me Slim said, *She's got grit, I'll give her that.* Such a begrudging compliment, high praise from a surly packer, but I'd have none of it. Damned grit! Fucking tenacity! I'd happily trade pluck for sheer strength, for technical prowess, for usefulness of any kind. They say I'm scrappy, determined, tough. Yet surely everyone had guessed my secret, which is that it wasn't innate, which is how many times I wanted to veer off the trail and hide in the brush, which is the only thing that kept me from lying down in a pile was pride. Still, in the absence of anything but the famed tenacity, I had to cling to it. Whether or not it came natural, if I gave up grit, I'd have *nothing*.

Gabe and I spent summers together in six-day stretches. That first night off hitch, a week stretched ahead endless, long enough for the first day at home doing nothing, the exquisite luxury of laundry and showers, an elaborate meal in a real kitchen, sex and foot rubs, swimming in the river on a hot evening, renting a movie on a rainy one. Then, four days left for trips, cragging at the reservoir, nights out in the tent, or a bunch of day hikes, climbing peaks, remote traverses, guiding out-of-town visitors to favorite places. The last day meant town, for groceries and supplies, a stop at the bookstore, then home to portion out food and prepare meals together for the next go. We packed the truck the night before, snuggled in cool sheets with the pre-hitch feeling mounting, the dawning idea of work in the morning, so long ago now we forgot we had jobs at all. Six a.m. came and we slipped sweet notes into each other's duffels, buried treats in the bottom of daypacks, snuck a quick kiss at the barn. On hitches, the occasional veiled radio contact, the "10-4, got your message, 253 clear" meant to us "All good on my end, I'd jump your bones if you were here," and the eager pitch to the stomach on day eight, hiking out with the adolescent quease, *This afternoon I'll see him again.*

Here's a favorite story in the trail crew canon: an east-side crew is doing rockwork on a busy trail, six or seven spread over several hundred yards. Two hikers approach, one lagging behind, so the first hiker stops near the crew, panting, hands on his fleshy hips, safari hat with a wide brim, bear bells jingling. The comment comes: *Who's the boss around here, anyway?* Somebody, let's say it's Kent, gestures down trail at Marcy. She's edging a rock step with a chisel. Near forty, she's been leading Glacier crews for more than fifteen years.

"Her?" The hiker pauses. "You're sayin' the *girl's* the boss?" Kent nods. Of course Marcy's the boss. Who else?

"The GIRL'S the *boss?*" the hiker asks again. He shouts back to his friend: "Hey Joe! Guess whut! The girl's the boss!"

Joe stops. "Whud you say?"

"Ah said, the girl's the boss!"

"Whud's that, the *girl's* the boss?"

"Yeah, I said the *GIRL*. Is. The *BOSS!*" It goes on, at top volume. Joe catches up, pink-faced and sweaty. They cackle longer, trying to get a rise out of Marcy, failing. When the men finally hike out of earshot, the crew loses it, rolling in the dust, tools helter-skelter. They can't breathe.

We choose certain stories for retelling, like any subculture; not every anecdote gets codified. Why this one? It's hilarious, for one, with the pleasure of reenacting ridiculous behavior: stories with dramatic potential get the most replay. Also, it gently mocks tourists, or better yet, lets them mock themselves, and if there's a uniting factor among seasonals, it's that we love to laugh at tourists. In a world where our status is tenuous and somewhat stigmatized—hourly wages, little recognition, no guarantees—we have the power that emplacement grants. Most of us are not "locals" by strictest measure, but no matter how short our time here, whether we hail from Kalispell or Kansas, we aren't visitors; for now, we belong.

But in this case, even the tourist is incidental. "The *girl's* the *boss*" is the part that matters, the relic, the fox's grapes. This simple phrase gestures toward a complexity we rarely talk about but instinctively know: the subtext of rank, who answers to whom, the realigning assumptions about gender, and the distance left to go before we're all so equal, we don't think about it anymore. There's something perfect about this story, the hiker's disbelief, and the truth of what he finds so difficult to grasp. Despite the parody, the ignorance even, the story's truth stands: the girl *is* the boss. While the crew howls, Marcy smiles, taps her chisel until the shard falls away.

The dictionary says argillite is sedimentary rock, fine-grained and made up of hardened clay particles. Geology says argillites are mud turned to stone, compacted silt, kin to shale, slate, schist. Art says the Rockies' argillites are pink and green (iron oxidization, science interrupts), bright in rain, colored in Gauguin's palette. Traildogs say argillite is plentiful along the trails that skirt the passes and ridges of the Lewis Range; unlike many sedimentary rocks, it doesn't split easily, but when it does, leaves angling planes ideal for tight-jointed rockwork. Experience says at the top of the last rise before Comeau Pass, the trail winds across a bench where rocks look dropped from sky like huge dice—hulky blocks you can climb up on for lunch and look over the three miles of trail below, down to the tiny chalet, out past Lake McDonald to the Apgar Hills, to the North Fork. History says that Precambrian Belt sedimentary rocks were displaced during Tertiary time eastward onto Cretaceous rocks by the Lewis thrust fault. The rangers say the park has been the setting for at least ten periods of glaciation. Hazy late afternoon says it's 90 degrees down in the valley, so sit a while longer on the rocks in the sun, let your hair get hot while the breeze dries sweat on skin. The wind says *sun water dust rest stone.*

Packers are cowboys; ours were Sheldon, Slim, and Greg. Slim was tall and skinny and hard as chert; Greg, round and jolly with a huge belly, a handlebar mustache, and a redneck twang; and Sheldon, the fairest, quiet and dapper, with sandy hair and a singsong mumble. Sheldon wore a white felt hat and, on days off, fancy western shirts tucked into pressed Wranglers. Greg usually sported a summer straw, and was prone to expressions like "cotton-picker" and "sumbitch."

Slim wore a black hat swiped right off the villain in a fifties western. At first it was his foul mouth that caught you off guard, and later when you'd come to expect the cussing, his high, girlish laugh would do the same.

Glacier has a lifetime's worth of mountains to climb. My first was Lincoln Peak, just above our Sperry cabin. Anyone who knows Lincoln will smirk; it's hardly a peak at all, just a bump on a ridgeline punctuated with craggy outcrops and a window-size hole in the rock where sky peeks through the ridge from the other side. I had climbed a few peaks before, scrambled a scree pile in the Sierra as a college student, snowshoed low summits in the White Mountains, seconded a six-pitch classic in Yosemite. But I hadn't been alone in the mountains much, not enough to trust my judgment. What was too steep? Which way was best? Where was the danger?

From Lincoln Peak you can see Gunsight Mountain farther up the ridge, at 9,000 feet, and across Comeau Pass from Gunsight, Mount Edwards at 8,900 feet, and massive Jackson, visible to the southeast, one of the five 10,000-footers in Glacier. I would climb those three several times each over the course of my hitches in the district, but few summits in the park are as memorable as my short hike up Lincoln. A windy evening, a little rain spitting. Reba below in the cabin eating dinner, tourists at the chalet milling about, Gabe up the divide at Granite Park, and me, alone on that tiny bump, part tentative, part brave, squelching my vertigo, daring myself against the wind to tiptoe along that unfamiliar skein of sky.

Reba gave me my first trails nickname: #2, like the pencil. Lanky with a fuzzy blond eraser on top, I was second on the crew, so it fit, the slight mockery ensuring I'd remember that I was not #1. (As if I'd had the slightest delusion.) Mitch called me *Half Scoop*, a riff on Laura Ingalls, earned one hot afternoon in a rocky fill pit where I could hardly fill my shovel. *CB* was common, suggesting a trucker's handle. *That girl,* the packers' favorite. Later, *Stretch,* for my long stride, *Throttle,* for my tendency to gun lagging diesel engines on a cold start, peeling out like a teenage boy. *Snick* was bestowed upon me by backcountry skiing pals, for the Snickers I ate whenever we were out longer than ten minutes. *Trouble,* because, supposedly, I was always asking for it.

The Sperry crew spent at least one hitch per season at Lake Ellen Wilson, a turquoise tarn so cold you'd shout when swimming even on torrid August days. Once Cassie and I paddled to work in an inflated one-man fishing raft we'd hidden in a manty load—two of us and our daypacks and rock tools jammed in between the rubber gunnels. We moored the raft under a cliff band, scrabbled up scree to the job site, and relished the coolest commute in the world. By 5:30, though, the up-valley winds kicked in, and like a freeway at rush hour, the evening trip took more than two hours, our rock-work-weary arms hardly able to paddle against the gusts. I watched ospreys and golden eagles coasting on the drafts above, the same wind that stopped us short boosting their flight to acrobatic levels. After that, the raft stayed at camp. Instead, we'd hike the twenty minutes home from work and take turns drifting out in the lake, Cassie in a bikini with the straps pushed down to counteract her farmer's tan, and me in a sports bra and the worn-out Carhartts I'd chopped the legs off of with a pulaski, having forgotten shorts.

The storms off Lake Ellen Wilson were intense. One hitch, it poured for seven of eight days. Cassie stayed high and dry on an air mattress so thick she'd wedged it inside her tent half-inflated and blown it up the rest of the way from inside, but Bernadette, the newest laborer, had a puddle on her floor that soaked her sleeping bag and she worked the last two days with borderline hypothermia. Ellen Wilson could be such a bitch.

On day eight, we'd break camp: lower the coolers from the bear pole (wilted bits of lettuce, limp string cheese, a slice of iridescent roast beef afloat in melted ice), flatten the tents, secure the tools in their special boxes. While waiting for the packers to inch down the long, steep descent into our camp, we'd take a dip in the lake in preparation for the scorching nine miles between us and the truck at the trailhead. On the hike out, the string of mules not far behind, the trail passed a tiny kettle pond much nearer the Sperry cabin, nick-named Lake Willie Nelson. Coming from Ellen Wilson, we laughed remembering hitches where we'd parted the algae from the top of this pond in order to swim. The raft would have filled half of it. Could we really have been that desperate?

What tourists say to a female traildog: *How'd a pretty girl like you get a job like this? What, are all the men too lazy? I wish I could have done that when I was young. My, you seem strong! Well aren't you something. I've always thought a dirty girl was pretty sexy. Who carries your tools up here? I'm gonna divorce my wife and marry you both. Can my boys have their picture taken with you? If your mother could see you! Can my girls have their picture taken with you?* For shame!

Midsummer, after a grueling hitch—long miles, heavy rocks—I looked down at my body and could see that it had changed. I had muscles: me, the shrimp of my family, the one with thin skin and angular bones. Over the first season of trailwork, it felt as if I had finally shifted from girl to woman, not with gentle rounding, the fatted ass and softer weight that many women describe, but instead with a taut curve of shoulder into bicep, the imposing loaf of thigh muscle above bony knee. My body felt purposeful and competent in a way it never had, as if it could take control, set the terms. I could hike twenty miles at a quick clip, move uphill bearing burdensome loads. I could lever large rocks, carry with one hand what used to take two arms close to the chest.

That summer, I showed off my arms for anyone. I parodied the strongman's pose, inviting irony to take the edge off my pride, but in a tank top at the bar, I flexed when asked, let total strangers squeeze my biceps. I'd never been drawn to the passively feminine wiles, and in my new arms I felt the intoxication of latent power, the knowledge that I didn't just *look* a certain way, but could force something to happen—lid from a jar, hand off my ass—that I could take the world into my own hands, give it a firm grip, kick it in the balls if I chose. Women have long been told that our bodies are to be presented, arranged for viewing, and that our power comes through flirting, a psychological dominance that stands in for physical strength. Goodbye to all that, which had never suited me. I felt power *in* my body. By itself.

I pondered explosive behavior out of context; I looked at my hands and wondered what they were capable of. Could I break a spirited horse? Chop a board in half with my bare hand? Wring somebody's neck? The violence surprised me, and to any onlooker, I would have seemed still laughably slender, no one to run from in a dark alley. Yet what I imagined I was capable of had changed; I lifted without thinking, spurned the grocery bagger's assistance, reefed on tight lug nuts, lit into a task without fear of failure. In trail-work, this meant I could quickly get in over my head, because I was by no means invincible (few people are, though Max seemed close, and kept me striving). Sometimes I got a log into my arms before I realized I couldn't go anywhere; with the rock bar, I could convince myself I was indomitable instead of just aided. Though I had long admired tenderness and vulnerability as much as strength, that summer I relished the bravado of muscle, the swagger of *look what I can do*. This is why the nouveaux riches spend their money so quickly, I thought. It's hard not to use wantonly a thing you've always wanted, slightly out of reach.

By now, I'm long used to my body and its rhythms, the way it's shaped and remade by a task. In a summer with lots of uphill hiking, my quads are hard as sandbags, and it takes a bit to raise my heart rate, steady as she goes. After a month of rock projects, my lower back twinges in the morning but my abs are something to write home about. Log work shoves my lats along my spine, brick-like but tender to the touch, and my hands are coated in pitch. On a front-country project with power wheelbarrows, backaches heal and arms revert to noodles.

In my midtwenties, growing strong, I couldn't foresee the aches and cracks and surgeries and convalescence that would come, couldn't know that time and labor would do the same thing to my body that it had to others, older or longer at work than I. But I was learning a lesson I'd carry with me through the invincible periods and the hobbled-up times, one of the many things manual labor taught me that my library self did not know. I learned that my body can do good work. That if I am patient, if I note its limits, tend its frailties, and push past them when I have the hunch it's right, my body is not just a partner I can trust. It's actually me. Both a tool and a home.

Cassie taught me the Montana Cowgirl's Mating Song while hiking up the Sperry Hill in the heat. A perfect tune for the Dew Drop Inn or Packer's Roost, here's how it goes: tip back your head and shake your hair loose down your neck. Hands on slightly cocked hips. Now, tap the rhythm with your foot, a horse's drumming can-ter, and sing loud in a monotone, raising the last syllable an octave: "Get it up, get it in, get it out, don't muss my hair-doooooo!" Go find a dance floor and try it. If that doesn't get you bum rushed in a cowboy bar, nothing will.

Glacier has about 725 miles of trails, many more than most national parks, but almost three hundred fewer than the peak 1,000-plus miles of the park's early years, before the road, when most visitors traveled by foot or horseback. In those days, the Civilian Conserva-tion Corps (CCC) and local wilderness rangers and explorers built the trails network fast and furious, with painstaking artistry in some places and get-'er-done, bare-bones efforts in others.

The old-time rangers also did trailwork, which back then consisted of roaming with an axe or crosscut and blazing trail or clearing blowdown. Nowadays, miles of trails and constant use mean that trail crews do very little new construction; our bread-and-butter work is drainage and tread maintenance, brushing, and logging out winterfall. But once in a while, a washout or flood or persistent beaver colony would require a reroute, and out would come the dusty survey tools—the Abney level, the grade stake, the clinometer—and the trail crew would put in new alignment.

Neither Cassie nor I had ever surveyed trail when our foreman gave us a perfunctory tutorial and sent us up the trail to Gunsight Pass. When we zeroed out our clinometers outside the cabin, Cassie saw my eyebrows and I saw the spot where the top of her hair puffed up from her head. Out on the trail, trying to tie in a switchback corner with the prevailing grade of the miles of trail above and below, 12 percent was harder to manage than we'd guessed. We spent hours peering through the clinometer, one-eyed, while the other person tried to hold the stake and mark the spot and keep blowing dust out of her eyes. The alignment finally staked with wobbly pin flags in talus, we grubbed in the working tread, whipping up a cloud of fine dust that didn't settle until we left the site each day. Our eyebrows were devilish, skin two shades darkened and powdery to the touch, white T-shirts striped with sweaty dirt rings, lips chapped and sore.

At the end of the hitch, we hiked the finished trail. Halos of dust floated up from our feet. The grade was steeper than we'd meant it to be. Maybe our "zero ground" hadn't been level at all, or the clinometer got dropped and knocked out of whack, or one of us read the degrees instead of percent, so the finished product was somewhere between the 5 percent of a wheelchair ramp and the 32 percent of the upper Cutbank Pass section, an ancient Blackfoot thoroughfare and a calf burner for any hiker, even Max. Next time, we swore, we'd be better at the survey part, having learned from a mistake or two on this one.

But there was no next time. I never held a clinometer again for trailwork in Montana. The brush grew fast, trees fell every winter, and drains clogged with the rocks kicked up from horses' shoes. Maintenance versus construction, the constant seesaw—many trails desperately needed reroutes, which fixed problems for good and ended the constant annual repairs. Yet, there was rarely money for the large-scale fix: Band-Aids are cheaper than surgery. Even Band-Aids eat up time, though, and every year, because of diminishing funding and smaller crews, we lost a chunk of the historical miles. In the shop hung pitted black-and-white photos from the trails' heyday, thirty-person crews clustered around a crosscut, the days of mass tourism still outside the frame. Those hearty young men in stagged pants and suspenders (and one grinning woman with braids) could not have imagined the day when our tiny crews would work as hard as we could just to keep trails open, dreaming of where we'd put new trails, even while the old ones disappeared in the undergrowth.

What we want to say to tourists: *Yeah, we saw that bear who ate a hiker yesterday. Well, you're paying to vacation here and I'm getting paid. I'm not a ranger. Would I march into your cubicle and ask to take your picture? I agree, best job in the world. No, I can't spare any water because I'm working six more hours and I need it. Yeah, they take our leg chains off out here. No, we don't pick up the mule shit. In the winter, I ski. You're welcome, it's my pleasure. Nope, not a ranger. Yep, been to college. You're old and pudgy and sexist and how do you think your wife feels standing right next to you while you propose to me? No pictures, I'm on the lam from child-support payments. I probably can't get your son a job, sir. In the winter, I write. In one million acres, do you have to take your snack break in the middle of my work site? I'm not a fucking ranger!*

It is beautiful, isn't it? It is so beautiful.

———

The Sperry cabin had a mouse problem. Or, I should say, the residents of the Sperry cabin had a problem with mice. A sticky night in mid-July, sleeping atop the sheet on my bunk, I woke to a mouse on the run from the tip of my foot up the length of my buck-naked body into my hair, where it paused in the tangles long enough for me to grab it and chuck it at the wall as hard as I could. Cassie woke up to my hollering and laughed at the thought of a mouse trapped and horrified by my knotted, gritty hair. (My old buzz cut would have been easier to navigate.) In the morning, a greasy spot on the plywood but no signs of mouse. It was probably licking its wounds, along with WD-40, in the tool cache. We thought we'd seen the last of it.

But the next evening, our dinnertime soundtrack was skittering feet in the walls. Cassie and I were not prone to shrieks and *eeks* over rodents. We dutifully cleaned up the mouse shit on the first hitch of every season, bandanas tied over our faces to prevent the dreaded hantavirus from roosting in our sinuses. We dealt with dead voles found in the outhouse without drama. Still, we postponed the inevitable task for hours, hoping the mouse would go away and we wouldn't have to kill anything. (It's much easier to dispose of dead pests than to kill them on purpose.) But with bedtime approaching, the dirty deed was unavoidable. We had to take back our home.

We carefully prepared the traps; the wooden one with a plastic bait platform shaped like a cheese seemed the most deadly. (Gabe's crew nicknamed theirs *Fromage de Mort*.) Before bed we placed the trap in the center of the cabin floor, peanut butter smeared on the platform, and that night I woke to the *snap*, tried to tune out the clatter and squeak, fell back to sleep pretending that my comfort didn't demand a small death. Cassie was a fish-eating vegetarian and in the morning as she fried croissants in butter on the iron skillet and I cleaned out the trap, I teased her ethics: if she killed an animal, she might as well honor its spirit by eating it. She poked out her tongue at the mouse and me, so I carried it to the rocks by the tail and slung it into the woods, stiff ballast that hurtled above the scrawny trees. On the cliffs across the creek, I saw the huge male mountain goat that patrolled the area, a handsome specimen we'd nicknamed "Big Balls" for the swinging sack he proudly displayed while perched on rocks in silhouette. The irony was blatant. So long, crappy mouse. Hello, beautiful goat.

Context is everything. Had the mouse stayed outdoors, hauling bits into its nest to feed its young, we'd have thought it tiny and cute. But for all our desire to beckon animals close enough to witness, distance dignifies. The habituated family of goats that practically trampled us in order to lick our urine off the trailside rocks was pesky, despite majestic looks. The pika that tried to drag away Cassie's lunch box was menace enough for me to huck a rock at it and knock it out, as if Goliath had the stone. The grizzly bears that broke into our tool cache and punctured the fuel cans and chewed on the bar oil did not seem wild. The marmot that tore holes in a left-behind fleece at the job site triggered one crewmate to brandish a pulaski and threaten, "I'll make a sweater out of you!" They were all too close, too much. The real irony is this: what made those animals seem less wild was us—our cabin, her lunch box, my piss on the rocks. The closer our lives edged, the more complicated our relationship became. Adoring, annoying, adversary, companion, wild, pathetic.

On the cliff across the drainage, Big Balls foraged tundra plants, looking regal. Somewhere in the scrubby forest below the cabin porch, the dead mouse lay in the duff, awaiting something hungry. I went back inside for my croissant.

Gabe and I spent summers in eight-day stretches apart. Wednesday mornings came and we'd head into the woods for another long week of shit work with crews we were slightly sick of, six days off not long enough to get back the enthusiasm. Morning goodbyes were rushed and tense, running late, and the breakfast spat over *You finished all the granola* or *Why didn't you put my boots on the dryer last night* went unresolved for a week before we could revisit *I'm sorry* with enough time for it to mean anything. The first days were lonely, best companion several watersheds away and no one to talk to about the thing with my sister, worry over this winter's work, the pressing urge to get a dog. No one to cut some slack on the day my period started, no one to rub my shoulders and say, Of course your ankles aren't fat. The scheduled radio rendezvous fell through, the transmission cut off, or it felt rote and intensified the faraway. We'd come out of hitches to a reunion fried and crabby, or the six days flew by—washing Ziplocs, paying bills, stockpiling groceries, never just a quick trip to the store for what sounds good, always the bags of apples, cases of Clif Bars, enough pasta to choke a horse. No time to be alone, visitors leaving, coming, leaving, and the pressure, *be sweet, feel loving, give him a massage,* only two days until we're gone again.

"Split my finger open like a grape." I've heard that phrase, and it's perfect: the thin membrane, slow yield, then wetness. I split open my right middle finger while working on a retaining wall nine miles in the backcountry. The rock hammer lay just out of reach, so I used a small rock to pound in a larger wedge, and *wham.* Three miles above the cabin, it was nearly quitting time anyway, so I didn't have to suck it up and finish the day. Cassie packed a bandana with snow from a nearby drift and I held the finger above my head, wrapped tight, blood running down my arm. Good thing the hike was downhill, because I was unsteady on my feet, my face pale and clammy. Hikers parted for me and turned to watch as I stumbled down, trailing bloody splotches on the rocks behind me. Outside the cabin, I retched. Inside, humming nonsense to keep from screaming, I cleaned the pulp of skin and flesh in a bowl of warm water, then splinted it, took four Advil with chocolate milk for the throbbing, and passed out on my bunk. The next morning the grape had swelled to an unripe plum, the kind you pick from a backyard tree, skin taut, and I could feel my pulse in it for the rest of the hitch. I cut the middle finger out of my glove for the bandaged digit; my grip on the rock hammer was loose and awkward. It hurt longer than I'd have guessed it would, the nail obliterated, sore to the touch for months, and years down the road still prone to frost nip.

When we got out of that hitch, I heard that Sheldon had busted his finger when the packstring rodeoed at Lower Nyack cabin, and he loaded the mules one-handed and rode home eight miles without mentioning it, as the story goes. (The reason there's a story at all is that he passed the crew on the way out; someone noticed blood on the mannies and asked about the hand clutched in his lap.) Stoicism is admirable, and it should be obvious by now that I'm no hero, but for Pete's sake, Sheldon, not even a whimper, no subtle gambit for a sliver of sympathy, the story dragged out like an ornery mule from the barn? Maybe alone at the cabin he yelped loud, kicked the porch, hopped around, and cussed his head off. Without any witnesses, we'll never know. If a cowboy complains and there's no one there to hear it, did he make a sound?

A Zen saying captures the music of the barn coming home from a hitch: "How refreshing, the whinny of a packhorse unloaded of everything!"

The Sperry Trail leads to Comeau Pass, terminating at a fifty-foot set of narrow stairs blasted into the headwall by the CCC crew in the 1930s (from back in the day when a depression could get you a government job in the woods). Every spring we installed a rope handrail, tightening the turnbuckle at the top to support a tired hiker's weight, and then we removed it in the fall before winter turned the stairs into an icy chute. Such rock handiwork is evident through out the Sperry district; trails wind past decades of drystone masonry. Rock walls ten courses thick with a keystone the size of a couch, a squared chunk of pink rock that it took five of us to move, climbing turns with stairs on a slight batter, retaining walls that bear up slopes of scree. Countless hours of work over even a single season, let alone five, let alone twenty.

One summer Cassie and I hiked out of a hitch we'd spent building rock stairs and came back six days later after a hundred-year rainstorm blew through, a toad-strangler that blasted the alpine trail network to pieces. Currents of water rushed through switchbacks leaving crevasses that took ten minutes to drop into and climb out of again, more topography than trail. If I hadn't seen it the week before with my own eyes, I'd never have believed water could change something that quickly. The rocks we'd cached for our stairs were gone, as well as the section of trail the stairs had climbed. We paired up on the rock bar, four hands and 250 pounds reefing on debris the size of kitchen appliances—Refrigerator Rock, we named one, taller than me by a foot. We leveraged precarious rocks over the ends of switchbacks, hooting as one-ton boulders catapulted like tumbleweeds into gullies that swallowed them up. We spent days grubbing, prying, digging through fill ten feet deep, cutting our hands through our gloves on rough edges, falling into our bunks at night too sore to move. Talking to tourists, we shook our heads: *Never seen anything like it.* Even our foreman, working trails since the seventies, agreed it was epic. It seemed as if every single piece of sediment on the whole mountainside had traded places with something else. As if heft were weightless. As if permanence, fleeting.

Winston Galt was the maintenance man at Sperry, with a trim mustache reminiscent of Nazis and a kindly, helpful air that put them straight out of mind. His voice held a southern twang so distinctive he didn't need a call number on the radio, his accent a handle on its own. He drank Coors Lite, which you could smell on his breath, fighting Doublemint and spicy mouthwash. Win tended the Park Service buildings surrounding the chalet and monitored all things mechanical. He tracked oxygen levels in the million-dollar compost-ing toilet facility, tightened what was loose, kept things fixed.

Win kept an eye out for our two- or three-woman crew with his gently solicitous deliveries: a package of propane mantles, ex-tra toilet paper, a new radio battery sent up on the pack string. We didn't need Win for much, but when we did, it was great to have him just a shout away. Some nights we went up to the comfort station, where he lived, for a few beers and a game of cards. His building had plumbing, while the trails cabin did not. Win always invited us to take showers—our T-shirts dirty, hair smelling of fumes from chainsaw or rock drill. We usually poached one shower per hitch, the maximum we could allow ourselves without selling out the traildog dirtbag ethos. Win couldn't understand this. "Why on earth not go to bed clean?" he'd say, stroking his mustache. It was hard to explain.

One night in late season, I woke in the Sperry cabin to a pound-ing headache and the insistent bleep of the CO_2 detector. Disori-ented, I stumbled around in the dark trying to shut off the propane lines and rouse the others. We fled up the hill, dragging our sleeping bags to the closed-for-the-season chalet, where we slept on the porch in fresh air. The next day Win replaced the cracked radiator coupling that had caused the leak, said the reason we didn't die was that the cabin was a mile from airtight. With the door closed against cool fall air, it could have been a death trap, but those cracks under the walls, the gaps where warp lifted frame from floor box, the spaces we stuffed with dish towels too gross to use—the cracks saved us. Win cackled at the thought of a cabin being too crappy to kill you. He invited us up for dinner that night. I took a shower. We played hearts and drank whiskey and toasted our narrow escape.

Wild is head back hollering at the sky, a moment that contains the full world. Wild is not tame, not bound, not constrained, con-stricted, condensed. Wildness is big or it is small, but it is open—open mouth, season, door, heart.

———

Traildogs in Glacier were rabid for skiing, especially telemark skiing, with its free heel and dropped-knee turns, perfect for the big, open bowls and treed powder slopes so prevalent in Montana's backcountry. Lots of people worked as lifties in the winter, at Big Mountain, the local hill in Whitefish, or resorts in Bozeman, Colorado, Wyoming, Utah. Several trails guys skied for the US Telemark Team, and nearly everyone who'd been in Montana more than a couple of seasons had caught the powder bug.

Reba brought her tele gear to the Sperry cabin the year I worked for her, sweet-talking the packers into lashing skis on the outside of a load and hiding the boots in her canvas duffel. A midwestern kid, broke from college loans, I'd never downhill skied before and looking up into the peaks where the slivers of white seemed so high and far away, I wondered if Reba's was just wishful thinking on the part of a self-described powder addict. But the first time we worked at Comeau Pass, Reba hiked up after quitting time and she skied those lines, then stashed her gear in the bushes so she didn't have to carry it three miles uphill every time. Marmots chewed the liners of her very expensive plastic boots, but she swore it was worth it. I explored the kettle ponds at the pass and poked around in the talus slopes at the foot of Mount Edwards, watching her bounce through turns on the soft summer snowfield above. It seemed worth it to me.

The next season, Cassie told me she alpine skied (who didn't, growing up in the resort town of Whitefish?) but she didn't telemark, and anyway, she said, she wasn't very good. As a kid from Michigan, I'd stomped around on fish-scale skis in golf courses and city nature preserves, and nothing had yet prepared me for going downhill, fast, in mountains. But I was getting comfortable hiking on steep snow; skiing seemed at least theoretically possible. Reba, who had upgraded to shaped skis and plastic boots that year, gave me her skinny old sticks and a pair of leather telemark boots, because she knew I wanted to try. I really wanted to try. Too shy to poach a lift off the packers, Cassie and I carried in a pair of skis for the two of us, splitting the load, the pictures of which later elicited laughs from our backcountry ski friends—*one* ski each?

On the first run, it became clear to me that although Cassie made parallel turns instead of tele turns, she was a "not very good" skier only by the improbable measuring stick of ski towns, where children run double black diamonds by the time they're five. Humiliation loomed. It was too late to back out, so I tightened my boots, pointed tips downhill, and fully epitomized the popular ski term "yard sale"—a crash-and-burn tumble where sunglasses, hat, gloves, poles, and pack get strewn over snow in bargain-basement fashion. Cassie laughed, despite promising not to. I couldn't blame her. I'd rarely felt so uncoordinated, splayed at the bottom of every run. We kept this up for a few hours, and that night I was as sore as if I had been beaten with a tire iron in a Tarantino movie. That was my first taste. I loved it.

A few years later, I was the crew leader who hiked my skis and boots up at the beginning of the season to the disbelief of my newbie laborer. I stashed them at Comeau Pass, praying marmots would stay away from my secondhand gear, and made turns after work in the evening before heading down to the cabin for canned stew, just as Reba had. I started by inching along the lower slopes of Gunsight in a nervous traverse, then skinning midway up the snowfield and snowplowing down. Eventually I could drop my knee into shaky tele turns to control my speed, falling every two or three turns, leaving cartoon craters in the slushy snow. I still wasn't good, years away from even the barely intermediate status I now hold, but I was mostly upright, at least. I was beginning to get what it would be like—snow an element in which I could thrive.

Most years, my mid-July birthday fell on a hitch, and I'd work the crew long days to bank hours so I could take my birthday afternoon off and ski the glacier. Once, my friend Brent hiked in to help me celebrate. With his far-superior skills to coax me, we skied a whooping run from the top of the snow-covered glacier, a soft corn slope that toed out into hard ice, our edges skittering over the open slots of narrow crevasses, until I bailed in a chicken-shit fall and cut up my knuckles deeply enough to leave a web of little scars, another accessory on my hard-knocks birthday suit. I chipped out a piece of the bloody ice and sucked it on the hike back down to the cabin, where Brent made monster burritos and margaritas. *Happy birthday to me. I know how to ski,* I sang to my past self, the eager girl who watched from the sidelines, and to my future one who'd look back at these golden days, older and wiser and stiffer. *Happy birthday, dear me.*

Halfway through a hitch, seeing Gabe approach on the trail brought pure glee, especially as a surprise. Visitors know to bring treats—the paper, extra chocolate—and visitors who love you best of all know to bring really good treats. Once, in a heroic gesture, Gabe packed in ice cream buried in an insulated lunch cooler at the bottom of his towering pack. It was a scorch-hot day and the ice cream had melted to a chocolate milkshake in a carton. I could have swallowed the whole thing, but sharing seemed appropriate—some for Gabe the courier, some for our friend Peach, who hiked in with him, and for Cassie, as hot and dust-covered as I was. After they finished, politely refusing the last sludge, I ran my fingers around the edges of the carton, finally tore it apart at the seam to slurp every last drip, and came up with the tip of my nose sticky and brown. To this day, the best ice cream I've had.

The rock bar's right-hand machine is the Pionjar, a Swedish gas-powered drill, pronounced *poon-jar* (good for a snicker) or *pun-jar,* like a glass receptacle of bad jokes. A dense powerhead that will drill or pound with the flip of a lever, with detachable three-foot bits for either function, it holds a special place in the heart of anyone who's worked in rock. When you want one tool that will drill holes and break rock off the grid, the Pionjar's your man. We used it sporadically in Glacier, to set a turnbuckle in a rock staircase, sink rebar for bridge abutments, prepare holes for blasting, until suddenly one project—say, an outhouse hole six feet through bedrock, or a repair of the craggy Highline Trail—and then we used it daily for weeks.

For all its iron bestiality, the Pionjar is a delicate machine. With a chainsaw, you can change 2,500 feet in elevation and never adjust the carburetor, but drop the Pionjar one switchback and the idle chugs, and if you tilt it too far, the engine will flood. In hard granite the bits dull faster than disposable razors, and the fumes kicked out by the 12:1 mix (four times richer than saw gas) made us vomit in the bottom of the shitter-to-be. Starting the thing cold is equal parts mechanics and sorcery, and carrying it, well, that's another complaint altogether. All this to say, when it runs, it's all worth it. The carbide-steel bit boring through bedrock, a perfect cylinder left behind, ready for rock bar or feathers and wedge: there are few things in life as pleasurable as the right tool for the job.

In open areas across the West, bear grass grows thick: in meadows and clearings beneath trees and the broad gullies of avalanche paths. There's something alien about bear grass, a swath of it or a single flower alone. It grows on a tall, reedy stalk, sometimes curved, the head a burst of small white flowers like those of a hyacinth, looking like one bulbous bloom from a distance. Also called squaw grass, elk grass, turkey beard, soap grass, basket grass, bear lily, or quip-quip, the Blackfoot name is *eksisoke*. Locals claim that bear grass grows in seven-year cycles, some years almost nonexistent, and others, white as far as you can see. The heavy heads grow little nipples on the top of the blooms, bringing to mind adolescent training bras. Native people used bear grass for basket weaving; elk and goats forage the stalks in early season. In contrast to the murky reek of the namesake bruins that use its leaves to line their dens, bear grass smells all lily, an un-bottleable perfume.

———

When Ira joined the crew, he greeted us all the same way. Stood at attention, stuck out his hand like a karate jab to the gut, and shouted, "Ira J. Schwab, US Marine Corps, Slippery Rock, Pennsylvania!" He was the new guy on Gabe's crew and we worked together off and on all that summer, long enough for Ira to gift me with more hilarious turns of phrase than I'd ever received from a single person. The phrases stuck because Ira said them over and over, and his booming voice made you take note. (He'd gone deaf in his machine gun ear, he told us, and we should feel free to tell him to pipe down, which we did, to no avail.) He introduced himself with the same exuberant spiel to anyone I ever saw him meet, from the chief ranger to a tourist on the trail. People startled at his forthright bark, but his boisterous charm warmed everyone.

Many of Ira's greatest hits had military origins. He called Gabe "m'leader" and followed him within five feet on the trail, stopping to pee when Gabe did, or waiting, spine straight, eyes straight ahead, for him to finish. When Gabe told him *Go on past, I'll catch up*, Ira would holler, "I stick with ya, man, yer m'leader!" Every night on hitches, Ira ate too much and moaned, "Man, that put the *hurts* on me!" Another common mealtime phrase, "Gabe, I'm a freakin' *huge* fan of yer beans and rice!" which he'd say every time Gabe made them (once a hitch).

Ira was new to the alpine realm and he took notes on our gear and the little tricks we'd accumulated over the years. A pair of gaiters for work on snowfields, a CamelBak for clearing days, a Tupperware lunch box to keep saw gas fumes out of the sandwich—Ira would respond to each innovation with, "Man, I gotta *get* me one a them!" His raucous laugh could scare you if you weren't prepared. He slurped his cereal, and, built like a Pionjar, was by far the strongest person I've ever worked with, even vying with Max for sheer brute force. Generous beyond measure, Ira praised all good ideas equally, tapping the side of his head with his index finger, a little too hard: "That's what I like about ya, man, yer always *thinkin'*!" For himself, he saved good-natured scorn. If he screwed up, he'd shake his head and bellow, "I warned ya, guys, I'm sharp as a marble!"

What Ira lacked in quick, he made up for in determined. On one hitch at Lake Ellen Wilson, Ira hiked to Comeau Pass after work, twelve miles round-trip, because he wasn't sure he'd get to see it otherwise. On the way back to camp, he stopped at the Sperry Chalet kitchen and bought each of us a slice of still-warm cherry pie. He hiked three miles to camp with a stack of Styrofoam containers balanced in his huge arms.

Years after the last time we saw Ira, Gabe and I still use his phrases weekly. I'm a freakin' *huge* fan of Gabe's beans and rice, for example, though they put me in the hurt locker. When perusing some eye-catching gear in a catalog, Gabe says wryly, "Man, I gotta *get* me some a these!" But Ira's most useful phrase was one he'd say apropos of nothing at all that summer he fell hard for "GlacierPark," and one we still quote on almost every trip into alpine country: "Guys, I'm gonna *die* in these here mountains!" It sounds like a death wish, but really, it's the opposite, a hope for longevity among friends in high places, life turned up full volume.

Four years in, Reba left trails to become a nurse, Cassie went to law school, and I inherited the Sperry crew. The transition to leadership had nerve-racking aspects (would I remember the right tools, time the projects well, bring enough fuel?), but I knew I was ready to be in charge. Where I'd once had questions, I now had opinions. Where I used to ask someone else, now I could figure it out myself. I had the confidence to say what needed doing, and the courage to admit when I didn't know. I was ready.

I'd have a new laborer on the crew, like I'd once been, and I'd teach her what I knew, and keep on learning what I didn't. Really, I looked forward to it, except for one thing, the most terrifying part of being a leader: the barn. The packers. Especially Slim. No more intermediary. Just me driving the truck, me parking at the barn, the same old scene I could picture: crew unloads, throws down ammo boxes full of food; shovels and pulaskis; and tarps, tents, and bags. The monologue begins: *Yer late! Whassall this shit, gonna be in there a gaddam year? Hey Christy, whatever the hell yer name is, move yer outfit, Sheldon's gotta pull in there. Tell yer guys to stand back. Them mannies are still wet, get the pile, it's inna barn. Max came outta Fifty Mountain late yesterday, pourin' like a sonafabitch. Take one end a this! Charley tell you guys they ain't given no more overtime? Gotta get in there fast 'cause I ain't working for free, cocksuckers. You seen the drift lately? If it's rotten we ain't goin', I'm not losin' a string for fuckin' trailwork. Carry yer own gaddam skis!*

The night before my first hitch as a leader, I sweated and twisted, my stomach an empty bucket, the sheets in knots. Then the day came, with nothing to it but a little shouting. After a few rounds at the barn with no major mishaps, I got over it. Terror aside, insults notwithstanding, trail crews and packers go together like whiskey and Coke. Can't you see how much we need each other? Without crews, the packers would have no one to transport, no reason to keep the barn running. Without packers, crews would spend all day carrying loads, barely enough time for maintenance, let alone projects.

As added irony, the stock that enabled our work also destroyed it, the impact of a mule hoof exponentially worse than a hiker's boot. For their unmatched capacity to damage tread, horses and mules have earned the description "four shovels and a stomach," and we joked that if it weren't for the mules that carried us to our job, we'd have no work. Still, the thought of banning stock from western trails developed by their passage is sacrilege. There's a whole culture in the handling of these animals, and the use of them for travel, that few want to see die out.

Packers may come on strong, but most of them are softies. In

Slim's case, they'd hired a *gaddam girl*, and he got over it. Despite the gnarled anxiety in my guts while driving to the barn, despite the fact that no one could make me feel like more of an idiot than Slim, I wouldn't have sacrificed the packers for anything. Ours is a wonderful fucking symbiosis.

CHAINSAW

Mechanics The modern chainsaw has an air-cooled two-stroke engine. Fins on the flywheel circulate air, eliminating the heavy radiator system and coolant flush of a four-stroke. A two-stroke engine's piston makes twice as many power strokes and generates double the horsepower of a four-stroke with comparable displacement. It also spews twice the fumes and noise. A chainsaw with a four-stroke engine would be far quieter, with fewer emissions, but way too big to carry. Such are the physics of compromise.

Inventor Andreas Stihl, the German engineer who patented the first modern chainsaw, devised his idea while working as a shill for a German sawmill. On sales calls, he encountered loggers in the Black Forest felling and bucking trees with crosscuts; this prompted his design for an electric prototype in 1929 for what would become the first gasoline-powered saw in 1954, both produced by Stihl's eponymous company. At first, loggers hated the newfangled saw and the men who hawked it, fearing their jobs would become casualties of the mechanized age. But the saw got lighter, faster, and more powerful, and these days, it's hard to find a sawyer who doesn't wax a little worshipful for Andreas, or a forest that hasn't felt the tooth of his innovation.

Science Combustion requires three components: air, fuel, and spark. Air and fuel pass through filters to get to the engine's combustion chamber, venturi and carburetor doing their part on the way. Spark comes from the electrical system—ignition switch, wires, pull cord, and the mysterious magneto, a tiny current generator that fires the spark plug. The three basics make a saw run. A clogged filter, improperly gapped spark plug, bad fuel mix, or a loose wire and— nothing. Tick off the possibilities—*air, fuel, spark:* how troubleshooting begins.

Teeth All saws, from the oldest one-man pull saw to the latest-model chainsaw, are united by one characteristic: staggered teeth with a cutting edge that cleaves the wood's grain, and rakers to guide the bite. The origin of the motion has moved from biceps to sprocket and the configuration of the teeth has changed, but the cut is the same—wood removed, chips created, a severing.

Repairs Carry a saw kit any time you hit the trail. Inside a saw kit, find a minimum of: one combination tool (a screwdriver-wrench, called a "screnech"), an extra spark plug, one round file, one flat file, two bar nuts, old toothbrush, carburetor screwdriver, sharp chain, clean air filter, ear plugs. For hitches, include: sprocket, bearing grease, extra pull cord, fuel filter, e-clip, star wrench. For dropping trees: wedges in a few sizes, hard hat, falling axe.

Loyalty There's an argument in woodswork: Husqvarna vs. Stihl, the two most highly regarded professional saws. Like Ford vs. Chevy, the defenders and detractors of each are as strident as politicos or sports fans. Really, they're both good saws, and it mostly comes down to what you're familiar with. If your dad drove a Chevy, chances are you will, too. I learned to cut on a Stihl, so it's my default. Stihl-heads say proudly, "All these years and she's Stihl running!" But older Stihls without a decompression button are notoriously hard to start. If a Husky fan comes upon you reefing on the pull cord, he'll scoff, "Stihl yarding on that thing, huh?"

CHAPTER 3

Middle Fork: Forest
(How the woods become a home)

The Middle Fork of the Flathead River flows east to west, tracing the southern edge of the park and cradling bears, martens, hikers, and trail crews in its mostly unbridged grasp. With Glacier to the north and the Bob Marshall Wilderness to the south, the river splits the region up the middle, a child's crayoned line across the map. The Middle Fork converges with the North Fork downstream near the town of West Glacier to form the Flathead proper, the South Fork flowing out of the Bob to join up a little ways west in the town of Hungry Horse. The Flathead River routes through Flathead Lake, and makes its way, via the Columbia, to the sea.

Like North Fork, the Middle Fork district in the park takes its name from the river, which is fed by creeks that trickle south off the divide. The Middle Fork is home to rapids that rafters love; big, shallow pools where cutthroat trout linger; and eddies meant for summer basking. The creeks bear with them the distant mountains' argillite, carried to the river bottom, where it is hewn to bright cobbles by the current.

To access most trails in the Middle Fork, you have to ford the river. There are few bridges in the district, managed as wilderness, and the river separates the road from the trails. You can avoid a crossing by starting at the bridge on the western end of the Boundary

Trail in West Glacier, or twenty-five miles upstream at the Walton ranger station, but trail crews can't afford the time to begin a Middle Fork hitch with a ten-mile hike just to access the trail we'll be working. We ford the river.

When you step into the current, wild pulls against your legs, the road, only yards away, as invisible as morning is from lunch. Far from the major tourist hubs, the trails in the Middle Fork are quiet, the sounds of breath and footsteps amplified. Day-hiking potential is limited. The first stretch of each drainage is heavily forested, with few big vistas until you reach the high passes or small lakes 12 to 18 miles in. The average hiker usually goes elsewhere, where the bears are easier to spot and views give more bang for the buck. If Sperry and Granite are the pretty extroverts twirling in the middle of the action, the Middle Fork is the wallflower, subtle but lovely upon close inspection. If you put in the miles, suck it up through bad bugs, boggy tread, and overgrowth, the Middle Fork will offer up the secret heart of the park, a pulse beneath your feet. The tourists who throng the road corridor don't plow through brush, or dip their toes into glacial runoff. The river keeps out the riffraff.

Like most of the great loves of my life—mountains, fiction, winter—the chainsaw seduced me with equal parts freedom and danger. I don't remember chainsaws in my life before trails, though I'm sure my dad had a small one for bucking the limbs that came off backyard oaks in a windstorm. But my first week on the job, when Sherri the shop tech took me to the gravel lot behind the trails sheds and showed me how to start one, I listened.

Sherri explained my starting options—the standard style, powerhead pinched between the knees, one hand on the handle bar, the other on the pull cord; the logroll, where the bar is shoved over a log and the pull cord yanked back; and the ground start, choice of weaklings and fraidy cats, where the saw is placed on the ground, a boot through the handle to pin it in place, and the cord yanked upward.

Negligible upper-body strength, slight terror—you can guess which start I chose.

I still couldn't do it. It was an old saw, Sherri reassured me. She went to the shed and brought back a newer model; a compression release made the pull start easier. I couldn't start that one, either. "Keep pulling," said Sherri, "you'll get it." So I pulled. I pulled until my wrists were sore, till the cord handle snapped my knuckles and made my eyes water, till a blister opened up on the meat of my palm. I pulled like my life depended on it, and got only the dull sound of the piston cranking slow, not even enough power to turn the engine over once. Sherri took the saw from me, flicked the on/choke switch, started it on the first try. She shrugged.

Back to the saw shed again, Sherri brought me the smallest Stihl, the 026, so much daintier than the 036s typically used for clearing that the guys christened it "The Lady Logger." I took it, too desperate to be sheepish or critical of the sexism, and I pulled some more. When it finally started, the roar startled me so thoroughly that I almost dropped the saw. I held on tight, stiff-armed, body arched as far as possible from the bar and chain, as if the thing I'd worked so hard to get running now made me want to run. But I didn't want to run. I wanted to learn how to use the saw to do something besides rev it in a parking lot. I could feel it from the first minute I held it—love. Danger and freedom, right there in my arms.

East from the confluence with the North Fork to west at Marias Pass, creeks flow south out of the Lewis Range and into the Middle Fork: Rubideau, Lincoln, Harrison, Nyack, Coal, Muir, Park, Ole, Shields, Autumn. Smaller feeder drainages include Pinchot and Elk and Fielding, and myriad tiny blue squiggles on the map. Anything without a name is, on the ground, pretty close to jumpable.

One of my first days in the Middle Fork resembles my firsts nearly everywhere in Glacier: out of my element, eager to get in, following along quietly until the former state gives way to the latter. This particular day found Reba sick and me shipped off for the day with Brook and his Middle Fork guys to get a jump-start on the heavy clearing in the Coal Creek burn. I knew Brook by reputation only. Thirtysomething, wiry, hyper, and flat-out hilarious, Brook was at the center of some of the most outlandish pranks and stories in the trails canon. He was drawn to drama, calamity, and excess. Brook loved attention. If he was on a search and rescue, he'd end up on the local news, and you could see why. He told a monologue worthy of a one-man show, complete with pantomime and imitations. He teased until the butt of the joke was ready to throttle him, stopped just before he was resented. His crews worked hard, hiked hard, drank hard, laughed hard. I was eager to see him in action.

On the south side of the river we sat on the rocks, unlacing our shin-high boots. I'd never forded the Middle Fork before, or any river of its size. The guys were loosening their belt buckles and dropping their pants, and though I'd brought sandals for the ford, I hadn't thought to bring shorts. Four of them stood in clownish boxers at the edge of the river, kicking water at each other, swinging their arms in the cool air. Clearly, I'd have to strip, too. I briefly considered fording in my pants. Stupid. The river was midthigh. The heavy cotton canvas would take all day to dry.

"We always ford in our underwear," Brook reassured me. "Don't think twice about it." I dropped my pants slowly, pulling my T-shirt down as far as I could. I tucked my rolled-up Carhartts under the top of my backpack. We tied our bootlaces together and slung them over our shoulders. Brook and Mike carried the saws, the rest of the guys the other tools, the unwieldy Dolmars of saw mix knocking against their knees. I had only a shovel in hand, the very least you could carry and still hold your head up. Mike waded in. I hung back as if finishing something, fussed with the straps on my Tevas.

"Have you done this before?" Brook asked, noting me sidelong, and I shook my head. Posturing was pointless. They'd guess as soon as they saw me stumble through the current. Maybe I'd fall in, drown, even. Brook gave me a quick overview, kindly, with no teasing, and then gestured me to go ahead of him. The icy water at my ankles kept just at bay an awareness that I was walking in my underwear in the middle of a line of strange men. At twenty-three, I was not particularly self-conscious about my body, didn't "hate my butt," as was the common refrain. Even so, it was disconcerting. A vulnerable promenade.

Soon I was in above the knees, and current pushed water waist-high, obscuring clear view of anyone's rump. I concentrated on facing upstream, one foot placed solid before moving the other, shovel handle triangulated in front of me like the third leg of a tripod. In the thickest part of the current, the water coursed between my toes and I sensed what it would be like to lose my footing and be swept quietly downstream. When the water shallowed, I ran for the bank, where the guys shook water off their legs. We stomped and howled as feeling reentered numb flesh. Brook laced up his boots without putting his pants back on, doing a funny little jig in his logging boots and undies. I glanced around. All of them, the same, no pants. There was a shallower ford of Ole Creek a ways up the trail, and anyway, their boxers were soaked, Brook said, and would dry while they hiked. They nearly convinced me to do it too, those varmints, but I was wise to them, what was necessary, how far they'd push, and I held my own.

I hid in the brush and shucked my undies, pulled on Carhartts over bare ass, and hung the wet bikinis over the handle of the pulaski strapped to my pack. (Could the proverbial mother ever have guessed, when urging clean underwear, that this scenario, not an unexpected trip to the hospital, might be reason to heed her advice?) I took my place in the middle of the line. I had to laugh at the sight of the sawyer hiking ahead, underwear stuck to his skinny white thighs. I was glad to be covered up, despite the chafe of cotton duck against damp cheeks. No matter how much I liked these guys, no matter how much I longed to be part of the gang, damned if I'd be the story they'd crow out later over beers: *We got her to walk in her underwear for hours!*

Al was the oldest of all of us and, at forty-seven, craved a nightly dose of Vitamin I(buprofen) washed down with PBR in order to keep getting up in the morning. Gabe was on Al's crew his first year, along with a guy named Mick. On Gabe's twenty-fourth birthday in June, he noticed the age relation: "Hey Al, Mick (twenty-three) plus me (twenty-four) equals you (forty-seven)!" "Don't ever say that again," said Al, his handlebar smirking.

Al also said that day, "Gabe, you're the workin' man's thinker; or is it the thinkin' man's worker?" and like the best birthday gifts, it was well chosen, and it fit. Al meant that Gabe sees beneath the surface; he looks twice, points out a thing and makes you see it new. Gabe is contemplative in a job that thrives on movement. He's an ace at his work, competent, capable, part of the gang, but also somehow beyond the gang, skirting the edges in the quiet: he notices *that bird,* asks *why do it that way,* thinks *is everyone okay?* and *of what the world is made.*

Trail crews are full of bright people, PhDs and autodidacts, all kinds of intelligence represented: kinesthetic, spatial, naturalistic. But very few people are the workingman's thinker. My crewmates rib my ten-dollar words, I talk about books and play trivia games, and still, I am too boisterous, too impulsive to be in that class. Eager for the next thing, I forget to notice this one. But Gabe, he puts his head down, gets the job done, and misses nothing. Like Zen carpenter-monks whose labor was their spiritual practice, Gabe is attentive to his work, and in it, everything else. He moves with a certain stillness, just digging, measuring, just working, and watching.

The trails season begins in May, with "logging out." Clearing trails of winter downfall can take months, and is among the most satisfying work we get to do. Long miles, constant cutting, a duet with a beat all its own. A saw team consists of two, the swamper and the sawyer. The sawyer hikes with the saw and saw kit and does the felling, limbing, and bucking, leaving a load of debris behind. The swamper follows the sawyer, carries the gas, bar oil, and a falling axe, and tidies the mayhem in the saw's wake. A good sawyer can leave behind even a fast swamper in little time. The sawyer's work is glamorous work, the pace frenetic yet deliberate, but without a swamper, the trail would remain impassable. Swamping is not a technical skill, but it's the hardest labor on trails, lifting and hauling huge log rounds, dragging limbs through brush, and hiking fast in between, trying not to fall too far behind. A swamper sweats buckets even in cold, and must remain psychologically hardy to follow in the shadow of the sawyer, a nearly impenetrable wall of work always just ahead. Usually swamper and sawyer switch jobs every tank of gas or two. The sawyer will say he'd rather keep cutting if asked, but really, the tradeoff is nice. When the saw disappears, you fall into the quiet smell of wood, the task of cleanup predictable and important. Absent the aggressive glamour of the chainsaw, work takes on a purposeful cadence, a solo effort metered by the rasp of a dry throat (always thirsty), a growling stomach (always hungry), heart pushed against skin.

My favorite trails sandwich: soft bakery bread, brown, not too seedy. Heavy mayo coating both slices. Extra-sharp cheddar cheese, sliced thick enough to see your teeth marks in, and deli-cut ham. Pickles separately, added on site. Sandwich double-wrapped and laid at the top of the Tupperware box, protected from saw fumes but not smashed by the apple (Fuji: crisp, not too sweet). At lunch break, potato chips from a Ziploc on top of the ham, then pressed flat with the bread, providing crunch without sog: workingman's lettuce.

Any traildog who's worked more than two seasons has heard the question *When are you going to get a real job?* In your early twenties, critics will cut you some slack: there's plenty of time to get serious. Parents smile and indulge, thinking, *This, too, shall pass.* But linger too long at an eccentric job, and questions begin. Relatives at reunions ask, "So you're still doing that, huh?" College pals who praised the quirky choice right after graduation begin to drop hints about grad school.

I couldn't exactly blame the skeptics. I hadn't planned this life for myself, and the ins and outs of it still surprised me, too. But while I had firsthand experience to convince me it was right, my folks could only take my word and hope there was more to it than what they saw from the outside: moving every six months, no security, intermittent income, what seemed at best like a tenuous perch on the roost of adulthood. I knew they were proud of me—my dad openly admiring of a job that had me out in the field all day, using my hands—but there was an undercurrent of slight dismay: our daughter, who wanted to be an archaeologist or an NPR correspondent when she grew up, the girl who meant to go on for a graduate philosophy degree, is doing *what*? Again? My mother asked if I ever thought about being a professor anymore (not really), and if my winter job paid enough (no). An aunt asked if I had health insurance, *tsk*-ing when I admitted that I did not. The prodding felt rude at times (who asked an investment banker how much she made?), but I knew that beneath the concern lay a persistent hope for my happiness. I wished they could see what I could: happiness too easily confused with orthodoxy.

Just when it's clear to seasonals that people think we're flighty and resistant to our true callings, someone will sidle up, with a "real job" and a salary, and whisper, *I envy you.* Including high school friends, distant cousins, and seatmates on airplanes. No sooner has one person at a dinner party back east finished shaking his head over *How can you live with that kind of insecurity?* then another comes over to say she'd move to a park tomorrow if she could. Many of the envious have good careers, some even jobs that they love, but describe feeling restless. Or, they want to try something new but can't because of the stability, the kids, the bills, the 401(k), the economy, the degree, the expectations. *Oh, I couldn't*, they say when I offer to put in a good word for them at hiring time next season. *My husband would never move there my folks paid for law school my kids are at a weird age we just finished the house.*

It would be tempting, in these scenarios, to agree with the enthusiast, that yes, I'm lucky, brave, noble, and happier than most. But as fervently as I defend myself to critics, I am just as resistant to the airbrushed longing. It's true that there are legions of us in the seasonal workforce sharing the woods—smoke-jumpers and naturalists, raft guides and researchers—many of whom are, if not blissfully content, at the very least enjoying our work day to day. But. I know deeply fulfilled accountants, happy real estate agents, and miserable traildogs. I have felt the restless squeeze of discontentment, even in the woods. My worries and roadblocks, when they appear, are as crippling as anyone's: what if Gabe needs an MRI for that knee injury, or worse, surgery? Where will we live this winter if last year's rental falls through? Could I even take the GREs anymore? Am I wasting my life?

Something interesting connects the two responses—both the critics and the admirers of my seasonal career find it novel, in part because it's temporary. Although rehire is likely for skilled employees, it's never guaranteed. To some, a seasonal job is not a real job because it isn't permanent. But my worries, and yours, confirm the opposite: nothing's realer than impermanence. I work with elements—rain, mud, metal, sun, rock—always in flux, no more or less immutable than the figures an accountant balances or the health a nurse works to promote. Even in the most secure professional circles, people get laid off, change jobs, lose interest in one field, learn another trade late in life. As witnessed in the past few years, corporations collapse, industries shut down, and economies falter. Nothing's too big to fail. One of the many things I love about trailwork is that in its seasonality, it is honest. No false assurance. Security only in the moment. Take the rest it as it comes.

And though I covet good health insurance and being laid off is stressful, impermanence is the fickle siren that draws me—many of us—to this career. I love working as hard as I can for a time, and then being cut loose, free not from work itself—other tasks and habits beckon—but free from the burden of being completely defined by a job. My career thus far has been as a seasonal worker, and I'm proud of my membership in that group. Traildogs are shape-shifters, opportunists, freelance experts. Our work's parameters are weather, budget, season. Temperature, health, light. Now here, now gone.

An autumn hitch at Ole Lake, crew camped on the beach. The Middle Fork is under no-open-flames restrictions; the summer's been hot and dry and all of Montana is a kindling pile. Smoke hangs in the air from wildfires in the Bob Marshall to the south. After dinner, always eager to flout whatever rules are most pertinent, the crew builds a contraband fire on the beach exposed by drought, and drinks beers, crunching the empties against their knees. The crew leader disappears, unnoticed. Minutes later, a flash down the beach makes the guys look. There's Brook, standing on the widest strip of sand with his back to the crew, feet planted wide, head tipped skyward, fists in the air. He's at the center of a fiery anarchy symbol, flames knee-high before they shrink to a smoldering ring. A can of saw gas sits just beyond the perimeter. The crew watches Brook stand unmoving in his pose until the fire's out, smoke rising from the beach. He drops his arms and stands still in the dark. In the morning, the anarchy symbol is black and ragged in the sand, as if it were traced with a huge crayon by a maniac. Which in a way, it was.

How to fell a tree: first, size it up. Thump the trunk, listen for rot's dull thud. Scan the upper half for lean, for twin-tops, widow-makers, a strong wind visible in branches. Check your escape routes, safety zones. Then take your saw in both hands. The chain should be sharp, yesterday's work. Flip choke on for a cold start. Pull cord until engine fires, one (choke off), two, three times, don't flood. Feather trigger, throttle to full rev, listen—high whine, low idle. Choose your lay, check your sights. Begin face cut: bottom cut, one-third the tree's width. Check sights again. Match slant cut to face cut, protect your holding wood. Aim for smooth edges, exact angles.

Take a deep breath. Look up again. Branches feather the sky, clouds, a squirrel high up plans its exit. Any wind?

Shout, "Back cut!" Begin a few inches higher than the bottom of the wedge and cut evenly. Keep saw close to body until there's a sliver of holding wood, holding. If the fall lags, pound wedge with butt of axe. The tree will lean forward, grain against gravity until the tipping point. Shout, "Falling!" Back away, eyes on it. The trunk hits ground solid, busted branches fly up, grouse burst from brush. Breath comes back to the mouth hard. Woodchips in your eyes, sweat-greased earplugs, pitch on hands, the sweet smell of saw mix, needles hot in sun, heartwood exposed to air for the first time in fifty years. Then, the limbing, the bucking, low crouch to flush the stump, teeth dogged in, the powerhead so close to your face you breathe in saw mix like greasy air.

I love trees, big, old stately trees, limby and thick-barked. And I love to fell trees. How can I weigh the sides, check the balances: old growth against my truck and our travels; chlorophyll against my bookish dreams? What we love against the cost of loving. I have a recurring dream in which I am dropped off by a small plane in a forest of the biggest trees on Earth. The grove is thick in my nostrils, trees on my tongue like the body of someone else's finest wine. I smell them. I taste them. I cut them down.

Half the fun of living in the woods is eating, and communal meals cement a crew. A good meal scarfed down by five hungry people who've busted ass all day is both balm and bond, easing past tensions and betting against future ones. On hitches we took turns, one person cooking for the gang each night, with rotating dish duty in round metal tubs. Cabin meals were five-star—appetizers, a woodstove pie. Backcountry meals were simpler, but the mules packed in Coleman two-burners and coolers with ice so we didn't suffer. Abby made rich desserts, Max ruled at Dutch oven cuisine, trout jumped from creeks onto our plates. The default meal was burritos, or any version of innards you could wrap in a tortilla and eat with both hands. (With Indian filling instead of Mexican, we coined *currito* long before the franchises.) Carbohydrates were critical—pasta, a loaf of bread, skillet potatoes. Frozen homemade soups and stews served double purpose: they chilled the cooler for the first half of the hitch and thawed into a one-pot meal a few days in.

Dinner was for refueling, socializing, chilling out, and competitive eating. We were ravenous and truly needed calories, but we also ate to outeat each other, quantities that would disgust in any other context. No cook wanted to leave crewmates hungry, which led to overestimated quantities and, often, a serving left in the bottom of the pot. Unfinished food was a pain in the ass; leftovers were hard to store in the packed coolers, and thrown away, food stunk up the trash, which, hoisted in Hefty bags from high tree branches, got heavier by the day. We needed a garbage disposal. On some crews, the same guy—a skinny twenty-two-year-old boy, usually—always cleaned out the pot. But a crew without a designated bottomless pit rotated the task among members. If you never offered to clean the pot, you'd be resented for shirking. Worse, someone would call you a wuss, your general worth weirdly calibrated to your (non)appetite. This tradition produced a strange, proud relationship with gluttony, summed up in the common trails refrain: "Being full is no excuse for not eating."

Good meals so frequent, the bad ones stood out. A new kid on a crew, eighteen and just out of high school, had never cooked for himself before his first hitch meal, which he called taco salad: wet iceberg lettuce beneath a lump of Grade C fried hamburger, chalky shredded cheese, canned salsa, and Fritos crushed atop the gray pile. Compared to Thai stir-fries and pan-fried pizza, this did not go over well. No one told the kid outright that his meal sucked, but traildogs specialize in stoic passive-aggression, and he got the message from our wordless picking and the way we slammed things around in the food box as we packed the next day's lunch. A village stoning hurts the worst. We got $12 per diem, for Pete's sake, and though we all liked banking the extra, a crewmate who went deliberately cheap was scorned. We weren't asking for king crab—he could have bought Grade A beef. In his defense, you learn fast at eighteen. He never made taco salad again.

At a hitch on Logging Lake, Bryce, an odd and pasty fellow who never quite fit in, promised fresh-caught trout for dinner. Eating late is a dinner foul in its own right; we're all starving at 5:30. We want to eat and be free before bed—to read, go for a swim, or a hike, retreat to the tent and privacy. So, when Bryce returned with a single fish at 8:30, which he bathed in cheap oil and supplemented with soft, raw "tahfu" (for the vegetarian), we barely contained our disgust. Making a crew wait for dinner was one thing. Making them wait for a gross dinner that they finished with growling stomachs was a crime punishable by the coldest of shoulders. We rummaged noisily through lunch stores, scarfing down a Clif Bar or carefully rationed cookies. Bryce lasted only one summer.

After five seasons of trailwork and five winters of patched-together jobs (surveyor's assistant, temp file clerk, legal researcher, deli prep cook, US census schlep, volunteer laborer, women's clinic counselor, nonprofit activist, newsletter editor, aide for disabled adults), I began to feel stirrings of discontent. My Protestant roots tapped deep, and I couldn't shake the idea of *vocation*, a heeling dog that walked too close. The niggling hunch that "work" was more than just "job."

Woodswork satisfied me at a level that nothing else ever had. It balanced me at a time when I had put too much faith in my brain. It authenticated me. But five seasons into my labor career, I had a tentative hunger, an appetite for something I wasn't quite sure of, though I thought it had to do with words. With language. With the slip of the hidden beneath the seen. I wondered about trailwork, how long it would be good for me. My philosophical bent prodded: is the work that I'm doing the work I want to be doing? Forever? Do I owe the world anything other than this hard and simple labor? Is there an itch in me, a passion gone dormant? I remembered old college professors I saw from time to time, who asked what I was doing with my life. I thought of my grandmother, who chastened me after years passed with no return to school. How to separate my own wishes from the expectations of others? The way I saw myself from the way I was seen?

That winter Gabe and I put in for the Peace Corps and I also applied to graduate school, imagining our options beyond western Montana and another season in Glacier. When I was fresh out of college, working in the woods was the challenge, and school off-puttingly familiar. Five years out, my trails job seemed like something I was possibly coasting on, and school the curious new. Classes, lectures, big ideas, I let the prospect of them thrill me again.

It's easy to make the split too simple: choose body, choose mind, a dichotomy that doesn't work even on paper. It did not feel simple at all. The thought of giving up woodswork, consigning it to the realm of "I did that once," rang a deep, unconsiderable loss. Trailwork was not a phase, a thing I'd say I did in summers when I was young. It had become a part of me, as grafted to my sense of self as childhood stories or future dreams. Yet I needed something. What did one do when the workingman's thinker was ready to become the thinking man's worker? Was there somewhere we could go to augment our life in the woods without leaving it altogether?

My grandmother's admonition—"Don't waste your gifts, dear!"—included a reference to the New Testament parable of the man who buried his talents in the sand. In the parable's context, a talent was a biblical monetary unit, but it's widely interpreted to mean a gift of any sort, including a talent as we think of it today. "Don't bury your talents in a hole," Grandma told me, and she meant, don't squander what you've been given. I appreciated her confidence, but I had to laugh at the allusion. She meant to spur me to a higher calling, to do right by my potential. But all I could think when I heard that phrase? If my talents needed burying, at least I could dig a hell of a good hole.

Glacier National Park is designated wilderness. Ask anyone—it's nature with a capital N. But as in most "preserved" places, traces of human impact—of culture—rustle beneath the pristine surface. In Glacier there are abandoned mine shafts on craggy passes, rusty machine parts along creek beds. Native tribal trade routes form the scaffolding for the trails network. The park's designation as wilderness owed much to the development of the railroad. Mossy foundation stones lie embedded in ground way off the trodden paths.

One of my favorite cultural relics in the park is the Doody Homestead, a dilapidated structure located off the Boundary Trail, a half mile downstream from the confluence of Harrison Creek with the Middle Fork. The ruin was Dan and Josephine Doody's homestead, built along Burlington Northern's Empire Builder train line before Highway 2 went in. Dan was a one of the first rangers in the park (fired later for poaching) and Josephine was a moonshiner and a "hostess" long after her husband's death. Approaching the structure from the forested trail, you can't see it until you're almost in it: two stories high and rotten, a staircase topping out to a punched-through upper floor. Rusted bedsprings and tin cans with antique labels, a collapsing double-seater outhouse visible through a glassless window. You don't even have to close your eyes to imagine miners and fishermen tipping back shots in the guestrooms, a curvy hooker doing the two-step with a top-hatted investor canvassing the Wild West.

Mixed in with the present—gusty wind in the grass and the *chip* of red squirrels— there's the past: twang of phantom honky-tonk, the smell of pork chops frying.

Evidence of human impact is another layer of this wild place, like the stratum of volcanic ash in the soil or the inland fossils that prove this arid forest was once a sea. Human history is palpable in the Middle Fork. Wilderness, the empty kind, is rare anywhere, and most of our places are not really untouched; we have always lived amid cultures on land. Old tin cans may undermine the claim of virgin wilderness, but they are relics that point us toward a candid way of seeing nature: not a distant diorama of a wilder place, but a home.

When I stand at the Doody Homestead, history feels concrete, but at the same time there's a spooky, ethereal vibe, as if it were haunted not by a person, not even by a specific psychological presence, but by a version of ourselves at an earlier time. I imagine what it's like to be native to this land, to know that your people and their stories have coexisted with a place for so long as to be inextricable, for good and ill—an autumn hunt rich in antelope meat, but the baby died later in a cold snap. A pass to cross for summer grounds, also an alley for enemy ambush. Food you ate because it was there. Seasons that triggered decisions, rivers that, some months, couldn't be got across, and so you stayed. Imagine it's no stretch to be interwoven with place: unbound by the present moment, terrain as physical receptacle for memory, geography as palimpsest, a layer always visible beneath the current story, home-making possible in all but the most inhospitable settings. Peel up nature, and there's culture beneath it. Scratch culture, and it's nature that will bleed.

Wild will fight for itself. Wild is unhemmed, cuffs dragging in the mud, fist balled up, thumping. Wilderness may require paperwork to bolster it, but wildness is wisp of instinct, a hunger silhouetted. Palm open. It is both cusp and center.

———

On hitches deep in the Middle Fork, the packers stayed overnight because fifteen miles in was too far to round-trip in a day. They'd tie off the mules to the hitch rail or trees and stay the night with the crew. On the trail, Slim ate cold fried chicken brought from home in his saddlebag and, at night, drank a half rack of Oly and bullshitted with the crew until he passed out near the fire and slept wrapped in a manta cloth, his boots for a pillow. A packer in socks made you feel a little uneasy, those bony, socked feet a secret you'd rather not know.

One rimy morning, world encased in fragile hoar, Slim stumbled around outside the cabin in his union suit, hollering, "I can't find m'gaddam pants!" Sleepy and cold. Staggering in baggy underwear. It was the most vulnerable he'd ever seemed.

Another time the packers stayed over, Brook came from the hitch rail gesturing to Slim and a few laborers about a mysterious mule. "Last night, Curly was hitched up on the far side of the rail, and this morning, he's on the other side."

"So?"

"He's in the middle of the rail, and he's short-roped!" He paused for effect. "He must have jumped over!" Brook cracked up. Tristan looked at him, his blue eyes round. "Cool!" he said, but Slim glared. He hated it when the mules did anything out of the ordinary. "Cool?" he withered. "There ain't a gaddam thing *cool* about it!" This phrase serves, in any context, as the perfect way to express disdain.

For centuries of work in the woods, including the logging of this continent's great forests, the crosscut was the felling tool of choice. A five-foot-long flexible saw blade (with a curved back for felling or a straight back for bucking), a toothed edge, and a handle mounted on each end, the two-man crosscut dropped big trees with more control and efficiency than an axe, with less likelihood of the tree falling backward and crushing the sawyer (the leading cause of beaver fatalities). Crosscuts still get plenty of modern use, in wilderness areas where mechanized tools are forbidden, in remote settings where a constant supply of gas and oil is not feasible, and in instances where a noise ban protects wildlife—nesting eagles, migrating songbirds, denning wolves.

The crosscut is a beautiful tool, perfectly engineered for a sawing duo and its single task. Using a crosscut takes muscle; cutting earns you big arms and lats and the kind of soreness that results in one of the tool's nicknames: the misery whip. But it also takes delicacy; don't overmuscle it or the saw blade will buckle or bind, and don't fight your partner—let the push stroke gently float away, make the pull stroke true and hard.

Across the highway in the Bob Marshall, the Forest Service uses crosscuts solely; the Bob's wilderness designation prohibits motorized maintenance. The history of old woodscraft is beautifully preserved in that reliance, but there's a cost. Trail crews in the Bob spend all summer logging out deadfall, with barely time enough to get trails open for traffic, let alone repair damage or upgrade structures. The trails are historical and quiet, but hammered. With trails budgets as they are, it's only a matter of time before work overtakes workforce. Slowly, more miles of trail succumb to lack of maintenance, eventually too impacted, obscured, or degraded for ordinary use.

The park, though it contains designated wilderness, has a chainsaw exemption for trailwork, and our crews did most clearing with power saws. Even with mechanized assistance, keeping the trails open was an annual challenge. Back in the crosscut days, the trail crews were three, four times as big as they are today. If we were to use only crosscuts now, half of the trails would never get cleared, resulting in greater resource damage. So, we trade off. A little historical value sacrificed for a little modern access. Hikers appreciate it; the growing burden of industrial-scale tourism demands it. With a burgeoning population seeking respite in nature and an ever-shrinking agency budget, the days of sustainable land use are long gone, so what option is there? No matter our preservationist bias, for these months we're laborers, not lobbyists. Short a major change in policy, there's nothing to do but fire up the saws.

Forest Service crews like to play superior, and sometimes I think they are, calibrated honestly to the slow, steady drone of handwork, what's possible in a day dictated by their own limits. But although there's less vintage cachet to the chainsaw than the crosscut, running a power saw is an art, too; this is clear when you watch someone who's really good at it. Even without nostalgia to buoy its value, skill is compelling, and moving wood is good work. There are places where it's best to do it by hand, and places to do it faster. Whether in the Bob or the park, a long day of sawing is a wearisome and admirable thing, and work does what it does—helps keep cynicism at bay. Visitation numbers and crew budgets and land designations fall away; crosscut or chainsaw, the things that have always been true remain true. Don't cut through holding wood. Stand uphill of a log when bucking. Keep the teeth out of the dirt.

Five of us stand in the parking lot at the trailhead, shovels and pulaskis over our shoulders, awaiting the crew leader. A man approaches the trail and passes the cluster of us, looks us over, keeps walking, then, just before heading into the woods, he stops and asks: What are you looking for? We glance at each other, blank. No one gives a derisive snort, or leaps to the usual explanations about maintenance, about drain dips and turnpikes. What *are* we looking for? It's a damn good question, isn't it?

Glacier National Park belongs to the traditional territory of the Niitsitapii. Translated as "the real people," the Blackfoot Indians of Western Montana call these mountains the backbone of the world. The Blackfoot traditionally used Glacier's passes as travel routes and rarely lived in the mountains, steep as they were, glaciated and inhospitable. Some peaks have sacred purposes—vision quests, celebrations—but home was always the plains, where long vistas made enemies easy to spot and prevalent game surrounded the settlement. The current towns of Babb and East Glacier mimic that historical range, lying just east of the divide on the Blackfoot Reservation. To an outsider's eye it's a desolate and hardscrabble place; rustic, undeveloped, perched on the edge of the gust-scoured plains as if it's only there until the wind moves it again.

In my six seasons in Glacier, Dwight was the only Blackfoot I worked with for long. He did trails for years and his nickname was "The Surgeon," for his prowess at chainsaw repair. He was a quiet guy who spoke with the distinct lilt of Blackfoot speech, and when he laughed, his upper body ratcheted from the waist.

Dwight had a drinking problem. Many traildogs binge-drink on days off, and most can't go a night without beer. But Dwight came to work hung-over, checked out. He smelled like liquor distilled through flannel. He was often late; once, still drunk, he passed out at lunch break, pale and damp-faced. His crew leader held it against him, as was his right. There was tension. The leader felt his hands were tied: if he came down hard on the only Native for being late, would he be racist? Was giving him a pass because he was a Native any better? The whole thing made him nervous.

It made me nervous, too. I wished Dwight didn't have a drinking problem. Partly because being around drunks of any race makes me uneasy and sad. I wanted Dwight to be able to look his leader in the eye. I thought I was rooting for him: *There's not much on the reservation, Dwight. Don't get fired.* Now it's so clear to me, the condescension I missed back then—I'd assumed my elective career was a job he felt lucky to have. I never asked.

I didn't know much then about addiction's vice grip, or the burden of only-ness. I never asked Dwight how it felt to come from the rez to work in the park. I never asked him if he liked his job. Under that, if he liked us. And under that, if he liked me. I wanted him to like me. It would mean that I was a good white person. But Dwight didn't offer much, a reticence partly cultural, partly personal. Who could blame him?

I remember a joke I heard, maybe twice, in those days. How do you starve an Indian? Answer: hide his unemployment check under his work boots. This falls into the category of despicable jokes prized by a group of people who find nothing too dirty, too shameful, too rude to laugh at. Sexist jokes, politics jokes, pedophile jokes: trail-dogs tell them all. We push too far. In our way, we're snatching after some of the nuance that "correctness" stifles. We're eager to see difference, tension, to name it the only way we dare. (We're weeding out the easily horrified, who won't last long on a trail crew.) Some jokes, especially when told to or by the target, can be liberating. When I screwed up on the work site, I could trust one of the guys to say, "Guess you'd better give the boss a blowjob." That pissed me off. But it also made me laugh. We all howled when the only queer guy on the crew told jokes about butt pirates. There's nothing like rapping on the wooden head of taboo.

When I think about the starving Indian joke, though, I cringe. I don't recall it being told in front of Dwight. Humor can be a great equalizer, but maybe that's true only if you already feel equal, and all the conventional wisdom about racism said Dwight couldn't possibly have felt equal. But maybe he did. Maybe Dwight felt better than us, and we couldn't look him in the eye. In any case, the subtext of the joke was clear: Indian=lazy=worthless=drunk. Reality made it more ridiculous than funny. For one thing, most of us collected unemployment checks. And Dwight wasn't lazy. He could hike fast, and he was strong. He wasn't worthless; he knew things a lot of us did not. But I couldn't gloss over drunk. It stunk up the cab of the truck. It frayed the crew bond.

In the years since I knew Dwight in Glacier, I've learned that addictions of any kind—work, sex, the private ones we don't even admit to ourselves—have, in many cases, less to do with genes and race than with a thing broken and the urge to mend. Add to that very ordinary pathology the distinct wounds of genocide and its parody, the guilt-built pedestal, and brokenness becomes tragically explicable. A Tlingit writer I know said to me once, "History has done its work and left us here, and sometimes it seems like such a great divide." Like many western whites, I wish I could undo history. Like many humans, I wish I could return to a time I did someone wrong, meet that person again, and make it right. I am not even a footnote in Dwight's biography, I know. I make too much of myself, thinking about it this long. Why? In part because, as that same writer, large of heart, said next, "The only way we can go on is together." I want to believe her. I want to be believed.

How can we go on together, Dwight? You could tell me the jokes about white people: there must be a book full. I could say I'm sorry for laughing at a joke that did you wrong. You could make me foolish, as I have done to you. We could mock the tourists instead, those hapless wankers who think I can't carry the saw because I'm a woman and you must know Chief Joseph because you look like their postcards. I want us to laugh at it together, this stupid script that neither of us wrote but both of us star in. I want us a fucking standing ovation.

That's what I want, but here's all I know: Dwight drank too much, had a great laugh, and was a hell of a sawyer. I get it. He was not then, and is not now, my Indian. And neither of us needs any applause.

Sierra Club volunteers came to the park every summer to do trailwork service trips. Predominantly men and women in their forties and fifties, middle- to upper-class, these dedicated conservationists pay hundreds of dollars to visit the park and do some good, and they usually got sent to do good in the Middle Fork, which always needed charity. Twelve volunteers per trip, they came with their own crew leader and a cook. They were good citizens, many of them interesting folks with golden intentions. But none of them, even the leaders, could do trailwork without serious guidance. So the park placed a pro crew on the project, to model the pace and the standards and do QC.

It wasn't kind, but we always complained about working with the Clubbers. From a distance, they could be a little eager, almost embarrassing in their earnestness. Some admired us too cheerily, claiming that ours was "real work." A few were insufferable, arrogant do-gooders with a sense of urban entitlement out of synch with woods culture. We were grunts, they thought, and they could easily master our trade in no time flat. Any dummy could dig, after all, and they were architects, psychologists, engineers. To be fair, to them, I'm sure we seemed unkempt and young, cocky and woodsier-than-thou.

But, over the course of a hitch, the work usually schooled us in each other's real ways. We let down our guard and grew to like some of them, the ones who could laugh and cuss, who ribbed us and didn't take things so seriously, and they began to like us, even our crass mouths and bravado. We shared pride in the job we were doing, grounded in our bodies made tired by work. We traded trivia on trips back and forth from the fill pit, surprised at what we knew in common (Battle of Normandy, Johnny Cash's first hit single, how many digits of pi). We asked them questions over dinner about their cases and clients, about living in San Francisco, Chicago, their pets, their kids. They asked us if we'd gone to college (some yes, some no), what we did in the winters (ski, travel, serve coffee, more trailwork, write). We plowed through our usual gut-bomb dinners, and they delighted in their forsaken city diets, packing food in like they'd earned it.

One volunteer per trip managed to preserve his disgruntled superiority, bemoaning the work, the weather, the bugs. The biggest jerk I've ever met in my life was on a Sierra Club trip, a type-A hedge fund guy from L.A. who thought so highly of himself I'm not sure what tempted him into service at all. He disdained advice, did things wrong just to do it his own way, patronized the women, had a short temper, broke things. After my first few olive branches got snapped and handed back, I turned cold out of spite. I gave him tedious jobs and my evilest eye. On the opposite end of the spectrum was a delightful older woman—a veterinarian, I think—and her grown daughter, both of them proud of their blisters, the fact that by the end of the week they could tell pulaski from mattock and chisel from adze. I cheered their prowess and told them our jokes (not too dirty). The woman and her daughter, and that unhappy man, stand out in my mind as clear reminders—there are all kinds of people in all kinds of places. No archetypes, villains from the city, saints from the woods. Flagging a cab or chopping a log, it's pretty simple: sometimes we like each other, sometimes we don't.

Justin, Kent, Gabe, Sam, Max, and I had been clearing every day for a week. We'd drive to the trailhead listening to eighties rock on B-98 ("the Flathead's best rock-and-roll!") and then load tools onto our packs, three saw teams to cut the epic downfall left by the past winter's winds that blew hard through a burn. We shed our morning fleece by 9 a.m., sweating long before the day found its heated center. At lunch on the last day of that week, every one of us fell asleep. We woke in a collective rustle twenty minutes after break should have been over, tripping over ourselves to hustle, one guy with a puddle of drool on his sweatshirt, my backpack buckle imprinted on my cheek. It's the only time I remember Max spending a second over thirty minutes on a lunch break.

Few trails jobs kicked my ass like long days logging out trails. We hiked, depending on the density of downfall, sometimes four miles, sometimes twenty. The weight of the saw, the work of cutting, and the focus it took made for profound weariness. I loved those days, even in the early weeks of the season, out of shape and vying not to be last in line, even at the end of the season, burnt out and stiff, even in the rain, even in a burn when the bark was compressed powder and cutting made us cough, left a thin film of ash on our skin. I loved those days. I loved them because I loved running a chainsaw, and I loved them because I felt free. Free to work hard and talk shit and eat huge lunches, free to laugh with the guys, even those I had nothing in common with after 5:30, free to be confident and at the same time have so much left to learn. Free to run a saw without being "a woman who can run a saw."

The knife edge of work flayed off the silly posturing, the eyeball and swagger between men and women in the regular world, where a girl unloading a chainsaw from the back of a truck elicits a leering whistle, when entering an engine repair shop brings on the size-up from the shop tech that men do not get, the one that says, *How much does she know?* When you're cutting with a partner, swapping back and forth all day, breakneck, and then, when you're both exhausted and there's still the hike out to the truck, and the miles seem long but bring 'em on, there is no energy for *Isn't a girl with a chainsaw sexy* or *Does he think I'm competent?* There is energy only for the necessary: *Did he drop the rakers* or *I wonder if she has any water left* or *Take this thing, please, it's killing me.*

The packer Greg refused to walk more than the distance from the barn to the stock truck or the string to the hitch rail. He rarely led the mules on foot. "Walkin'? Hurts too damn much," he said. He couldn't touch his stiff knees, let alone his feet. He complained cheerfully, thumped his melon-belly with both hands: "It's hard work draggin' this pup around." Once, Reba asked, "Greg, you ever try yoga?" He looked at her, cocked a bushy eyebrow. "Nah, I don't eat that stuff. Too sour."

By late summer, the Middle Fork is clogged with vegetation. The long drainages (Park, Nyack) spend 15 to 20 miles in the trees before trail pops into the open alpine. Every so often there's a burn, an old-growth clearing, or open spots along rivers with cottonwoods, but mostly, miles and miles of lodgepole, Doug-fir, spruce, larch, pine. In July, brush takes over the lowlands: blueberry and mountain maple, devil's club and cow parsnip, alder and willow and yew tangled in a cat's cradle. A trail that's been neglected more than five years turns from pathway to tunnel. Head off the trail two feet to take a piss and you could be gone a while, searching for cut log ends or that brighter swath of light to guide you back on trail. Whoever first said, "Can't see the forest for the trees" had surely been lost in woods like these, knew this about the big picture: perspective is critical, and easily obscured.

When a crew brushes a trail, we cut vegetation back five or six feet off each side, and when the job's done, the mess raked up and dragged away, we hike back through the swath with saws and brushers over our shoulders, sticky and satisfied, the itch of cow parsnip on our forearms, devil's club spines embedded in our fingers. Yet, despite the open view of the trail snaking into the distance, the weary muscles that tell us we've made a dent, we can feel the greenery sneaking back in as we pass, a sinister behind-the-back enemy: too slow to catch in the act, too fast to feel we've conquered anything.

On September 11, 2001, we were up Harrison Creek working on a bridge, a bunch of remnants from different crews assembled for the late-season project. It was clear and cool with starry nights, elk rutting, and the trees turning their seasonal stunts, the kind of weather and place in which you just feel lucky to be alive. On September 12, Sam and Mitch hiked in to join us, and we looked forward to their arrival—the paper, extra chocolate, new jokes. They showed while we were having lunch in the sun, one gabion abutment finished, the log stringers ready to be hauled across the span. Sam pulled the paper out of his pack. Mitch said *bomb* and *plane* and *terrorists* and *dead* and *New York.* The rest of us looked at each other: are they screwing with us? This remote, so easy to play *War of the Worlds,* to invent some disturbing news we couldn't disprove until we got out in a week. Those guys were jokers. We wouldn't put such a caper past them. But there was the headline in the *Daily Interlake,* not prone to reporting beyond the region. There was the color photo, mostly smoke, and the headlines in large type. It looked real.

Like every American, I have a memory of 9/11, a flash my mind

returns to. Mine isn't of the towers, not the first collapse on live TV, or the second, or the hundredth. I didn't come out of the woods for another week, and then to our TV-less cabin, buffered from media and spin. To this day I have never seen the live footage of the falling towers. I've heard stories from friends, some of them New Yorkers who were on the N train or the Brooklyn Bridge when the planes hit. But I did not experience the news, raw and then, instantly, mediated. I was insulated from the unrelenting aftermath. In a defining cultural moment, an odd one out.

My days following 9/11 were full of sensory experiences incongruous with national trauma. The feel of water flooding my waders as we set the footings for the bridge. The sharp sound of the rut. Late-summer sun warming my flannel. The strange experience of peace amid larger turmoil. The disparity was garish. How could those worlds—the one of steel and force and hate, and the one of antlers and dirt and camaraderie—be the same world? How was I so protected from the abject horror of the New Yorker, or the desperate loathing of the extremist? To what stroke of fate or luck or karma or blessing did I owe the fact that my memories of 9/11/2001 were of an unbombed world, inured from all but the ordinary harm of storms, food chain, flood?

I am thankful for that positioning, not to bury my head in wilderness at the expense of the human, but because that dichotomy—steadiness in the face of mayhem—reminds me that peace is possible. Reminds me that even amid terror and silencing, aggression and defense, there are pockets of life indelibly sublime, and that we can remember them, bring them to the fore, not to escape the reality of violence, but to counter it, to temper hopelessness and despair with wind, water, light.

Later, when I lived in a city and was consumed by the frantic marches for peace, letters to the editor, petitions, and arguments, I'd think back on that week at Harrison Creek often. It was a less tangible response than diplomacy or activism, but even years later, those moments outdoors in a world not of my making were both antidote and balm.

Over the course of that hitch, during brief moments of downtime between cutting and pounding and digging and cooking and sleep, I mulled over villainy and victims. I thought about people hating people, and terrorism, a distant but far more haunting menace than the grizzly bears that passed by our camp in the trees. War, the idea of it, filled every blank space in my mind. I wondered if it would happen, where it would happen, when. If we were on the cusp of something big.

By the time the hitch was over and we'd mannied our loads for the packers, the news was a week old. The world beyond Harrison Creek was moving from shock and mourning to analysis and revenge. Fall had blown in on a stiff wind, ice skiffed the creek's edges at night and sleet fell sideways on the hike out, coating the mules' hides with hoar. The bridge was finished. We left it to weather winter's snow load and next spring's melt. The elk remained, intent on mating.

We are always on the cusp of something big.

Autumn. Late season. Seven a.m. is cold. We huddle in the shop too long, shifting in our boots while the rigs warm up in the dark. By eight thirty, the truck's parked riverside and we're wading, legs wet below the knees. In morning light, larch trees blaze gold, lit hills roll into deep fall. Traffic sound fades, summer folk long gone home, the river now low enough to ford for the first time in months. Sharp nights, earlier stars, a new bluish-black tint to midnight, the color that expects dark dreams.

The current's strong here, midriver water low over rock. Tools heavy on the shoulder. Shoulder heavy in the socket. Air comes in the mouth cold.

Summer has worn out. The saws need work (sharpen chain, grease the bearings, carburetor's running lean). The body's hinges rust, quiet. Thoughts turn to winter's tasks. The mind balances between the work of now and the preparing for soon.

Ten yards away the far bank waits. Beneath our feet, rocks slip against each other and demand a patient step, a sure foot, each of us focused on this lurching pace unchanged by what will later come. Autumn's balance is preserved in this: the wide-legged stance midriver, then a turning.

On the last day of my last season in Glacier, I turned in my keys, signed out at headquarters. Tools clean, trail reports written, evaluations over. I swung by the barn to say goodbye to the packers. They don't hold much truck with ceremony, you can imagine. The hope for closure was mine, more likely to end in awkward foot-shuffling than the hearty hugs and good wishes even the most stoic of my crewmates could provide. So near quitting time, I found the packers hidden in the dark barn, sitting on stumps in the tack room. Greg raised a Mountain Dew: "Wish it were an Oly!" Sheldon crossed his legs, picked at the tooling on his boots.

These guys had known me for six seasons, and by strictest traildog standards you had to put in seven before you even got your "dog year." (Less than that earned you the derisive label "hobbyist.") But I'd stuck around, and they knew me, first as "that skinny girl," then as "the one who goes with Cassie" and finally by various mangled versions of my given name. Still, without the salve of task, no mules to load or miles to cover, there wasn't much to say. I made a few lame stabs about the fall weather when Slim interrupted: *So I heard ya ain't comin' back, that's what they all say. Yer not back when it's next year and you ain't here! Kent says yer leavin' to go to school, go write gaddam books?* I smiled. That's the hope, I shrugged, but who knows? Grad school was, from this vantage, a destination odder than the moon. To the crew, I'd joked that MFA stood for "My Fucking Art." It seemed most gracious to suggest that my leave-taking could just as likely result in failure—silly me and my dreams. But Slim wasn't finished: *I'll*

*tell ya what I wanna know, whattina hell ya needa go ta school da write
books for? Ima write me a book, call it* Switchbacks and Cocksuckers*!*

Any awkwardness in the room evaporated like spilt white gas
and we cackled at the thought of Slim writing a book at all (the picture of him hunched over a desk in his black hat a "true crack-up,"
as Cassie would say), and then, what title could be more perfect than
the one he'd chosen? *Switchbacks and Cocksuckers*, my God! Who
knew how long he'd been thinking of that, waiting to try it out loud?
We laughed a while, all four of us, even Slim, who usually didn't care
for a joke on himself. Then he got serious: *Yer district looks all right
this year, see who fucks it up when yer gone. Anyway, we got work to do,
them new mules getting' shoed in Kalispell, Greg's gotta pick 'em up and
the stock truck shit the bed. You'll prolly be back next year like the rest of
'em, I been trying to leave this crappy joint for years.*

On my way out, I passed through the paddock to pat my favorite animals, and Greg shouted at my back, "Well, you been around
long enough, maybe we'll name a mule after you!" Slim laughed,
getting my name wrong one last time: "A mule named Christy! Put
that in your gaddam book, why dontcha?"

Such tenderness! With my back to them, I blushed. In a field
where transience is a given, where short-timers' faces are quickly
forgotten from one season to the next, a mule named for me was
sweeter praise than any "good luck." I've never checked back to see
if they actually did it. It was enough, for those minutes, just to think
they might, to be considered, to belong so completely to a world I
was leaving behind.

Every cut has a kerf. Picture a sawhorse, a two-by-four across it, the
saw partway through. The line where the wood will split in two is
the kerf. A log across the trail, the saw dogged in, a chain-width gap:
that's kerf. When the cut is complete, the kerf disappears. Writer
Thomas Glynn describes the kerf as "the channel in the wood the
saw rides in"; while Richard Manning writes "that's the path the saw

makes into sawdust—the path is waste, not lumber, so some of the strength of the original tree dies on a sawdust pile." It's a pragmatic point, but how can kerf be waste? Kerf is the critical negative space of wood, as present in every severance as water is present in air or a pause is present in a line. Kerf is no commodity. It cannot be sold, held, or used. If Derrida were a carpenter, kerf would be the *trace* of sawing, the invisible evidence of what has passed. To the builder, kerf is a shorter board, a penny tax on every cut. To a student of Zen, kerf is the path that disappears behind you as you walk on it, the way you can only see by not looking. It's the between of the before and the after, this thing and the next. To the wood, kerf is gone.

Two days before I got on a plane for grad school in Anchorage, I hiked in to visit Gabe and his crew hitched out at Harrison Lake. I forded the Middle Fork alone and ran into Gabe on the north side, heading for me. We hugged where the river met the woods, then hiked back to camp for dinner with the crew. The next morning, Gabe got up early for work and I slept until the sun hit the tent, drank a leisurely cup of tea. I lay on my back on fir needles and held in their smell until I had to gasp breath. I made Gabe's lunch for the trail, spreading peanut butter on both pieces of bread to keep the jam from soaking through. I moved slow, then fast, then slow again. Holding on, letting go.

Two weeks earlier, Gabe and I had gotten married in Polebridge, up the North Fork. By then we'd been together eight years (common-law married in Montana), six of them working trails. We fell in love in college amid stacks of books and late-night conversations about art and ethics, but we stayed in love in the woods. We made a life together of hitches and birthdays in tents in the pouring rain, and conversations, while hiking, about ethics and art. Glacier seemed the only place we could make vows worth keeping.

Under the kitchen tarp at Harrison Lake, the wedding seemed far off, already grafted into other memories of the North Fork, twined in with fourteen-hour workdays and weather to remember. Before the ceremony, my friend Rochelle knelt at my feet painting my toenails. A hasty ritual; as always, we were running late. The day before, I hiked out of an eight-day hitch in filthy clothes to a yard full of wedding guests in tents. Half an hour before, I was cruising the gravel road in my pickup, tending to the last details of a rural wedding—generator, weed whacker, extra fuel. I thought I was to be the only bride this century who didn't bathe before her vows. But I squeezed in a quick shower in the one cabin with plumbing, the water pressure too weak to blast the larch sap from my forearms. I sat in my chair before Rochelle, trying not to fidget. The guests waited in a half circle down by the river in the cottonwood grove. My sister braided my damp hair with wildflowers from the meadow in front of the cabin—a daisy, a sprig of valerian. I twisted in my seat and Rochelle slapped my knee.

"Stop wiggling," she said, stabbing the air with the wet brush. "I'll get it on your dress." I hiked the skirt above my knees and closed my eyes, felt her fingers on my toes, gentle over the bruised big toenail, the callouses. By the time Gabe and I entered the wedding circle, ushered within the cluster of our families, the polish was dry and we were ten minutes late. My fingernails remained pale, unpainted. My hands were not the soft, gloved hands of magazine weddings. Veins pushed up against the skin. A swollen sliver in the thumb. Creased knuckles faintly brown.

Just above the flood plain of the North Fork, beneath the faces of the mountains we'd called home, Gabe said his vows to me. I told him mine. The peaks to the northeast were as much witnesses as the guests shifting on their slab log benches—Numa Lookout, family, Rainbow Peak, fellow traildogs, old friends, Brown's Pass. I looked down at our feet, both sets in sandals. My toes were already dusty, the nails pink. I wiggled them, flashed their ceremonial shimmer. I was thinking what you'd imagine: there's this man I love, these people I love, witnessing our covenant. And something more: these mountains I love, the dirt under my nails. Some echo of *I trust myself.*

After the wedding, Gabe and I left on separate hitches, and this stolen overnight at Harrison Lake was the closest we'd get to a honeymoon. I'd head to Alaska the next evening. "Our life is a honeymoon," we'd joked at the wedding. We were kidding at some level, but sitting on a stump around the fire at night, it felt a little true. Like a honeymoon, our Glacier days were charged with feeling, rife with tenderness and laughter, and also little spats and lost chances and the sense, sometimes, that we could be missing something. The novelty of "married," put off for so many years, felt unmistakable, and it struck me at odd times—at lunch with the crew trading riddles, standing shin-deep in a lateral, wiping mud from my eyes. I watched Gabe in his suspenders and logging boots, same dear face, reddish beard, smile lines around the eyes, and tried the word: *husband*.

Midafternoon the next day, Gabe lined out the crew. He'd leave to take me to the airport for my evening flight, then hike back in to camp for the rest of the hitch. We had to hurry; I hadn't even packed yet. We forded the Middle Fork together, the slow water up to my thighs, a burned-out chainsaw heading back to the shop on my shoulder. The familiar view from midriver was wide-open, and Heraclites, rarely considered since college days, came to mind. "You can't step in the same river twice" hit me hard as I realized I would never return to this—to Montana in my twenties, the life I accidentally made here and loved, this steadiness in moving water with tools on my back. This exact balance of what I knew and what I did not know.

Hours later I'd pack my bags, by nightfall I'd be on a plane from Kalispell to Anchorage, the next day in a fiction workshop. That day, I would be outside less than an hour, riding my bike to the university on asphalt trail. Smelling like shampoo, not saw mix. My muscles, used to moving, urgent and sore. No one there would know about packers, or how to sharpen a saw. *Get over it*, I told myself. *You're a student again.* As if I hadn't been one for years.

So I threw myself in, and it felt right. Still, in the midst of class discussion about the elements of fiction (character, setting, tense), a discussion I had craved, I would nonetheless be struck wistful by how quickly things go from present to past. I'd think of Gabe, who would join me in a month when the season finished, for now still hitched out at Harrison Lake, his tent a heap of damp clothes, dirty boots. The way the larch would smell if the morning was warm. Startled, how that place—my *here* for so long—had turned overnight to *there*.

BOAT

Commute In forests and mountains, you get to the trailhead by truck, to the job site with boots and mules. But if the trails are surrounded by water, not land? If you are in Southcentral Alaska, where the Copper River Delta and Prince William Sound entwine so that land appears to float? No more trucks, boots, stock. Steady yourself, crouch low. Step into a boat.

Ocean Craft The seventeen-foot Boston Whaler is known as "the unsinkable legend." A flat-bottomed utility boat built for fishing, day research, and hauling tools or crews, the stripped-down Whaler is as ubiquitous seaside as Subarus in ski towns. It's not a luxurious boat, but a Whaler rides seas of three to four feet, is tough to tip, light and sturdy, and tucks trailered in a corner of the yard. Pair it with a ninety-horse Evinrude and cruise semiprotected waters, even if you've hardly driven a boat before. It's a ship for fools.

River Raft Rubber inflatable, all grown-up bath toy. With puffy gunnels, dry bags wedged between coolers and seats, a raft bobs on river waves like an optimist. A finger *thwack* to the rubber tubes will bruise a nail but leave no imprint. On long trips, it swallows the extra gas can, a box of cheap wine. Durable, buoyant, chubby yet sleek. Like a grade school buddy: unflappable, in primary-colored clothes.

Vocabulary Hull, gunnels, rudder, ballast, tiller, keel, paddle. Double letters mimic the symmetry necessary for flotation. Boat words, as with many words for work, sound deliberate. Saxonic. Deck, motor, oar, bow, stern, davit, fore, aft, transom, cockpit. The emphatic syllables, the grit of language distilled to convey essence—grunt, heave, float. Latinate words, too—navigate, triangulation—describing action more than thing. How many words for boat are there? Vessel, raft, ship, dinghy, craft, skiff, barge, dory, punt, ketch, shell, launch. The current or the tides a propellant they share, inescapable momentum, water as surface, as engine, as fuel.

Measurement The sea's maps are charts, showing depths and shoals, cliffs and islands, shipwrecks, beaches, buoys, and harbors. Measure waves in feet, bottom of trough to top of crest. Wind and boats both travel in knots: one knot, a nautical mile, is 1.15 miles per hour. Do seasoned boaters convert highway speed-limit signs in their heads? *Forty-five miles per hour, how many knots?* When traveling on water, your own speed matters as well as the speed of the medium, an extra dimension. On ocean, neither water nor vessel is still—always the rise and plunge, wave in, tide out. On rivers, current flows in cubic feet per second, the volume of water traveling past a point at a certain time. Sometimes it seems that the raft stays put and, beneath, the water moves.

History The Eyak have lived at the mouth of the Copper for ten thousand years. Today, Alaska's smallest Native tribe numbers fewer than two hundred members, the old Eyak village incorporated into the town of Cordova. These indigenous residents of the Sound were kayakers, the palindrome *kayak* an Aleut word, related to the Inuit *qayak,* meaning "hunter's boat." *Baidarkas* and *umiaks*, too, one double cockpit, one wide and open like a canoe. All used for fishing, hunting, and hauling passengers and cargo between land sites. Like the axe handle, each kayak was built to fit the user's body, the width of cockpit based on the hips, the length on the span of outstretched arms. Though open skin-hulled boats no longer troll the Sound for salmon or seals, every modern paddler and her kayak—fiberglass, plastic, or wood—pays homage to the Eyak, a people who befriended the sea.

CHAPTER 4

Cordova: Coast
(Where I meet the sea)

Late August, I arrived in Anchorage as a loyal Montanan. I came north for grad school, I told new friends, and because Alaska interested me. But not to stay. In November, the Intermountain West was still my home, and everyone knew that after my Alaska hiatus I'd return to my beloved dry plains and low wooded hills, to the Rockies' craggy divide and the complex scent of western trees. (They probably wished I'd go so I would quit talking about it.) In January, I still had no intention of slighting Montana by falling for a new home place, especially one as obvious as Alaska, like the high school boy head-over-heels for the prettiest cheerleader. I also thought that trailwork was behind me. It's a natural time to move on, I said. Grad school had shifted my focus to writing. A new path would emerge.

By May, I ate my words in two helpings. In spite of myself, I was warming to Alaska, almost contrite, as if cheating on someone I still loved. And also, I was going back to trails. I remembered Slim's old rejoinder about seasonals: *You ain't quit until it's next year and you ain't back.* School let out, we were broke, and all I wanted, despite my earlier pledge to step off the seasonal treadmill, was to get back into the woods. To let my brain release, feel my body's rhythm become primary again. And so, when the applications we'd filed in midwinter "just in case" resulted in job offers, Gabe and I accepted.

Instead of West Glacier, the town of Cordova. Instead of the NPS, the US Forest Service. A new crew, new foreman, mountains and water we'd never laid eyes on.

In a guidebook I read that Cordova was a working fishing village in some of peninsular Alaska's rainiest and most rugged terrain. The Cordova Ranger District managed the Copper River Delta, a chunk of Prince William Sound, and the eastern edge of the Chugach National Forest, the second-largest parcel in the Forest Service system. I knew the Chugach range. In Anchorage, I'd hiked and skied its western edge all winter, those snowy faces visible even from the university's library windows. "I ♥ the Chugach," read the locally popular bumper sticker, and puffy-heart them I did. But I knew only a sliver of them, the arc that cradled my urban home. I dreamed of work and play in a slice of the range that butted up against an unfamiliar sea.

You don't end up in Cordova. You have to mean to get there. Surrounded as it is by ocean and mountains, your options for arrival are a tiny plane for a short flight across the Sound from Anchorage (fresh-baked cookies the in-flight snack), or the state ferry—Alaska's most heavily used public transit—which arrives every other day from Whittier or Valdez. You can't drive to Cordova. You could walk, overland, if prepared for perilous crevasse fields and icefalls, and you'd arrive weeks after you'd begun, itchy with devil's club spines and the mental fatigue of a month of route finding. You could kayak, if you had time, or take a private boat, if you owned one. (If you knew how to maneuver it against chop and fetch, if you weren't a little afraid of the sea.) No matter how you get there, what strikes you upon landing in Cordova is water and mountains. And birds, and fishy air thick with salt you taste on licked lips.

In Cordova, you need all the names you can think of for rain. Pour, drizzle, dump, shower, deluge, gush, storm. Torrent, flood, piss, downpour, cats and dogs. As important are the words that follow rain: damp, drip, wet, mold, puddle, muggy, dank, clammy, humid, mist. When the sun comes out, the air clears as if it has been pressure-washed and the whole place glistens like it was just made. Rotting rubber boots and pruned fingers are small penance in exchange for those first rays after weeks of gray. You forget the vocabulary of wet, turned suddenly to a language you learned while traveling for a brief time in a foreign place: where was that again, how did you say hello?

Moving from Anchorage with everything we needed in boxes in the back of our pickup, Gabe and I drove south along Turnagain Arm and through the second-longest highway tunnel in North America to emerge seaside in the town of Whittier, where we boarded the twice-weekly ferry to Cordova. It was pouring rain, hood-up weather, confirming the local joke, "It's always shittier in Whittier."

It was my first time on a large, ocean-going ship. I was a landlubber, recent transplant from the Rockies, born in the Midwest, raised by the Great Lakes, which looked like oceans but tasted fresh and had no discernable tides. Though I grew up sailing a twelve-foot boat with my father on summer vacations, I knew nothing about big vessels, and had never been "at sea." The ferry was my introduction to the boat culture I knew would permeate Cordova, and I studied that ship as if I'd be tested when I got off. I wandered the ferry for nearly the entire seven-hour ride, along narrow hallways lined with porthole windows, up flights of stairs with textured-metal steps to prevent slippage. I leaned too far over the railing at the bow, sea spray on my face, and made myself dizzy with vertigo. Walking the uppermost deck, I imagined a plummet into the water from high up, like Jonah cast overboard, or a pirate walking the enemy's plank. I huffed diesel fumes, flicked open and shut the empty cleats, and fingered chunky knots tied with ropes the size of my wrist. The wake off the stern was as wide as a two-lane highway.

Most of the birds ganging the air and floating on the water were unfamiliar to me, except for the horned puffin, which thrilled me beyond words. Two French birders scanned the horizon avidly, once pointing out a group of floating whitish birds they called *ghee-moh*, heavy French pronunciation intact. It was several minutes before I realized it was a guillemot they saw, which we Americans called a "gill-a-mot."

I visited the captain's cabin, as wide-eyed as a child on her first airplane ride, hands outstretched for the pilot's gift, the plastic wings clipped to her collar. I wished I dared ask him to roll out his charts, to let me hold the brass instruments and borrow some prowess by proxy. I had a hunch, where we were going, that I'd need it. Eventually, like most boat rookies, I lay down on the flat-nap carpet beneath the seats of the enclosed observation deck, trying to quell my stomach in the worst heaves of the open crossing. I took deep breaths and rallied mind-over-body fortitude to the task at hand: *do not puke.*

Remember the work boots, the list of leather favorites? Upon moving to Cordova, new rules applied. The midshin lace-up boots so associated with Montana trails would mold in one week of work in a rain forest, so they were consigned to the closet, where they molded anyway. To replace the sturdy Danner's, there was the brown rubber boot called the XtraTuf, purchased at an Anchorage Army supply store before arriving in Cordova, at the urging of our new foreman, Steve, who all but refused to hire us unless we got off the ferry wearing a pair. "They're cheaper in the city," he said. "Trust me, you'll want them."

My first week in Anchorage, I'd heard a new friend refer to her "Tufs." I thought then it was a joke, her own silly name for rubber boots. But no. XtraTuf is a brand, Tufs their affectionate nickname, and good luck wearing any other boot in Alaska and holding your head up. (The boot is so universally associated with the state that Miss Alaska's regional costume for a recent national pageant included a specially commissioned pair of brown rubber XtraTuf pumps.) Tufs are first choice for fishermen and cannery workers, for biologists and dip-netters, for day hikes and yes, for trailwork. They're so ubiquitous in coastal towns that the foyer of a house with a potluck going on is piled with Tufs, and people Magic Marker their names on the vanilla-colored stripe around the top in order to ensure they'll go home in the right pair. With a tight-fitted calf and tapered toe, these beauties provide far more stability than the rubber boot from childhood puddle walks, with handles at the top and a fit like a bucket. You'd rather not lose them.

Tufs aren't perfect. A heavy object dropped on the flimsy toe hurts, and running a chainsaw in wet weather seems sketchy, at best. Even with good insoles, ten miles on a trail in Tufs will make you foot-sore. After a few weeks, the neoprene lining stinks of mold and fish guts and gull shit and foot funk. But, in places like Cordova where it rains for days, weeks on end, in places where ordinary footwear disintegrates in months, Tufs hold up better than anything else. Feet stay warm and damp instead of cold and soaked. A small victory.

Gabe and I showed up to the yard on the first day unsure what to expect. Ten minutes in, the differences were clear. Our West Glacier trail staff was multiple crews, more than thirty employees, many of them expert lifers. In Cordova, there were twelve of us, Gabe and I the most experienced. Gabe had a couple of young guys on his crew—Bryant and Dale—and mine consisted of Randy, the leader, and Trent, a husky eighteen year old from rural Minnesota, John Deere cap low over his eyes. Randy had been hired before I applied, so there was no leader job for me, which rankled. He had worked several seasons in the Bob. We smiled and shook hands, fellow Montanans. I looked around. These were our people. No Cassie, no Kent, no Brook. No packers. And for the first day, no rain.

When Steve hired us, he made Gabe the leader of the "easements crew." He assured Gabe, "It's awesome, man. It's kinda weird, but it's awesome. You're gonna love it." What was *it*? Gabe would get a boat, he knew, and a brief small-craft training (good thing). Easements had something to do with Alaska Native land, and it wasn't like regular trailwork. That's about all we could figure. We pieced together the history bit by bit, a complicated and sometimes maddening issue typical of so much Alaskana—no way to make any sense of it until you see how it works on the ground, and even then, good luck.

Federal 17B easements have their root in the Alaska Native Claims Settlement Act (ANCSA) of 1971, which revoked Alaska Native claims to their indigenous lands for a one-time land-and-cash buyout and resulted in the formation of autonomous Native corporations. At $963 million and 44 million acres (10 percent of Alaska's total acreage), this was no small real estate deal, and the politics of ANCSA are muddled. Seen by some as progressive, the act was a clear improvement over the reservation mentality that had typified the United States' previous attempts at "compensation" to Native people for their displacement. But it was still typically rapacious, a policy that, spurred by the wet dream of a pipeline economy, forced subsistence cultures into a structure they would not have chosen, and triggered internal battles over extraction versus preservation. Better or worse, there's no noble way to see a land grab.

The on-the-ground outcome of ANCSA is a patchwork state, with federal public lands and private Native lands as enmeshed as our cultures have become. Many parcels selected by Native corporations during ANCSA border the waterways that grounded their historical settlements, especially river and ocean access critical for fishing, hunting, and transport. Non-Native Alaskans use these waters, too, and have subsistence rights that are different than Natives' but legally equal. Where tribal parcels abut lands managed by government agencies and owned by the public (both Native and non-), access and trespass issues inevitably arise. That's where easement corridors come in—no-man's-lands, with ownership retained by the government, where all parties agree that the public may pass through in order to use public lands without violating Native corporation private property rights. Ideal? No. Fair? Sort of. Complicated? Yep.

The Forest Service has a mandate to provide access to the public's lands. If it fails to, it can be held legally accountable. Because the USFS is already the target of complaints about "locking up" acreage, it's important to the agency that it maintain at least hypothetical access. The result is paper trails, in a way, marked on maps as byways but often undetectable on the ground. Because of their remote locations and arduous going, many easements are used infrequently, if ever. The trailwork has this same jury-rigged quality, if the term "trailwork" even applies to these passages, which seem less like trails—absent walking tread and structures—and more like swaths, paths of least resistance cut through brush so that a user may have technical, if not comfortable, ingress. They're cleared every three or seven or fifteen years, and even then, bushwhack style, as if done with a machete. This leads to the somewhat demoralizing fact that on the easement crew, most of the work is done so it can be said that the work has been done.

Even without the satisfaction of a necessary and visible result, or an obvious user group to appreciate the labor, all in all the work was taxing, and pretty darn fun. After the first week, Gabe christened the easements crew "Indiana Jones Trails." You were far more likely to grab a thick vine and swing over a rutted gully, or get lost in brush up to your eyebrows, than to clean out a drainage structure or trim wayward limbs. If classic trails mythology lionizes Paul Bunyan and Bob Marshall, easement heroes are Tarzan and Indy. For a person who gets satisfaction from intricate tasks seen through to completion, easement work can frustrate, as the main credo is "Blaze through fast, cover the miles, and call it good." Gabe is a meticulous worker, unused to slipshod methods and imperfect results. At first, it chafed him. But, it was his job. He learned to pull his hat low over his eyes and crack his whip.

I worked with the easements crew on several hitches, and despite the grueling and often tedious quality of the work, some days passed like a ten-hour adventure. No spectators. No bureaucracy. In some cases, no human had passed through the spot we worked in decades. Hours flew by as we slogged through insurmountable geography; like kids on unsupervised summer afternoons, we made up games: we were being chased, we were lost, or about to discover a secret stash—national treasure, a crashed fixed-wing full of pot. The crew fought when the endless rain made us pissy and glum, but we bonded over the hilarious and punishing motions of the workday, the headers into brush, the foot wrenched out of a sucking mud pit, boot left behind. We did what it took to the best of our ability, performing a slapdash job with enough nods to the artistry recalled from other tasks to preserve some sense of honor, and enough grit to get out alive. Steve was right. It's kinda weird, but it's awesome.

Prince William Sound is a geologic wonder that is rarely described without superlatives. Oldest, longest, coldest, most diverse, best, clearest, wildest. In the decades-long aftermath of the 1989 Exxon oil spill: most delicate, most fragile, richest, most heartbreaking, at greatest risk. A 10,000-acre inlet off the Gulf of Alaska that laps at the southern coast of the state's mainland, the Sound is a saline depression born of plate tectonics and eons of glaciation, home to the array of northern maritime wildlife: sea lions, puffins, seals, whales, pelagic birds of all kinds. Kittiwakes by the thousands nest in rookeries. Murrelets and guillemots bob on the waves in rafts. Cormorants hunch on rocks; oystercatchers patrol beaches, protecting their hidden eggs.

Where birds live, of course, there are fish. All kinds of fish. Schools of swirling herring and eulachon have been integral to native diets and are critical calories for predatory fish, birds, and mammals. The eulachon, (or "hooligan," following its phonetic pronunciation) is an anadromous fish so oily it's called "candlefish" because when dried, strung on a wick, and lit, it will burn. Fishing has been a lynchpin of Sound communities since the first Eyak fished from kayaks, and in today's economy, fishing is a commercial industry, a sport for tourists, and a subsistence pastime for residents of coastal towns and villages. Halibut and salmon are the cash crops, the catches that draw most commercial boats and seasonal tours to troll the Sound. Halibut is a type of flounder, a deep-sea flatfish with a migrated eye atop the head. They can live at depths beyond two hundred feet, along with harvestable rockfish, cod, and the occasional ill-tempered and unappealing skate (perfect for fish sticks). Catching a halibut is no rush, akin to hauling in a sheet of plywood, but its meaty flesh and delicate flavor are incentive enough.

On the other hand, an ocean salmon run is a hoot. Five species of salmon spawn in the Sound in summer. Salmon gorge themselves in the ocean to prepare for the long haul to their birthplaces, where they'll drop their eggs and sperm. Bright and lively, they arc above the waves with the vigor that attends reproductive rituals. Gulls and eagles hover, waiting for an exhausted fish, a seiner's slurry cast overboard, the easy protein snag.

The Sound is destination for all manner of boats: bowpickers and gillnetters, cruise ships and cargo barges, Kleppers and purse seiners and Zodiacs. Its countless coves, fjords, passages, and arms are particular paradise for kayakers. The semiprotected waters confer safer travel for small crafts than the open seas of the Gulf of Alaska; frequent landforms and the sinewy curves of glaciated topography give respite from fetch, tempering the winds that billow over open water. On Prince William Sound, you could poke around in a kayak for decades and never visit the same place twice. Even at a faster traveling pace, say a twelve-glaciers-in-twelve-days push or a months-long expedition, the breadth of the Sound is difficult to fathom. From the air it looks like a shape-shifting amoeba, organic limbs snaky on all sides.

Like any ecosystem of such scope, the Sound encompasses contrast, with ecotones—places where distinct biological communities abut each other—at every turn. Forest slopes to shoreline, shore meets tide line, tide line drops to shallows, shallows deepen. Bus-size whales slip beneath boat keels, beginning or ending migration, while microscopic plankton drift the currents, awaiting direction. In a day of paddling you might glide beneath the ice-aged face of a glacier, katabatic winds watering your eyes, and half an hour later tuck into a plate glass cove with swampy kelp draped on the water, plovers after bugs at the shoreline, a torpid sea otter tailing your boat. Batten down hatches for a long crossing, and as you weave between grimy container ships bound for Japan and cruise ships decked with toasting retirees, the Sound seems the world's crossroads. Then find land again, duck into a long, slim arm where your buddy's boat is the only one visible, and the sea seems like a private away you've entered via wardrobe.

The lure of the Sound is wide cast. Tourists and Alaskans alike wax eloquent on its "extensive charms," its "lifetime of exploring possibilities." True as they are, these accolades can ring as hollow as a chamber of commerce brochure. Longtime Sounders, those who have worked and explored the waters for years, speak of Prince William in intimate tones, tinged with possessive humility. They've seen the panoramic vistas on a day trip, and have also lived weeks out in damp fog under head nets to keep out mosquitoes, or been turned back from a destination by a wind that lasted days. They've admired the photo-shoot puffin colonies, and have also held crude-soaked birds in their gloved arms. They've hauled out fish-heavy nets and also mended them at night in oil-lamp cabins, puked in the cockpit while riding queasy swells, and fallen to sleep in narrow berths, cradle-rocked with cramped knees. Such an old-timer is a partner to the Sound, like half of a long-married couple who have shared the span of years, only to realize how much they still don't know.

I stood at the dock, on the beach, admiring veteran paddlers and fisher folk and researchers, their gravitas, their matter-of-fact allegiance to those waters, their confidence with the sea's moods. In contrast, I felt flighty and naïve, a giddy newlywed who'd barely dipped her toes into the cast shadows of true love's depth. My gaze was on some uncertain future, an anticipated history, romantic, and for the time, still unmade.

Coastal brown bears made Montana's grizzlies look like marmots. The first time I saw one on the Sound, I was tightening lag bolts on a bench near the Alaganik Slough, looked up and caught sight of what must have been the biggest male in the Cordova district. But when Steve joined me and we watched it feeding on sedges along the slough's bank, he said it was just a juvenile. He'd lived in Cordova for years, and he laughed and called me easily impressed.

Unlike the smaller inland bears, opportunistic omnivores with a hankering for the occasional carcass, coastal browns bulk up because most of their summer and fall calories come from salmon. Spawning stream banks are littered with half-consumed fish, tails and back-bones left behind as bears rip out the bellies, rich with eggs and organ meat, and the heads, thick with brains. Eagles and gulls peck out the eye sockets of abandoned skeletons, and always in search of more, they trail bears on land, sea lions on the water, and fishermen in their orange Helly Hansens filleting on the dock. My naturalist friend tells me that in the course of an average salmon's spawning ritual, it benefits 136 species. Like the biblical catch made sufficient for 5,000, most salmon feed more than one mouth.

And not just ursine mouths, or avian ones, or the rooted mouths of moss and trees. Coastal people take cues from coastal bears, growing full on what's near. A midsummer potluck dinner in Cordova offered: sockeye salmon fillet, king salmon croquettes, pickled silver salmon with onions, pink salmon dip. Mountain goat meatloaf, salmon roe, black bear steaks, moose burgers, salmonberry jam, blueberry pie, salmon milt on crackers. In one Crock-Pot, there was stewed alligator brought back from someone's trip down south, the only meat on the table not shot, caught, gutted, or wrapped in Cordova within the last nine months. Except for half a package of hot dogs, which the kids, like scavenging gulls, scarfed down with $4-a-bag white-flour buns.

In Glacier, hitch transport was a string of mules, the end of a back-country stint signaled by the chuff of horsey breath and the smell of sweaty flanks beneath pack saddles. In Cordova, hitch transport was a boat or a bush plane, both signaled by a mechanized roar and the odor of fuel. I definitely missed the mules, but there was something heady about packing tools under the prow of a silvery dinghy in a stiff wind, buckling up float coat as an extra layer of warmth for the ride home, or tossing duffel into the rear of a fixed-wing flown by a salty fiftysomething woman who'd been piloting small craft in Alaska since she got her license at age seventeen. In this new country my hiking prowess, nurtured over years of long miles, was barely necessary. The memorized knots and hitches, all the rules for safe passage on trails with stock, out the window. In land this massive, passage home meant rocketing through sea spray, the *thwack* of hull on swells, or humming below the clouds with the quilted earth below confirming what I'd already guessed: the usual scale is useless here, everything farther, wilder than I imagined.

The five kinds of wild salmon that navigate Alaska's waters are commonly known as king, red, silver, pink, and dog. Their other names are chinook, sockeye, coho, humpy, and chum. To remember the correlations, make up sayings: Chinook is a name fit for a King. If you're Socked in the Eye, it turns Red. Coho glitters like a Silvery jewel. The parts you use for Humping are Pink. And everyone knows, a Dog is man's best Chum.

All spring in Cordova, Gabe and I vacillated between delight in the unusual place we'd landed, and grim comparisons to "how it was in Glacier." We took to mocking each other gently, waking in the morning to sheet rain on windows, shoveling in cereal with a whine: "This isn't how oatmeal tasted in *Gla-cier*." We parodied ourselves, but here's what we meant. Glacier meant friends, people we'd known for years. Cordova meant co-workers, often testy, missing home (like us). Glacier had seven-hundred-plus miles of trail; Cordova Ranger District had about thirty. No more eight-day hitches, long miles of sawing, those body-busting ten-hour days. Cordova hitches were shorter and rare; mostly, we worked eight hours local, and returned to an overheated apartment every night, where I played Scrabble with our white-haired landlady, Rose. Delicate and proper, her lacy living room downstairs belied a steely past. She grew up on a fox-farm island in the Sound and ran her own bowpicker for years. This is what we meant: Glacier was ours. Cordova belonged to others.

Also, there was the Forest Service. It's an honorable organization in many ways, and the Cordova district was full of excellent folks. But the rumors we'd heard for years about the "Forest Service mentality" were true. A laxity, a sluggishness pervaded the agency. Paperwork for everything short of a bathroom break, drawn-out weekly meetings, ridiculous regulations. At the shop in the morning, where was the old urgency, the rush to see whose crew got out the door first, which person could carry the most tools? Though Glacier trails sometimes felt like boot camp, all stoicism and hike-till-you-drop bravado, I missed that sense of purpose, that pride in being "industrial athletes," as a ranger once dubbed us. We worked *hard*. In Cordova, one crew leader lobbied to "park and disappear" on gruesome weather days. He'd have napped in the truck with the heat on and the windows steamed up long past the end of lunch break. The Glacier guys would rather have died.

You've heard the stereotype of the lazy government worker leaning on the shovel, which fries me, since I've never sweated more blood than I have for the feds. But in Cordova, it fit. People leaned. They said, "Good enough for government work" and "We get paid by the hour" and "Job security." Not that all the folks we worked with were lazy. Many of them worked hard, had solid skills and good spirits. Our foreman Steve busted ass when he joined us in the field, and seemed unaffected by the damp cold that made me whine. But crew chemistry is inexplicable; something was missing. That underlying adrenaline, the push that made you work till you couldn't stand up, and the satisfaction that went with that kind of effort. I couldn't find it. Sometimes, trying to infuse the morning, the day, with that kind of vigor, it felt like swimming upstream.

Even compared to a cherished job left behind, though, Cordova had plenty of charms. Glacier gets about one million tourists in six months, most of whom come through in cars, and popular trailheads are jammed by 9 a.m. Cordova sees a fraction as many tourists annually, spread out over ocean and forest in boats, on bikes, in rubber boots. Without the cruise-ship traffic of Alaska's deepwater ports, it's blissfully free of the RVs and tour-bus hordes that flood the rest of the state, buying up key chains. Glacier was a distinctly seasonal place, where everything shut down come September. Cordova's local population drops by half when the summer fleet leaves, but still, it feels like people's working home.

The idea of home kicked me out at the knees that summer, balance awfully hard to find. Despite my penchant for the new adventure, I realized I was not so different from most people, looking over shoulder at the thing I'd left behind. Cordova was magical, one of the most vivid places I'd ever been—sea smell, bird noise, craggy peaks, wide sky. The work was novel, the commute over ocean thrilling. But it wasn't home. Cordova intrigued me, seduced me, but in the end, did not enfold me. I couldn't relax into its pace and expectations. With hindsight I see that, like a bad breakup, it wasn't Cordova; it was me. Glacier ushered me through a coming of age. Like a first love, Glacier occupied a place in my psychic geography that couldn't be usurped by the grandeur of the next place. To really love Cordova, I needed time.

What did I even mean by home? One place I'd left but not forgotten. Another place I lived in, and even loved, yet it wasn't home, either. I was adrift in questions. Can two places both feel as deeply like home? Could home be somewhere you never lived again? Is it wrong to love two places at once? (If not, why did I feel so torn?) Does being rooted require geographical monogamy, the fealty to place that was once common? Is home where you are, or how you imagine where you are? Can you build a home out of questions, stockpiling them like a beaver dragging sticks, until you have made a structure around you safe enough to crawl into and rest?

On the Sound, weather changes with sunrise and sunset, moon phase, seasons, the tides. Ocean turns from chop to glass in minutes. You might predict it if you've read your barometer right, or heard a forecast, but change will sometimes catch you unaware. Before crews board the Whaler each morning, we file a float plan. The National Oceanic and Atmospheric Administration is the federal agency in charge of, for all practical purposes, weather reports, and we use their forecast. The acronym, NOAA, combined with the computerized male voice that delivers most reports, births the colloquial reference to the invisible weatherman as Noah, and upon hearing his digital pronouncements, through echo and static, how can we not think of Genesis, Noah sky-turned, awaiting the deluge and making notes? "Winds out of the southeast, 10 to 15 knots," he drones, robotically. "Seas, three feet." No flood in sight. Work-worthy weather. Two by two, and we're off.

The forecast was shit. Today bad, tomorrow worse. NOAA predicted heavy rain all week. But a hitch was scheduled. Across Orca Inlet, work needed doing, a landing on a beach we'd never been to, and the weather could always clear. (Ha.) In Cordova, canceling plans because of rain meant you'd never go anywhere. We all wanted out of town for a few days, craving a break from the monotony of day work, wet rides in damp trucks, the nickel-and-dime tasks that can spend a week. A hitch beckoned, and since hitches were infrequent, it was welcome, even in the rain.

So, we went. And it rained. Water dripped in tin pans under the tarp's edge so fast, it took ten minutes to collect our daily drinking water. It poured for five straight days. It never let up for even a second, not a tiny lapse before a new squall blew in, not a general lessening in the middle of the night, not a slivery break in the billowing gray above us, not one single shred of unfiltered light. It seemed as though nothing had ever mattered as much as weather. The sound of rain was a constant drone, an aural Chinese water torture. Every day I thought about quiet.

The work was bloody wet—hiking through thick brush, sometimes over our heads, we ran chainsaws all day with arms above our waists and pointing upward so the water funneled down the cuffs of our raincoats, soaking the armpits of our poly-pro tops. At dinner under the tarp, we peeled off rubber raingear and hung it from the guy lines, not to dry, impossible at 40 degrees in saturated air, but at least to air out the odor of an Italian meatball sub on a moldy bun. After scarfing down cold stew from cans, too chilly and numb to bother with real cooking and dishes, we'd take hot drinks to our tents, shucking the fly from where it was plastered to tent skin like a wet T-shirt worthy of Fort Lauderdale. Inside, we swapped wet Capilene for the drier pair, kept in a Ziploc inside the sleeping bag, somehow still damp. The wetter set went to the bottom of the bag (synthetic—a down bag would kill you) in hopes of drying it slightly before it went back on in the morning. The temptation to keep the dry pair on was great at 7 a.m., just to prolong relative comfort, but after work when there was nothing dry to change into, you'd regret it. We pulled on the damp stuff, each howling from our separate tents.

The ten-hour workdays passed in a hallucinogenic state borne from no-end-in-sight and the dreary brain of borderline hypothermia. We tried not to look at our watches, the faces too fogged to decipher anyway. On day five, our foreman motored across the inlet from Cordova, the lights of which had been mercifully obscured from us by a ridgeline between camp and the beach. As we loaded our gear to the gunnels and boarded the puddled Whaler, Steve told us this low-pressure system had dumped a record amount of rain in four days, which is saying something for a place like Cordova, whose regular rainy days would set records anywhere else. And to top that, said Steve, we were the only ones in the field all week, the only ones in the entire district who went out—the cabin restoration crew, the wildlife techs with planned oystercatcher surveys, everybody else bailed. He wasn't out here, Steve, but his crew was—*we* were—and he was proud. We'd been crabby and wet and miserable for five days, but by the time we pulled away from the beach, damn it, we were proud, too, and by the time we entered the harbor and docked the boat in its slip, by the time we heaved our sopping gear to the dock in fish-gut pools, we were high-fiving each other, stomping in puddles on the pier, arguing over what to get on our pizzas at the bakery whose warm glow beckoned across the jetty like a lighthouse calling sailors in from a storm.

Living in Cordova, I became a birder. Of course, I'd noticed birds before: admired fishing osprey on Montana lakes, listened for the call of the violet-green swallows nested in the eaves of our West Glacier house. Still, except for the obvious sightings anyone would stop for, most birds passed above my radar. But when you hunker at the confluence of Prince William Sound and the Copper River Delta, you start to notice birds. How can you help it, in May, when more than twenty million individual birds pass above your head, when you get out of your truck at a trailhead to deafening birdsong, the air full of ruckus and symphony? Some birds in Cordova are resident (crows, which I'd never seen elsewhere in Alaska); others stay for the summer (noisy passerines who sing in midnight light); many more pass through quickly, bound for feeding grounds in the Arctic. Sandhill cranes and Canada geese travel in huge flocks, while others—eagles, ravens—hover singly, or in pairs. During spring migration, that many birds in one stretch of sky make a hell of a spectacle.

I didn't become a birder because of any special inclination to notice. I am missing that innate watcher's sense that my birding friends have. I don't have a life list or an Audubon membership. I can't identify many songs or wing profiles, I have no fancy binoculars, I know only a handful of Latin names. I became a birder because to not be a birder would have taken far more effort. Professionals or dedicated amateurs would scoff at my use of their label. But I don't know what else to call it. I'm a person who has learned, taught by birds themselves, to notice winged creatures. I am a birder because once I started watching—preening crossbill, sandpiper's leggy steps—I could no longer quickly look away.

In Cordova, trail crews carry guns. Pepper spray is fine and good, but Forest Service regulations require that, in salmon and bear country districts, you also pack heat. This seemed absurd, since I'd worked among bears in the mountains for years unarmed, and never felt vulnerable to impending death by tooth and claw. But, rules were rules. Extensive post-9/11 security paperwork granted us firearms clearance and our crew spent a day in the ranger station learning safety measures, how to clean the barrel, the difference between a rifle and shotgun. (We'd use both.) Our training culminated in target shooting at the firing range, for me the first time since grade school summer camp that I'd shouldered a weapon. The kick of the twelve-gauge beat the pants off my preteen rifle.

In spite of my sneer at the silly requirement, I had to admit that the shooting range was . . . fun. Gunpowdered air, rifled slugs in my pocket, the satisfaction of a hit target while *boom* echoed through the lot. Six of us lined up, all firing, emptying, loading, round after round, a racket I'd heard only in Hollywood wars. We logged a few hours at the range each month, and Trent, our cowboy ranch kid, laughed at Randy and me as we overcame our tendency to handle the weapon at arm's length like a venomous snake. At first, Randy took the gun tentatively, but by the second week he cocked it like a bandit and hooted with a fist in the air at a bull's-eye. Though Randy would've liked to be immune to the gun's charms, it seemed no one, not even a diffident "granola," could resist the allure of firing off a shot.

Fun and games aside, even Trent in his NRA hat agreed that packing a shotgun on the trail—another eight-pound load to lug, awkward over pack straps, a shovel in the other hand, a chainsaw on the shoulder—was plain old ridiculous. Only certain wage grades could legally carry it, but Randy and I conceded it was even stupider for one of us to tote the gun when Trent, though a minor and the lowest on the totem pole, was the only one who could use it effectively in a pinch. We took the saws and Trent took the gun.

It wasn't clear exactly when that pinch would be. Not when we passed by the bears feeding on stream banks, oblivious to us, intoxicated by salmon. Not when we approached a beach for landing to find a bear on it; then we'd wait it out or moor elsewhere, not shoot. Certainly not if I was being bluff-charged by a bear I'd surprised. The prospect of dropping backpack and chainsaw, chambering a round, shouldering the butt, and finding any kind of accuracy with wet, cold fingers while a bear was charging seemed daft. In this situation a shotgun was a shortcut to confidence, a false one at that, side-swiping senses and alertness and notice. Gun strapped to your back, you moved faster, head down. It was easy to stop paying attention.

In the Tlingit's complex relationship with the grizzly, bear is cousin and the best way to head off conflict is to acknowledge him, speak to him with respect, and request co-existence. Such graciousness appealed to me, as did the advice, traced to several American Native lineages, that a woman lift her shirt to a charging bear because her breasts will indicate her sex and, since bears and humans have intermarried, remind him of their kinship. It sounds naïve to modern ears, tuned as they are to the realism of science and the pragmatism of food chain, but the tenor of these old ways of being with animals indicates a critical understanding about interconnection: vulnerability need not always trigger fear.

I wasn't offering to strip my shirt to save my crew, but if charged, I knew I would wield pepper spray with more confidence, and if that didn't work, could curl into a ball and take my chances easier than I could fire an efficient shot under duress. No part of me wants to die in a bear attack, a martyr to wilderness. A co-worker in Montana had been badly mauled by a grizzly and his scars and stories would have knocked the romance out of Alexander Supertramp and Timmy Treadwell at once. Still. If it came down to it, I'd rather exit this world made humble, not fumbling with a violence I don't fully comprehend. Maybe if I were a marksman, I'd feel differently. An old coot in a bar mocks me; he'd bring a pistol to a high school graduation. "Wait till yer charged, honey," he drawls. I guess I'll have to.

In any case, such nuance was outside the agency's purview, and in the Forest Service, rules are made to be kept, not argued over. The shotgun came along, deadweight, a John Wayne prop that failed to convey what was very clear to me and my crew: peaceful passage in bear country is far more dependent on the individual bear and how you meet it than the weapon of the day.

Wild is noise in a quiet space, a whoop in a churchyard, and wild is silence amid bustle, a hush to the burble of small talk, barrage muted. Wild is giddy and weeping, kicked up heels, and also a monastic pacing, back and forth, tempo unvaried, destination in. There is wild in storm, and in the eye of storm, and also, in the steady beat of rain.

Sea otters witnessed our daily commute. On bucket-dump days and limpid still mornings, otters floated behind the Whaler on their backs, tails poked out of the water like a whale's fluke, poised in what resembled nothing so much as a friendly wave. Luxuriously thick, otter fur can have up to a million hairs per square inch. It's spiky when wet, but despite constant immersion, otters never look soaked. A sea otter seems complex, its whiskered face dear enough to inspire children's plush toys, yet inquisitive, as if it doesn't miss a trick. An otter isn't all cuddles. On the hunt, it smashes the exoskeletons of crabs and urchins, and rips apart a sea lion carcass with ferocity. Two young males were observed having "rough sex" with a dead baby seal, eating it when finished. (Such natural history rarely makes it into the toy store.)

Notwithstanding the sex, as with most animals we're drawn to, the qualities we love best in otters remind us of ourselves. For one, they are highly individual, showing dietary preferences from animal to animal, and they are a somewhat rare example of a mammal that uses and hoards tools, in their case, rocks to bash open the shells of their prey. Some otters even save a particular rock for regular use, tucking it into a skin pouch under the armpit, as handy as my favorite pen slid into pocket.

Although they also exhibit solitary behavior, sea otters are social animals, grouping in rafts of a hundred on a stormy sea, eating off each others' bodies like a floating dinner table, dozing on their backs with pups asleep on their chests. Otters make remarkable eye contact. I passed one in a boat that watched me, so dispassionate yet intent, it seemed to discern something that I could not. Was my paddling awkward? My fly unzipped? Had I dropped my sunglasses in the water? It drifted out of view, taking the friendly smirk. If it's true, as Emerson said, that every word was once an animal, for their complexity, sea otters must be the root of many words.

The northern reach of the Pacific Coastal rainforest extends into the southern end of the Chugach National Forest, and its trees are the biggest ones on Alaska's main peninsula: Sitka spruce, hemlock, the occasional yellow cedar. Log work had always been an integral part of trailwork, and the tools and techniques were the same, but with trees of that size, the possibilities were new. On forest projects, we dropped trees for bridge stringers and milled them into decking for puncheon and running plank. To cross a narrow span, we could use a single log, snapping a chalk line up the middle and ripping it with a saw to make a Gadbury-style bridge, or adze a planed walking surface easily wide enough for a hiker, perhaps two children abreast. Imagine a tree this large—like the stumps in Northwest lore, big enough to build a house in—sufficient, not a component, not a material. A structure in and of itself. Which, of course, is also what it was before we cut it down.

Fifty miles down the Copper River from the Chitina Bridge, Gabe's crew had been out for four days on a work patrol, most of them wet. One afternoon, the sun gave a timid showing through clouds, warming the gravel bar where the rafts pulled out, shining in stripes on camp setup chores. One boat was still in the water when the sound of a plane droned overhead, a fixed-wing circling low, then lower, until a beach landing seemed imminent. Everyone looked up and a small package hurtled from the sky, landed on the beach with a bounce, and popped into the water. No one knew what it was, but delivered that way, as if chucked by the gods, it seemed important. A raft guide jumped into a boat, flipped the bowline off the mooring log, and rowed out to the package in one motion, before any one else had even thought to move. He scooped up the parcel—a brown-papered brick swathed in duct tape—and caught the tail end of the eddy that dumped him back into camp. His was a truly graceful feat, the motions instinctive and precise, but it was glossed over quickly in the excitement. The crew huddled around while Steve tore the package open. He thought maybe it was his wife, Donna, with their pilot friend. Her gift? A half-gallon container of softening chocolate ice cream. The rafter who made the quick grab became the day's hero. The thought of that carton carried downstream by the current, never tasted, was almost unbearable. Steve tore the cardboard flaps open and Gabe brought spoons from the kitchen kit and they thoroughly chilled themselves, inhaling ice cream in the 45-degree mist.

We'd been slogging away at rock steps for weeks when Steve pulled us off that project for a welcome diversion: fly to Montague Island with the cabin crew to replace the footings and build a new porch on a public-use cabin. Dan and Frank made up the whole cabin crew, but for this job they needed extra hands: Randy, Trent, and me.

We landed on the beach at high tide in a de Havilland Beaver and ferried two planeloads of gear a mile inland to the cabin. Tents, carpentry tools, a generator, piled at the foot of the stairs. The off-kilter cabin stood on rotting wooden piers and our work was clear. Dan, an ace carpenter, lined us out fast, taught us the quick tricks of 3-4-5 squaring and the hammer flip from one hand to the other. Jacking and pounding and rocking out to Hank Williams on the battery-powered radio, the work went smoothly.

At 5:30 sharp, the focus shifted: beach-combing. This cherished pastime thrives on coastlines that face the Gulf of Alaska. These beaches are littered with junk. Empty orange juice jugs and busted electronics, the flotsam of a plastic-based culture. But hidden in the wreckage are glass fishing floats from Japanese nets, treasures that drift across the Gulf to end up on the Sound's beaches after big storms. I'd seen them on local porches, blue, green, or clear, some the size of an orange, others big as a basketball, sometimes still wound in old bits of net encrusted with barnacles. Turns out, Dan was a float scavenger. As we traipsed to the beach after work that first afternoon, he explained their history, how many he'd found over the years, which beaches in which seasons brought the highest yield. "The rarest kind," Dan said, "is called the rolling pin." An oblong float the size of a bratwurst in a bun, with small grooves on each end where nets attached. "I've been looking for one since I moved up here," he said. "Thirteen years."

Ten minutes later, my toe hit a knot in the sand. I kicked at it and the glint of blue glass caught my eye. I unearthed it further and pulled out the oblong shape, brushed it off, and held it up to Dan. "Is this a rolling pin?"

"Holy shit!" he said. "Ho. Lee. Shit." He grabbed it and looked at me, turned it over, handed it back, shook his head. I offered it to him but he shrugged me off. You had to find it yourself; I knew this, even without being told. Thereafter, I was hooked on scavenging. The previous night's storm proved a lucrative one and three of us gathered more floats than we could carry. We tied the arms of our sweatshirts into makeshift sacks to get the loot home. I was the only one who'd found a rolling pin, and I remembered my childhood penchant for finding Petoskey stone fossils on the shores of Michigan lakes, when my dad used to crow, "Good eye, kiddo!" and I would thrill with shy pride. When we finished the porch, we lined up the floats on the railing and took photos with the sun glistening off their Japanese curves. Dan said it was one of the best single-day hauls he'd ever seen.

I found one more rolling pin that summer, on Hinchinbrook Island with a visiting friend. She found a rare float, too, a two-hander, wrapped in a piece of rotten net that stunk of fish. She didn't dare take it on the airplane, so she left it with me. The last week of the season I tried again to offer Dan one of my rolling pins. Glass-rich, with my lucky summer behind me, it was no sacrifice, and, as I told him, I loved the finding more than the objects themselves. Dan still refused, though he wasn't as bitter. "Unbe-fucking-lievable," he grinned. "Rookies."

The *Rubus* genus claims salmonberries, related to black- and raspberries, fruits with a honeycombed structure and a jolt of sucrose upon first bite. They're named for the color of bright-red salmon flesh, not the flavor, which was a relief to me upon first tasting one. The bushes grow all over coastal Alaska; in a good year branches are dotted with heavy-headed fruit you can pick just by running fingers through the leaves. If they aren't too ripe, berries fall unbruised into an open palm.

Downtown Cordova spanned five blocks between the harbor and our apartment. We did errands on foot and factored half an hour into every trip for foraging berries. My first attempt at canning resulted in salmonberry ice-cream topping: too runny for jam, too seedy for syrup. It glowed from squatty jars with earnest iridescence and gave me a pang of homegrown satisfaction. I presented a jar to my mother, an expert canner, with delight not just in the homemade, but in the specific, a gift signifying—in the jar, in the mouth—a harbor town's wall of bushes, July's warm rain.

John showed up at O'Brien Creek the first morning of our Copper River float trip looking every inch a rafter, and small-town Alaskan, and outlaw. Dressed in paddling gear with a ragged ponytail, a faded T-shirt, and an oddly capped gold tooth, he seemed like the perfect wing nut to usher a Forest Service crew one hundred miles down the third-biggest river in Alaska. My crew had disbanded when Randy left early and Trent went back to school, so I joined Bess, another loner, and Gabe's easement gang for the last hitch of the season. The Copper originates high in the Wrangells, flows past the Mentasta Mountains, and through the Chugach to empty into Prince William Sound about fifty miles southeast of town up Cordova's only road. Because there's public land along the river, and plenty of reasons to access it (rafting, salmon fishing, sheep hunts), easements pepper its entire, remote length. Lucky for the trail crew that meant a semi-annual rafting trip. It was more expensive for the district to buy the gear and maintain a certified guide on staff than it was to contract the service on an as-needed basis, so we had guides. Lucky for John and his sidekicks, it meant being paid to ferry us downstream, prep our breakfasts and dinners, and hang out on the beach and drink while we thrashed in the wet brush.

A ten-day hitch rafting the Copper River sounds grand. In many ways, it was. But on a private trip, you set your own pace, sleep late, play dice while waiting out wind, and crack a beer on board by noon. A work trip is different. We had to cover the distances between easement pullouts fast enough to leave us days for clearing in between, and we had to ferry along a boat full of tools and gas cans like a slow dog on a long leash, and we couldn't wait out bad weather, and we definitely couldn't crack a beer before noon. Not even before 5:30. Not even ever, according to stringent Forest Service rules about alcohol on government trips. Still, the float was a very cool bonus, and none of us, beer or no beer, would have turned it down.

We began the late-August adventure by boarding the state ferry to Valdez, off-loading under the first brilliant aurora we'd seen in months. Mitch and Allan, the other guides, picked us up and we drove several hours to Chitina, a tiny town on the Copper where we'd camp that night until John showed up with the rafts in the morning. Like most traildogs, we were proudly self-sufficient outdoors. Only one of us had been on a guided trip before. I didn't like the idea of it at all, the weird boundary barring the usual easy fraternity among seasonals. We were clients, and it would take a few days to distinguish ourselves—helping with the dishes, taking a turn at the oars, complaining about the feds— to show the river rats that we were allies, not a batch of government fat cats watching for a broken rule. We assured them that fat cats stayed behind with the paperwork. We were dirtbags, just like them.

By the end of the hitch, there was little worry about fraternity. During ten days in boats, we bonded with Allan, Mitch, and John over dirty jokes told standing up on the gunnels, an all-you-could-eat hot-dog roast, the sighting of a black wolf on the Bremner flats, a couple of epic weather days, and contraband whiskey and cheap beer. We trusted their river skills and were grateful for their presence in camp, the hot meals at the end of fourteen-hour workdays. They admired our work ethic, slapped us double high fives when we stumbled onto the beach at dusk with chainsaws on our shoulders, raingear shiny wet.

While we fell for each other, I also fell for the river. The sound of the Copper is a constant hiss, the glacial water so thick with silt it's like liquid sandpaper against fingers dipped in the river as you float downstream. This suspended material is called glacial flour— the river's origin on the glaciated slopes of the Wrangell Mountains means it brings with it rock and ice dust that impede the river's clarity. The size of the Copper River is confusing. John pointed off to the far shore: guess how far? It's a mile across, which I'd never have guessed until, paddling out on it, *Why does it take so long to just get there, right there?* The temperature of the Copper River is just above freezing. John said if you fell in it wouldn't matter if you could swim. The strength of the current, even in "still water," prevents much more than a controlled float, and if you aren't hauled into the boat quickly, hypothermia will kill you long before you get kicked out in an eddy. The opaque waters conceal so many victims, a great remote Hudson that would be a perfect repository for mobsters' collateral damage. We wondered who was beneath us that we couldn't see. A gold miner missing after a bar brawl in 1921? That kid who fell in at the Chitina picnic, rough-housing with his siblings on the bridge? The dip-netter who scorned a life jacket and ropes, and got pulled quietly under by three flashing fish in his net, a mother lode quickly turned to cement block when he didn't let go? *Poor suckers*, I thought. And, *May I stay in the boat.*

Near the Million Dollar Bridge outside Cordova, the Copper widens into Miles Lake, an anomalous river-lake formed by the retreat of the Miles Glacier. In bright sun and calm water, we rowed across the huge expanse, ringed by glaciers and full of iceberg chunks that bumped against our boat in the current. Our final campsite was on the edge of an exposed gravel beach, open to all that river, ice, and sky. It was prefall crisp. Dinner was a hodgepodge of leftovers and stashed treasure—no need to hoard Snickers or bacon—and Mitch

built his long-promised waxed-box fire, an integral part of any rafter's camp arsenal. Opening the top and bottom flaps of a produce
box (emptied of the fruit eaten on the trip), he created a combustible
chimney that channeled an orange flame twenty feet into the air. It
was incredibly impressive. We danced around the fire, barefoot and
whooping in the gritty sand.

Like the packers in Glacier, John refused to bring out alcohol
that should have been drunk on the hitch. So we drank. Midnight
came and John got out his flare gun—for emergencies only—and
shot off four blanks at the indigo sky. Such a cry-wolf violation of
USFS safety parameters might have been grave, had we been closer
to town. Luckily, there was no one who cared within fifty miles, no
officials to initiate a rescue even in dire straits, no bosses to see the
beer bottles all over the beach. Nobody to sneer when half of us
never made it back to our tents. Midmorning we woke blurry to find
John, arms and legs spread wide, collapsed on the beach beneath the
flapping tarp. With goldish sand in his stubble, a beatific smile on
his face, he was an angel come back from a bender. Not fallen, just
passed out cold.

My friend Chloe visited from Sweden, and with an Outsider at
my side, I marshaled my few months' experience into local status.
I showed her around town like an old hand—here were the docks,
the fishing boats, our Whaler in its slip. Here were the tide charts,
the weather reports. I fed her fresh halibut and berry pancakes.

A few days into her trip, Chloe, Gabe, and I flew to Hinchinbrook Island, southwest of Cordova in the Sound. When the pilot
lifted the red Beaver off the beach and left us and our small hump of
gear, the clouds covered the plane in minutes and we were alone for
three days, no way to go anywhere but where our feet would take us.
Which was plenty of places. We walked beach miles. We explored
the shell of a shipwreck and climbed limestone cliffs. We found and
hoarded glass floats, Chloe as big a scavenger as I, Gabe happy to

scan with us but blessedly uncompetitive when it came to our final sprint toward the found object, hip-checking each other to get there first.

Hinchinbrook is a remote island by any but Alaska standards, where a short flight from a small town means it's downright accessible. To us, the beach felt close to untouched, and yet, up along the tide line, chocked beneath driftwood stumps and burnished logs, debris coiled around itself. Every trace of civilization, dumped, could end up here. Cracked plastic buoys, a raincoat, scraps of net, one flip-flop, Happy Meal toys. The junk surprised Chloe. No one pictures garbage on the Last Frontier.

Late afternoon as we were heading home, the ocean came alive with pink salmon, leaping at the mouth of the creek we had to cross to get back to the cabin. We had no fishing gear; we could practically catch them with our hands. Still, they were faster than they looked, so we got creative. In log piles at the head of the beach, I found a buried section of net and a serrated takeout knife to cut it free. Chloe and I held the net, gating the width of the creek. Gabe waded upstream, forcing the fish into our arms like the loser in red rover. Only one got tangled. Most of the salmon darted beneath the net or found its torn holes. But one was enough. Alaskans don't go far out of the way to eat pinks, which, far inferior in texture to silvers, reds, and kings, are usually saved for cannery products, smoking, or dog food. But this one flopped on the sand, opalescent and firm. Ocean-fresh pink, one-minute-dead, over an open fire, is still worth eating. Gabe pinned its tail, Chloe thanked it for its life, and I cracked its skull with a driftwood cudgel. Back at the cabin, Chloe wrapped the fish in foil. Gabe and I rooted through the tide-line plastic and we built a fire from all the wood we could haul. Log rounds sanded by waves, the blade of an oar, a broken pallet. The refuse was damp and it smoldered, but it burned.

And now for our special feature: *Indiana Jones and the Bridge of Horror.* Midway through the Copper River trip, our five-person crew had covered four miles over four days, clearing an epic amount of brush and deadfall from the easement alignment. The ground was wet with fallen leaves and mud, and every half hour, one of us toppled, knee-deep in a hole, tripping over a concealed root, failing to notice that the ground, obscured by devil's club, dropped out from under our feet. At first, it was funny to see a crewmate disappear suddenly, head and shoulders visible above the brush line and then nothing, like they'd fallen through a trap door. At first, we hollered, "Man down!" and tallied who'd taken a plunge. Soon it was old news. No one commented. Pick yourself up, pull the chainsaw dogs out of your neck, and move on. Only a full-on face-plant or a bloody injury was worthy of mention.

We knew from our GPS data that the alignment would cross a few creeks. There are no bridges on easement trails, but previous crews felled a tree or cobbled together a rock crossing to make some fords easier. The first creek had a log spanning the fifteen-foot channel, but de-barked and soaking wet, it was too slick to walk across upright, especially in Tufs. We shimmied across on our butts, straddling the log and mantling with our arms. Staggered along the span, we passed the power tools over our heads, trying to pivot on the seat of our Hellies without losing balance or ripping holes. Our legs gripped the log tight to counter the slip of rubber raingear against the slimy wood. Later, when I looked at the photos of this procedure, it was hard to imagine how it had ever made any sense, that lineup of people sitting two feet above the current with chainsaws hoisted in the air, raindrops sweating on the camera's lens.

After the first crossing, which we surmounted twice daily, there were several miles without any major obstacles, only the constants of trail and work. By the last day, it looked like we'd make it to our GPS-ed termination point if we pushed hard. We were blissed out on the peeking sun and the high of impending completion, a rare luxury in easement land, when we dropped into a gulley and saw the final hurdle. Another river crossing. This one three times wider than the first, spanned similarly with a slick old-growth log, a whitewater hole just downstream. Intimidating, at best.

I charged up to the log with the brainless drive that sometimes overtakes me when a group is paralyzed. I have to just *do* something. We'll use the same technique as with the other bridge, I told them, undaunted by the wider span and the higher-stakes plunge I'd take if I fell in. Offering myself as bridge guinea pig, I sat on the log and began the shimmy. A few feet off the bank, I smelled an intense fishy odor, sharper than it had been since we'd left beach camp that morning. As I got farther out, the log bowed and the water level rose until it almost touched the bottom of the log and the soles of my dangling, splayed-out feet. It was scarier than I thought it would be. Then I noticed the fish, a layer of dead salmon trapped in the limbs on the log's upstream side. Spawned out and done in, they'd given in to the downstream push and ended up stuck and rotten, disintegrating under my boots. I'm not particularly squeamish, but I recoiled from the spooky fish carcasses with the instinctive clutch of doom I used to get as a child when I turned my back to go up the basement stairs.

I don't like to give up, especially not with the crew watching from shore, especially not on a task I asked for. I squinted my eyes and dragged on, butt muscles clenched. The odor made me gag. The heels of my Tufs dragged through the scaly debris, separating chunks of flesh from the skeletons. I made it to the far bank, barely, slipping as I stepped off so one leg dropped into the river knee-deep and water filled my boot. This misstep is called "topping out," and it means you owe the crew a six-pack. But no one had noticed. They were too busy cheering that I'd made it across without drowning. On dry ground, I jumped around and shook my freezing hands, shouting to bleed out the horror of the crossing. Worst, I still had to get back. It was late in the day and obvious by then that the crossing, which took me ten minutes unencumbered by tools, was neither efficient nor safe for a crew of five people with chainsaws and brushers. Not even possible for Bess, with very short legs and a low tolerance for risk.

After a brief foray on my side of the river, including a covert boot-dump, I was buoyed to report that in fact, the GPS-ed end was not in sight, there was no survey marker that I could find, and we likely would never have finished even by the following day, let alone this one. We'd already be pushing overtime just to get back to camp. (This made it easier to leave than if the finish had been right before our eyes but unattainable.) On the passage back across the log, all the limb stobs faced the wrong way, and as I wriggled along they jabbed me in the crotch. Once, I looked down too long at the hollowed-out eyes of fish and almost fell in. When I reached the bank, the crew slapped me on the back. Gabe concurred that the crossing was not in the stars for us. We found a spruce with low boughs downstream from the fish stench and ate a quick snack, stale Clif Bars and soggy trail mix. For a few minutes, the sun shone brighter than it had in days.

"That was fully creepy," said Bryant. I might have agreed, but I was too preoccupied with the moral dilemma I'd been mulling over since I'd rejoined the crew. When we arose to begin the hike out, I had made my decision, the honorable one.

"Guys," I confessed, "I owe you a six-pack."

Once, I called them "sea gulls." My friend, a birder, laughed and said, "You know there's no such thing as a sea gull, right? That's just a common misuse. What do you call a gull in a bay, a bagel?" Feeble sea gull, shot full of holes. Truth is, then, commonly, I did not know. *Now* I know, having lived momentarily at ocean's edge, woken to their daily complaint. Now I know legal sea gull names: Glaucous-winged Ross's Sabine's Mew Bonaparte Little Laughing Ring-Billed Black-headed Franklin's California Herring Iceland Black-tailed Thayer's Yellow-footed Glaucous Western Heermann's Ivory Lesser Black-backed Greater Black-backed Slaty-backed Gull! (Thank you, Mr. Sibley.)

I have floated through jiggling rafts of seagulls, pealed out of harbor in a rickety Whaler ducking from fecal seagull debris. I have cleaned halibut down by the dock, tossing heads and tails and bloody entrails to gulls in murkish harbor water lapping at the *Auklet*'s slip (old wooden trawler fish-gut hull). On drafts of seaside breezes, brave as eagles, sea gulls, fishing for salmon in the jaws of bears.

Regal sea gulls, kings of ocean edge I dub you: white pretty bird common and dull. Greedy shopper, haggler, always wants the best fish heads for nothing! Bird of my youth—free gull—wailing above the Great Lake like you owned the place.

High up above the sea's fall, I found a seashell at two thousand feet. What whimsy takes gulls far from tides and up toward passes on wind—lee, lull—to drop a shell near the summit of the peak we climbed on the last day before fall rains began?

Linked with liquid, salt and silt, boats and stink and salmon milt, fogged-up windows overlooking the sea, gulls run ocean towns. They let me stay.

Traildogs are adrenaline junkies. We take to the mountains full-throttle. We drive old trucks and station wagons with gear racks on top, our kayaks and bicycles and skis worth more than the vehicles below. On days off, we pursue backcountry adventures with the discipline and fervor that other people apply to stock portfolios or child rearing. There's always a map out on the desk, a trip plan in the back of the mind. The great outdoors can seem a giant playground, with unlimited equipment, and (in remote places) no lines for the slide.

In the Lower 48, this description typifies outdoor professionals and those who flock to mountain towns in search of what their homelands didn't offer—the freedom of the hills, and companions to travel with. The worst incarnation of this culture is the Boulder, Colorado, caricature, the *Outside* magazine marketplace addict for whom place is commodity and pursuit status symbol. But for many of us, climbing peaks and riding single-track is a treasured way of life, a spine we've strengthened to hold up lives we love. I don't say this scornfully. I have the truck, the rack, the kayak, the bike, the skis.

And I moved to Alaska with all this gear, lured in part by the notion of adventure's Last Frontier, whose geographical realities and mercurial weather would dwarf all but the smallest of my dreams. What I found in Cordova instead was surprising, a mentality, embodied by many of Alaska's rural inhabitants, that was not defined by an emphasis on leisure. Though Cordova is surrounded by craggy peaks and ocean, most local people did not spend their days on mountain traverses or paddling trips. People spent their days picking and canning berries. Catching and preserving salmon. Halibut fishing, mending nets, boat up on sawhorses for tinkering. Sheep hunts. A greenhouse to build. Watching birds.

The climate explained it some—the snowpack by the time we arrived was too rotten for late-spring ski runs, and rain shut us out of the high country plenty of days, a chill and muddy playground too grim for outdoor recess. Also, there was the languid pace of isolated, small-town life, where motivation is easily sapped by the relaxed ethos and days pass chatting with neighbors, helping get wood in, lending a hand. But more than that, Cordova's outdoor rhythms, as in much of nonurban Alaska, were dictated by the necessity of subsistence in a way I had never imagined in the Lower 48. Cordova is cut off from the road system and groceries are expensive, so most families supplemented the American diet with all the wild food they could bag, net, or shoot. Halibut trips were referred to as "grocery runs" and the vigorous, end-of-berry-season canning frenzy really felt like "putting up."

This Alaskan disposition is due also in part to the values of native communities, a more integrated part of the state's identity than anywhere else I'd lived. Alaska Native people's relationship to this geography has for eons been founded on the presence of nature, not the mitigation of it. It's easy to romanticize this too much, to make of every rural Alaskan a wise elder or a salty Sourdough, humble and self-sufficient. Yet, lots of Alaskans do live like this, for many reasons. Because they always have—subsistence not just a tradition, but a way of life in some communities, and because they *can*—there is space here, and the animals and plants that come with space. Because they want to—drawn by culture or principle or temperament to the effort and the meaning that a worked-for life confers—and because, sometimes, out of need, they must.

In Montana, we'd return to work after days off and friendly competition ensued among the crews. We narrated weekend escapades, vying for the gnarliest accomplishment: climbed five peaks in ten hours, skied the three bowls you can see from the pass, biked to Polebridge and back, hopped the border for cragging in Canada (yes, they searched the truck). In Cordova, our weekends were shorter, with little bragging. Caught a few fish. Went for a spin in the boat. Puttered in the rain, looking for critters. The scope changed, and with it, the assumptions about what nature should deliver.

At times, I missed the old days. I longed for the weather and the stretch of time to rage the peaks I could see through shifting clouds outside our apartment window. Some weeks, I yearned for a place where people pushed themselves to their VO2 max, where someone else's personal best could spur you to transcend physical limits of your own. I longed for the old me, who woke up chafing at the bit, ready for any distance, any summit, any plan. Instead, the truck sat parked, the skis in the closet, even the hiking boots mostly nixed for XtraTufs. Adrenaline, and the pursuit of the edge, seemed like a relic from a different life.

But I'd had those days. And I'd have them again. Despite the claustrophobia, the torpor, even, of that rainy summer, I am grateful for the lessons Cordova and its people underscored for me. A reminder that though soft-shells and front shocks and fat skis have their place, they do not themselves confer connection. Outdoors is not catalog or movie set, not just work site, not even sanctuary, no matter how nuanced my desires appeared (name the plants, still the soul). Outdoors is a place where salmon swim upstream to die where they were born, where bears eat the salmon so they can survive their winter dens, where humans move through calling loudly, intent on fish and berries and bears. It's a place to be reminded that, while sport is fun, while the rush of summits, linked ski turns, and belay stances are a joyful thing, they are second. Auxiliary to a world that is not playground but homeschool, where I am taught to settle in, over and over, until being outside isn't about endurance or leisure, but life.

I arrived in Cordova on the ferry, seasick and jelly-legged and curious. I left Cordova on a plane, an initiate into the cult of boats, but not a full-fledged member. Over four months spent seaside, I rode in or on a raft, a jet boat, a kayak, a ferry, a Whaler, a bowpicker, a canoe, and a wildlife cruise ship. I piloted, briefly and illegally, the crew boat, with Gabe's licensed hand ready to take the wheel, and the row oars of the raft on a mellow section of the Copper until, after about half an hour, my saw-weary shoulders went numb. I unloaded and loaded boats, backed the trailer into its spot in the yard (but not down the steep boat ramp at the harbor, in front of all the fishermen), helped repair the prop on the Evinrude, filled fuel cans, changed spark plugs, recoiled pull cords, and bettered my bowline, which I could almost do one-handed (not quite). Yet of all the tools I'd used for work and loved, the boat remained the most resistant. I knew it would take me seasons longer to become a true pro, comfortable on the water with chop and wind and passengers who leaned too far over the side and made my stomach clench. I wouldn't have that time. Our Cordova season was to remain singular, epic, almost mythic in status. The time I'd look back on fondly from farther inland, those months when I got my feet wet, and fell, tentatively, in love with the sea.

———

Rain gear. Foul-weather wear. PVC coat, stiff hood up. Sleeves gape. *Why don't they put a cinch on these damn cuffs?* Cotton lining soaks fast: rain in, damp sweat. Gore-Tex is pointless, waterlogged in minutes. *Why buy this crap?* Rain like this skunks technology. Fishermen's gear, off-the-dock our only prayer for dry. Helly Hansens. Grundens. Stove-pipe legged rubber overalls, suspender buckle click. Orange. Green. Yellow. Bright and thick, knees slick. Too hot to hike fast. Clammy cold when still. Clothes hardly matter, except wet cotton kills. Grit your teeth. Keep moving, steady, tough, outlast. Shiver. Brain over rain. Dry always comes.

XtraTufs were my Cordova souvenir, what I took with me from the coast to use everywhere else. (Thank you, Steve.) Statewide, Tufs are the badge of a local. If you see them on someone's feet in the Seattle airport, you can guess they're going home to Alaska, like you. In recent years, Tufs have made the leap from work prop to fashion statement, and like Carhartts on movie stars, they now crop up in settings unrelated to tides, dirt, or sweat. I've seen chic Anchorage girls sashay through town in miniskirts and glossy new Tufs, work boots recast as couture, ready for the nightclub. They're trying to own a place, I know, trying to stake the local claim, just as I was, getting off the ferry in my shiny pair. But the girls have missed the point. Tufs are ugly, more sweaty than *hot.* The thing that makes them sexy is what they've done, what they bear to prove it—fish stink, mud, moose dung mashed in the tread. Few of us are local, and those who are know best: we don't own anywhere. All we—or our boots—can say is where we've been.

SKID STEER

Terminology A skid steer is a compact earthmover with a hydrostatic
transmission. Left and right tires operate independently, granting
dexterity in tight quarters. Technically, skid steers are wheeled, but
track loaders are often lumped into the same category, and whether
a Cat or a Deere or a Kubota, people call it "a Bobcat"; like Kleenex,
one name fits all. Some call a skid steer a loader, but minus the prefix
"mini" or "skid steer," *loader* more precisely refers to a front-end
loader, the heavy equipment with an articulated front end and a lift
arm positioned in front of the operator's cab. (A Bobcat's lift arms pivot
from the side, tightening its footprint.) Loaders do the massive lifting
and digging, while a Bobcat tackles smaller-scale tasks, with far less
expertise required to operate one safely. Toddlers have the best name
for skid steers. "Auntie C," my three-year-old niece says with awe,
"you can drive a *digger*?"

Uses For trailwork, a Bobcat moves gravel. It loads a five-yard dump truck,
or a flatbed pickup, or power wheelbarrows, called toters, used to get
fill into place on a trail. Other tasks: moving vegetation for replanting,
cutting bench trail, spreading mulch, perfecting dirt work, hauling
brush, and plowing snow. But remember, and this is very important,
a Bobcat is *not* a man-lift. It should *never* be used to transport a crew
down the trail all piled into the bucket. You should *never* stand in
the bucket while the operator raises the arms so you can limb a high
branch on a tree, or hide somebody's ball cap on top of a tool shed.

Attachments The most common skid steer accoutrement is the digging
bucket, but a range of implements mount on the front plate for other
tasks: a snow-plow blade; pallet forks; a menacing four-foot auger

(making quick history of the posthole digger); a ground trencher with a heavy-toothed cutting rim like a chainsaw bar and chain on steroids; a six-way dozer blade; and a hopper, a one-yard-capacity wheelbarrow on a front-mounted tire with a mind of its own. At lunch break on a hot day, find a hose and spigot in an out-of-the-way spot and fill the empty hopper with water: *voilà!*—a grimy, shoulder-deep soaking pool for a four-person crew.

Expertise A competent operator in a skid steer is a thing of beauty if you concede that beauty can exist knee-deep in mud and laced with the smell of diesel exhaust. While a new operator relishes a simple task— fill a struck bucket and move smoothly to the dump site without losing the load—an old hand can practically brush his teeth with a skid steer. Using the bucket's flat bottom as a grader of sorts, a good operator can buff out just-unloaded gravel into a tidy parking pad or fill slope in minutes, or remove small trees with the bucket's corner in less time than it takes to fire up the chainsaw.

Accidents Skid steers are nimble and tough to tip, so an adept driver will try anything, convinced that his expertise and a Bobcat's capabilities can combine to solve all problems. Thus, it's usually veteran operators who get into trouble. Greenhorns are too timid to drive 30 percent off-level or back over a four-foot dirt berm. If you see a Bobcat buried to the tops of the tracks, leaning off-kilter, or flipped over (very rare), chances are the operator was an expert.

CHAPTER 5

Denali: Park

(How far north can I move?)

"Do you have jobs yet for this summer?" Ralph asked when he called in March. Gabe had spoken to the trails foreman in Denali National Park the year before, but he didn't have two leader positions then, and we went to the Forest Service instead. Ralph seemed nice enough. Heavy on the sales pitch, but nice.

"We're going back to Cordova if nothing else comes up," answered Gabe. At hiring time, we seasonals hold our cards close. "Is something coming up?"

"It never rains here," joked Ralph. "If it weren't for the winters, we'd probably qualify as a desert." Ralph guessed that, after a season in the rainforest, the desert would appeal. And he was right. Not to mention other stakes: much higher NPS wages (though proudly, we'd never yet taken a job based just on pay), and the siren song of a park that bewitches every mountain lover with its renowned peaks and ranges, a lifetime of trips in our potential backyard. We went all in.

After he outlined the housing and the season's projects, Ralph reminded Gabe that the job was a uniformed position. Unlike in Glacier, where backcountry trail crews lurked grungily out of view, unlike in Cordova, a remote Forest Service operation with no budget for sartorial excess, trail crews in crown-jewel Denali were clad in

Green-and-Gray. I'd seen this clause on the application materials, but with jobs in hand, the reality of *uniform* came home to roost.

I had not worn a uniform for work since I was eighteen, a hostess in a restaurant whose manager enforced a tight-white-shirt, black-skirt-well-above-the-knees dress code, a job from which I was eventually fired for standing up for myself and the brutally harassed waitresses. I am not partial to uniforms in any capacity, but even absent principles, how could I possibly work trails without the broken-in gear that had served me so well all these years, my security garments as comfortable as pajamas? The faded to almost-white Carhartts with reinforced knee worn through the first layer; the holey long johns; a red-plaid flannel for cool days and the lightweight oxford shirt for bug protection; the Patagonia fleece of late-eighties vintage with burn holes in the sleeves; my vast collection of caps, toques, and bandanas; the soft leather belt worn almost translucent where the pouch to my Leatherman hung. Chucking this treasured stockpile for the heinous polyester Park Service shirts with an arrowhead patch seemed sacrilegious. In Glacier, our trails clothes were holy vestments and we made fun of the rangers for their company getup. How could a traildog with any pride be caught in green pants and a green fleece—the pickle suit? And, God forbid, what if they made me wear the dorky flat hat with the badge? I felt as adamant and pissed as I did at five when my mother forced me into the kindergarten carpool in a vile woolen coat with toggle buttons that I never would have chosen.

Gabe talked me down, as only he could do. Great pay, two jobs, a place we'd always wanted to explore. He didn't want to wear the uniform, either, he said, but we should give it a shot. With Gabe so reasonable, I felt childish and vain by comparison. Begrudgingly, I buckled. I imagined climbing peaks in the Alaska Range. I imagined working in alpine tundra with bears and wolves all around. Every time I imagined myself in the uniform, I felt the immediate need to shower.

———

The word "Denali" has its roots in the Koyukon Athabascan language group. Several variations—*Denadhe*, *Dghelay Ka'a*, and the closest in sound, *Deenaalee*—all translate to roughly the same meaning: "Big Mountain" or "The High One." All were used by Interior Native people to designate the Alaska Range's highest summit, at 20,320 feet a rank clear to locals long before the area was mapped by whites. Most Outsiders (Alaskans' term for Lower 48 dwellers) know this peak as "Mount McKinley," the name conferred by explorer James Dickey in 1896 in an obsequious nod to his home state of Ohio's presidential candidate, William McKinley. When the park's current wilderness boundaries were drawn in 1980, Mount McKinley National Park was renamed Denali National Park & Preserve, but Ohioans have fought in Congress to retain their homeboy's claim on the actual peak, and so the "official" name of the highest mountain in North America persists on maps and in records. Pragmatists maintain that separate names for the park and the mountain make it easier to distinguish between them when speaking. But most Alaskans, Athabascan and otherwise, trust context to provide the distinction and choose to call the mountain by its older, more expressive name. Bequeathed Denali by the language that sprang from its heart.

I finished my semester in Anchorage in late April, eager, once again, to box up folders and trade laptop for shovel and Danskos for Danners. We sublet our apartment, piled into the truck, and drove north, past Eagle River and Eklutna Lake, into the Mat-Su Borough, off the Glen Highway and onto the Parks, which runs clear to Fairbanks, two lanes all the way. Across the huge Susitna, north past the Talkeetna Spur Road, through Denali State Park with startling views of the Alaska Range—Denali, Foraker, Hunter, the Moose's Tooth—across the Chulitna River, over Broad Pass. And farther north still: past Cantwell and the Denali Highway heading off to the east, along the Nenana River, north, north, north, until we turned west onto the Denali Park Road. Snow, long gone in Anchorage, still lined the shoulders. The air was crisp.

We parked at our cabin in C-Camp, the employee housing area, mostly empty. The big influx of seasonals was still a month off. Gabe had been at work a few weeks already, and knew what he wanted to show me first. We walked a gravel trail to the sled-dog kennels and met the ranger patrol dogs, thirty Alaskan huskies chained to posts outside their houses, leaping and circling and yowling in raucous choreography. I envied them their chummy, noisy pack—they were at home in the smell of tundra, the way the wind felt, from which direction it blew. I wanted to learn what they knew.

Tundra: the vegetation type covering a vast, treeless region in the Arctic where the subsoil is permanently or intermittently frozen. Tundra comes in two main varieties. Alpine tundra is dry with a thin root mat, similar to what's found high in alpine regions of the Lower 48, though in Interior Alaska it grows below two thousand feet. (The northern latitude compounds elevation, so high alpine characteristics occur closer and closer to sea level, until farthest north, along the coast, "alpine" tundra grows practically out of the sea.) Sphagnum tundra is lower, thick, wetter than alpine tundra, and mossy, with spongy floating muskeg tussocks in flatland black spruce bog or, on better-drained birch and aspen-forested slopes, a lush carpet you can fall to on your back like a child into a pile of leaves.

Grade school lectures drove home the fragility of tundra plants, how one footprint could cause damage lasting thousands of years. While true, especially of the sensitive alpine variety, this lesson belies the fact that the dwarf plants comprising tundra—reindeer lichen shaped like tiny white antlers; bottle-brush bog rosemary; the spicy intoxicant Labrador tea—are some of the most tenacious living things on the planet. Woody-stemmed and nonvascular plants alike survive six to nine months of frigid winter every year, bear the imprint of the moose's and caribou's heavy hoof, withstand bears digging for roots and grubs, and shrug off midsummer frost and midwinter thaw with equal aplomb. Though without a doubt fragile (and losing the battle with ATVs and horse hooves all over the state), tundra plants are the steely architecture of Alaskan landscapes.

Our first season's major project was tundra transplanting and site revegetation at Denali's new visitor center, under construction by a general contractor. In exchange for the GC's permission to work on-site during construction, park personnel had to abide by all rules and be on our best behavior. We were to think of ourselves as their guests. Obey speed limits and traffic patterns, wear hard hats, avoid closed areas, and always, always give them the right-of-way. Bend over backward, Ralph said. (Dirty jokes ensued.)

On the job site, things went well for about five hours. A few of us new to Denali were practicing our Bobcat skills in the mulch pile. Alec had driven one often, so he conceded practice time to Amy—a petite, butch toughie with a pale mustache and a ready smile—and me. The tasks were simple: scoop a bucketful, flip the arms back and forth to level the load, reverse, turn around, dump it back in the pile. Pretty elementary stuff, but thrilling if you'd never driven a Bobcat (I barely had). Amy was in the machine when a contractor's pickup bumped by and a passenger shouted out the window, "Hey, a shovel might be faster!" The GC guys ran D-9s and 950 Cat loaders, and to them "Little Bob," the smallest skid steer on the market, was a joke. Of course, I was indignant, since it comes so naturally to me. *She's just learning, assholes! So am I!* My middle finger flew up, unbidden. Gabe, who was in charge of the project, who assured Ralph we'd follow all the rules, dropped his head in his hands. Impudence within hours of our arrival, by his wife, no less. He beckoned me over.

"You just flip him off?" Gabe was always fair, never one to accuse.

I smirked. "I guess."

"You have to go apologize."

I hate apologizing for anything, especially if I was provoked. Gabe knew this.

"I was provoked!"

"If that guy is a dick and reports you to someone, we'll get kicked off this site. Ralph will throttle me."

The chance that said guy was, A) a dick and, B) planning to rat me out seemed highly unlikely. And no one ever throttled Gabe. No one really even got mad at him, except me.

"Come *on*. Nothing is going to happen. I won't do it again."

Gabe raised one eyebrow, a move I'd always been envious of. I knew it was futile. He was in charge, and by the letter at least, he was right. I stomped off, head down, toward the spot where the guys had parked.

"Wear your hard hat?" Gabe called after me.

Annoyed and muttering with a hard hat tucked under my arm is how I met the truck's loudmouth and target of my middle finger. I could see at once that he never would have tattled. "Are you kidding?" he guffawed when I told him my boss made me come apologize. "That made my day! I'm usually the one givin' the bird. It's nice to get it!"

Nic and I shook hands and exchanged names. He was in his early fifties, I guessed. A short gray ponytail stuck out from beneath his faded ball cap. About my height with a strong grip, a slight beer gut, and a weather-mapped face, the kind of guy you meet on construction sites all over the state, only jollier than average.

"Well, see you around," I said, after a minute or two of bullshitting. Nic got the last word as he yelled at my back, "You gotta admit, though, that's a dinky-ass Bobcat!"

On the drive home from work that evening, Gabe told me what happened post-apology. I had gone up to the shop to get more fuel. Minutes later, Nic arrived at the mulch pile and introduced himself to Gabe, who apologized, again, about the finger. Nic waved him off.

"That Christine, piece a work," he said. Gabe nodded.

"Man, she's feisty." A short pause. "She seein' anybody?" Gabe looked blank, Alec later told me. (He was watching the scene from behind the pile.)

"Um, yeah, she sure is," said Gabe.

"Really," said Nic. "Serious?"

"Um, pretty serious."

"How serious?"

"Uh, she's married."

"Ah. Serious. Local guy? Live around here?" Nic was angling for a loophole, an absentee husband, perhaps, some guy who worked on the Slope for weeks at a time. No such luck.

Gabe said, "She's married to me, actually."

Nic went crimson. "Is she, now? Sorry, man. Well, you got a good one!" He shook Gabe's hand, spun on his sneakers, and fled. Alec came rolling out from behind the pile: "Holy *shit*, dude! How'd you keep a straight face that long? I was dying back there!"

A month later, I walked into the break room for our morning meeting and who was sitting in one of the chairs, the FNG (fucking new guy), our just-hired trail crew heavy-equipment operator? Nic. I gave him the finger and he grinned. After I ribbed him for asking me out via my husband and he defended himself lamely, Nic and I came to a teasing peace. That year we discovered we had more in common than our impudent streaks. We dissed the uniform together, bet on the definitions of obscure words, and tried our best to offend with dirty jokes. Nic's favorite: "What's the difference between a blow job and a salad?" I walked right into it, shaking my head: *No idea.* Him: "You wanna go out for lunch sometime?"

For my thirty-first birthday that summer, Nic used a chainsaw and pocketknife to carve a six-inch wooden hand with the middle finger stuck up. It sits on the windowsill above my writing desk. When I look up from the page, there's the muse, giving me the finger. It's a piece of work, to be sure.

The development plan for the visitor center mandated landscaping of the two-acre site in time for opening the following summer and the construction of a bike trail connecting the park entrance with the new facilities. Ralph liked to take on challenges; a sucker for logistics, he could see possibilities where others saw obstacles, and he bet that our crew could kill two birds. A construction-reveg double whammy: remove all the tundra in the bike trail alignment and re-plant it on the VC site. Two tasks, one stone. Tundra revegetation on that scale had no precedent and plenty of skeptics, Ralph's favorite combination. Onward.

He leased a 950 Cat loader for the season, hired Nic as the equipment operator, required commercial drivers' licenses for three leaders, and turned us loose. Gabe and I took notes on the work expectations, tasks inconceivable to backcountry traildogs whose Glacier repertoire consisted of maintenance more than construction and rarely required a Skil saw, let alone a backhoe. The shovel-pulaski era seemed long gone, leaving us, after all these years, beginners again. The first weeks of work blended novelty and nostalgia and we thrived on the fast pace of large-scale construction while longing for those quiet, long-mile, backcountry days. Lunch breaks at alpine lakes? No way. Instead we lounged on the loader's giant tires and slumped atop the Knaack box, more like a construction crew with minicoolers and Cokes than a trail crew with CamelBaks and trail mix. The Denali gang was union equipment operators and recent local high school grads, a potent blend of handy and clueless. Alec was the only other classic "traildog," a seven-year veteran of Rocky, a hiking park with rockwork and alpine vistas, like Glacier. We bonded, of course.

The construction-reveg may have been different, but it wasn't boring. On the ground, we began with a rough trail alignment survey, then cleared the swath with chainsaws, and hauled the brush to the burn pile. We spray-painted parallel lines on the tundra to mark the sixteen-foot width of the trail, and to enable removal, we chopped lines through the root mass of the tundra mat with pulaskis and mattocks, grateful for handwork.

The timing of tundra transplantation is critical—once trees are cleared, the direct sun on tundra begins to warm the permafrost layer beneath. After the loader removed the tundra mats, the exposed icy ground fast melted into mud pits requiring chains on tires and logs laid corduroy-style under them just to keep the machines afloat. Flatbed trucks waited at the side of the road for the loader to deposit the sixteen-by-sixteen squares of tundra onto their beds, whereupon drivers transported the mats to predetermined sites on the VC complex, backing up mounded dirt hills and contours, lifting beds and draping the mats on the ground. Don't worry if you can't picture it. The whole thing took weeks to sink in, even while we were doing it.

The operation required people power: a loader operator, two or three on the ground cutting line and directing the bucket, three truck drivers, two shovelers to guide mats into place and mulch the edges. Miscellany ate up hands, too: haul brush, guy small trees, direct traffic as equipment crossed the road, and make constant runs to the shop for diesel can, shackles, tow strap, dunnage, chains, cell phone, hard hat, mattock handle, Griphoist, zerk grease. To keep things interesting, something was always getting stuck: truck, loader, puncheon, tools. Occasionally even a human went down big, by an inadvertent step too close to the edge of a mud pit or a calculated belly flop performed for lunchtime laughs.

Things changed daily. New reveg sites took priority over old ones. We ran out of mulch. Brakes went out, the power takeoff on the dump truck shit the bed, a rolled skid steer incited a safety shakedown. With complex logistics and a tight timetable, each day required innovative thinking and a ready store of cuss words to surmount inevitable glitches. Hurdles notwithstanding, it was great fun for those with a thing for big machines and playing in mud (most traildogs). Although I wasn't licensed to legally drive the Cat or the twelve-yard dump trucks, Nic schooled me on the sly on airbrakes and bucket controls. In the woods well out of sight, I lurched around in a twenty-ton machine like a giddy bull in a deserted china shop.

The project's end brought resounding success. We moved and transplanted over a square mile of tundra, the largest known such operation in the state. (Regrowth two years later at 80 percent.) The bike trail and the VC looked spit-shined and the finished product silenced the critics who thought we'd bitten off more than we could chew. Even the road crew, the guys who bemoaned us novices—a bunch of wing nuts borrowing *their* trucks, who forgot hard hats, traffic vests, seatbelts, safety glasses, those kids who *ran* back and forth on the job site—even they had to admit we done good. And the boss? Ralph leans back in his desk chair, arms in the air. He gets out of the office far less than he did when the project started, but that doesn't mean he won't get his share of the credit: "I *told* you we could do it!"

As always, new tasks meant new vocabulary. Large-scale mechanized trailwork brought with it the diction of road building. Who knew there were so many kinds of gravel? Pit run, aggregate, screened, three-quarter-inch minus, D-1, trail mix, washed, fine. And the trucks gravel comes in: ten-yard, five-yard, end dump, belly dump, side dump, some with a "pup" trailer pulled behind. Using heavy equipment meant hauling heavy equipment, and there were words for trailering (itself a new verb): tilt top, ball hitch, ratchet strap, low boy, chain binder. The words for trails mixed with the words for road and construction-site work until language blended into one fluid mass, and a shift happened: we traildogs seemed less the blue-collar cousins of rangers and more the woodsy siblings of trade laborers. The old rule, brought from Glacier's barn to Cordova's harbor to

Denali's yard, held true: the only way to enter a new world without humiliation or offense was to keep ears open and mouth shut. Quiet is better than stupid.

Nicknames ruled the crew's roster. It began with Alec, the crew leader from Rocky hired on with Gabe and me. He was an übercompetent traildog, the biggest goofball either of us had ever met on a job, an able mountain partner, and soon enough, a dear friend. Two days into the season, he admitted that his distinguished name, Alec, had long earlier been replaced with "Krusty" because of clownish antics and some unrepeatable high school legend involving his underwear. Krusty set the bar low and nicknames proliferated. Nic, the oldest of us, and an incorrigible womanizer, became Dirty Uncle Nic. Evan Owens had a puff of blond hair that went fuzzy in the slightest heat; we called him "Frowens." (His wife called him "fucking Owens," with great tenderness.) Pretty dark-haired Mara nicknamed herself "Elvis"—with her full lips and wide-set eyes, well, you could see what she meant. Felipe was "Flip," the biggest wiseass of us all (which was saying something). Jack Roderick came with the nickname "Nice Guy Jack" because of his affable way, but the new job let him re-christen himself and he chose "The Rod," whose irony he savored for its anti-nice-guy bluster. Gabe went from Gaberiferous, to Riferous, to Gaber, and me, well, nothing sticks, so anything goes. Nic called me a number of standards—Stretch, Throttle, sister, Trouble, *woman* (earning a punch in the gut). For any "lady" on the site, Nic used Gretchen, Matilda, Henrietta: whatever old-fashioned name came fastest to mind. Conventional wisdom says you can't choose your own nickname, and the more you resist one, the longer it'll stick. Krusty, like it or not, will have his for life. Even his mom back east goes, halfheartedly, by Mama Krust.

Of course, it was different. Glacier, eight-day backcountry hitches, with six days off; Denali, four ten-hour workdays, three-day weekends. Glacier, a modern two-bedroom we spent little time in; Denali, a one-room cabin without running water that we came home to every night. Glacier had one million acres with trails crisscrossing every USGS map quad; Denali had six million acres nearly void of constructed trails.

In Montana, we'd commuted half an hour from the park to town for staples; in Denali it was a two-hour drive north to the nearest grocery store. Glacier saw one million visitors in six months; Denali had four hundred thousand visitors all year. No more salty mule packers and telemarking stoners; now we had truck drivers and stoners on four-wheelers. Glacier, hand tools and familiar, backbreaking tasks; Denali, heavy equipment and a new challenge every day. Who could separate the rewards from the drawbacks after a while?

The Denali trails shop is a conglomerate of slapdash structures salvaged, borrowed, begged from other worlds. The power tools, workbench, and rehandling station occupy a dusty metal shipping container, the omnipresent Alaska building-in-a-pinch (commonly referred to as a Conex after the trade name emblazoned on its side). The saw shed is a plywood shack that contains chainsaws and their tack, a cabinet full of Griphoists, block and tackle, winches, and come-alongs. The walls are lined with miscellany: haul chains, tow straps, forty kinds of fasteners (carriage bolts, turnbuckles, all-thread). Then there's a passel of poorly organized safety gear: a metal trash can full of brain buckets, caution tape, orange vests, and traffic signs. A long, brown building with a rotting front porch holds traditional trails hand tools, hung in racks by their heads. Broken tools lean in a corner, awaiting someone on light duty.

Rumors of a new shop persisted. Ralph alluded to it. We helped clear the site (more tundra to transplant), but despite blueprint on the wall, I'd believe it when I saw it. What would we do with a brand-new shop, anyway? Who needed a concrete slab free of oil stains, unmarred drywall? A conference room, or God forbid, an ice machine? How on earth could we remain true to our grimy underdog status in a glossy shop, the structural version of new Carhartts? We borrowed tools and space from everyone else—a garage from the utilities crew, table saw from the carpenters, drill press and welding bay in the auto shop—and maybe they would have rather we stayed out of their way. But the back corner suited us, rusted and warped, falling down, out of sight, where we could thrive on getting things done however it worked: borrow, stretch, invent, replicate, brace, scrounge, reinforce, weld. Return. Repeat.

Back and forth from grad school to woodswork, my vocabulary changed. In cusp months—May, September—I used the wrong words in the wrong settings. My raunchy trails mouth carried over to the first sessions of fiction workshop when I was tempted to write on manuscripts, "This is total bullshit," and while vernacular does make for vivid writing, I couldn't pretend that "fucking awesome" was a useful phrase for discussing aesthetics. By the time months of school passed and art openings and poetry readings had given me more appropriate language for scholarly discourse, I'd be back to work again, explaining to my crew that the season's project would require a "paradigm shift," and parsing the ubiquitous grammatical errors in NPS memos.

It's true that some academics swear and some seasonal laborers have killer vocabularies, but the linguistic well I draw from in each arena tastes of different minerals. This necessity of dialect is satisfying, the way diction gets woven in with the spirit of the endeavor. There's no language bond like looking at a finished piece of trailwork and slapping your crew high fives with a "hell yeah!" just as there's true pleasure in crafting well-turned arguments and hearing the ring of complicated syntax. I like hauling up these opposite buckets; the challenge, when both modes are intuitive, is to blend them ably, to use the right words in the right contexts, to consider

audience, intent, relationship. In each realm, a quote from the opposite one guides me. For trails situations, pithy writing advice helps
translate wordy directions: "Say it plain." When in academia, a trails
favorite is a good mantra: "Obscenity is the crutch of the illiterate
motherfucker."

A ninety-one-mile road cleaves Denali's northeastern corner, the
only developed road corridor within six million acres. Beginning at
the north entrance and terminating just east of Wonder Lake at the
old mining settlement of Kantishna, the mostly gravel thoroughfare
weaves over passes and across river bars, paralleling the Alaska Range
through some of the wildest country it is possible to enter by road
vehicle. And with few exceptions (researchers, permitted photogra-
phers, park staff) that vehicle is a bus. Private traffic is prohibited
beyond the initial fifteen-mile stretch, leaving visitors these options:
an interpretive tour bus for packaged cruisers who want to stay put,
a shuttle bus for visitors who want to get on and off, and a camper
bus for backcountry users who just want to get out.

Traffic on the park road has been managed this way since 1972,
when the completion of the George Parks Highway connecting
Anchorage and Fairbanks doubled visitation to the previously remote area in just one year. In the forty-some years since, tourism
has morphed from large-scale to supersized, and it is only because
of foresight and a road plan that Denali's wildlife remains relatively
unharassed and its visitors' experience enhanced. As I write this, park
management is proposing more-lenient road capacity parameters under pressure from tourist-industry big guns and the constant march
toward growth: more buses, more rest areas, more access, more exceptions, more.

As a ranger at Arches in 1968, Edward Abbey lobbied to halt all
road construction in national parks, and to make existing roads accessible only by foot, bicycle, or shuttle (his concession to children,
the elderly, and the disabled). Abbey's hope has clearly not come

to pass; development in parks has exponentially increased since his death in 1989. Now the norm is the Going-to-the-Sun Highway in Glacier, choked in summer with bumper-to-bumper traffic and mountain goats licking antifreeze in sweltering parking lots, or the Valley in Yosemite, where a line of glistening autos flows at the base of the big walls like a metal river. Amid the grim realities of a burdened national park system and a public obsessed with the private vehicle, Denali's progressive road policy is a respite. To properly honor Edward Abbey, though, I should not use his name in the same paragraph as the phrase "policy is a respite." Abbey would probably say that policy talk is a respite for small and fearful minds. Though Denali's road is far better than many, I know that for Abbey, this is still too much. And though I love getting out into the park quickly, I know what I'm trading. When I tuck my monkey wrench into my pocket, I wince.

Some type of bus, or a cluster of them, passes any point on the road approximately every seven minutes. This is not the pinnacle of pristine, but it is amazing how different it feels than the usual road-bound park experience. No private cars means no parking lots outside of rest areas. No parking lots means no trailheads, and no trailheads means no throngs happily trudging in the same direction. Between buses, after the engine grinds away and leaves you behind, you hear water flowing, or notice the direction of the wind. It's possible, for six minutes, to imagine what it was like here before there was a road, and what it will be like someday, after the road is gone. Once off the bus, you can day-hike anywhere. With a backcountry permit, you can go anywhere and then farther. If, miles out, you turn back toward the band of road where you started, you may be able to pick out a green bus passing, a cloud of dust. But as the quiet draws you in and your route coaxes you forward, you'll forget about the buses. Until you reappear on the road's shoulder to wave down a ride two hours or five days or three weeks later, they'll forget about you.

Minimized traffic protects the visitor experience, but most important, it protects animals, allowing the creatures along the road corridor a semblance of ordinary life. Bears and wolves cross ditch lines, gyrfalcons and rough-legged hawks nest along the cliffs. From a bus on the park road, I have seen a father wolf regurgitating bits of carcass into the mouths of its five pups while the mother lounged in the brush; a bear running upstream in the Toklat River, current pouring over its shoulders; two grizzly cubs in a pullout batting at a traffic pylon; a heavy-antlered moose head breaking the surface of a kettle pond; three jaegers in jet-fighter formation; a wolf pair dividing and conquering a caribou herd, finally picking off the smallest, weakest calf that couldn't run quite fast enough; a fox with a rodent's head in its mouth. Others have seen a bear take down a moose in a river swollen with runoff, a wolf and a bear jockeying over a caribou carcass, a mama bear and three cubs sliding down snowfields, a boreal owl clip a snowshoe hare. On the bus, kids turn from their video games and iPods and watch. *It's like a nature show,* whispers a man from Ohio. Cynics gape. Stoics smile. Loudmouths go quiet, except for one loudmouth announcing how amazing it is.

The Denali road system isn't perfect; as the NPS caves more frequently to corporate tourism, there's great risk that small concessions—to capacity, frequency, cost—will have large repercussions on animal and human communities. Denali's bigwigs reexamine road policy under great pressure from the tourist industry to increase the number of buses allowed on the road per day. But it seems probable that Denali has avoided Yosemite's fate. The optimist in me hopes that people will always have the good sense to protect this place, and feels lucky for what I've received here. The pessimist in me knows that eventually, we kill what we love. The pragmatist in me hands the driver my ticket, takes a seat by the window, and watches, for new owlets in a nest above Igloo Creek, for bears on the braided Teklanika River bar, for the Toklat pack's wolf pups, chasing their own tails, not yet watching for me.

———

Speaking of wildlife. The first ten minutes in a Bobcat are awkward. The steering handles—or joystick on newer machines—feel strange. The cockpit is cramped. The foot pedals for bucket control are sensitive and prone to accidental activation by an errant boot (Gabe's size 12.5 monsters barely fit upright). Early on, the Bobcat bucks like a mechanical bull with all but the most tentative acceleration. But give it half an hour. By then, you can rocket across the yard, do wheelies, spin 360s, screech to halt. Drive into the sand pile at top speed and mound the bucket heavy, level the load, dump it on a dime.

The best way to learn to run a machine is from a cocky guy who's lived in Alaska for thirty-odd years, who's worked out west, on the Slope, for the mine, up north, on the ice, building the pipeline, the highway, on a fishing boat, for the union. Watch when he drives: where he flicks his wrist, not his arm, how he grips the throttle, loose, like a baseball bat in a pro's hand, not white-knuckled, like yours. Listen to what he says: *Grease the zerks. Did you check the plug? Split your tracks. Make a windrow. Feather it.* If you don't know what he's talking about, listen longer. He'll say it again. Bite your tongue when he calls you honey, sugar, or sweet cakes. He's kidding (mostly). Don't be defensive when he says you're slow, the bucket isn't full enough, you forgot to throttle up before you lifted the arms, you're doing it all wrong. He's right. You are. Don't tell him when you accidentally put unleaded into the gas tank instead of diesel and bugger up the works. Take a deep breath. Change out the fuel filter. Bleed the lines. Believe it: someday you'll do it right. Then he'll tell you, *Way to go, honey!*

Midsummer, my crew went west, out to the Wonder Lake gypsy camp at the end of the road. Five of us hitched out to work on a handful of trails between Eilson visitor center and the Wonder Lake campground. These stints were a welcome break from front-country

Bobcat-dependent work. I was eager for a work site on steep tundra slopes in full view of Denali's north face. Eager for tread work, the familiar twist of a wooden handle in my palm, the grunt of moving heavy things, the intricate pieced-together pride of rock steps and walls battered against hikers' boots and winter's weight.

Owens was the west-end crew leader, I his second-in-command. He'd been around Denali several summers and the logistics were all new to me, so I was relieved to follow his lead. Following Owens's lead was a hell of a ride. He talked a mile a minute, contradicted himself, interrupted, and gave us all (especially Chip) a rash of shit. Owens was generous: he shared his prized family recipe for smoked salmon, made us biscuits and gravy on the last morning of each hitch, and would offer the shirt off his back. And Owens loved to rant. It was less tendency, more full-on hobby. He had stronger opinions than an AM radio shock jockey and once he got started, his stream-of-consciousness monologues kept him as wired as a handful of amphetamines.

To shitty drivers on the park road: *Don't even try it, pal, I've got the right-of-way, seriously, do people think this is the fuckin' Autobahn with bears? Turn on your lights, jack-off!* On the federal government, particularly then-president W and his minions: *Unbe-fucking-lievable, bunch a idiots, who voted for that moron, they deserve it, that's all they can think to do is elect him again, I oughta move to Timbuktu, Canada's not far enough.* His most vigorous steam was saved for "the bus" out on Stampede Road, and anything to do with it, including Jon Krakauer, tourists on pilgrimages, and rich kids with poor judgment: *Goddamn Alexander Supercreep or whatever his name is, what a dumb bastard,* Into the Wild, *my ass, he died for Chrissake, we oughta blow that bus up before it turns into a monument!* Every rant eventually included his favorite expression of disbelief: "I mean *Jeee*-sus!" Owens moved away for a job Outside, but the phrase remained, homage to his blue-ribbon crankiness, a brand of loveable ornery we'd be lucky if we ever saw again.

———

The Denali gang was dirty. Dirty uniforms, dirty trucks, a filthy break room, packs that look like they'd been dragged behind the loader, nasty mouths, lunch boxes caked in mud. Four or five people had gas that could clear a room in seconds. Alongside physical filth, sexual innuendo was constant. I learned more explicit slang in three months than I knew in my previous twenty-nine years, and I never considered myself naïve. Any reference to length in inches elicited jokes about penis size. Ordinary words like "box" and "come" earned guffaws even if they were used four times in two minutes. It is sort of funny, the looming double entendre that yanks you to your toes, the sparring that keeps conversation interesting, but also exhausting, as when you gesture at a two-by-four and say "How long is that?" hoping for some answer beside "Longer than his."

At first, I considered myself a curious onlooker, stunned by this undercurrent of language I had never noticed, laughing from the sidelines. But before long, almost against my wishes, I became champ of the sly off-color remark, a habit so ingrained that I had to stop myself from snorting when a classmate asked for a "hard critique" or snickering at anyone named Dick. Sometimes I'm proud to be shockingly, unexpectedly bawdy. But it's a dubious honor, the repository for the dirtiest jokes, which, retold at the wrong dinner party, get me cold-shouldered faster than a sloppy drunk. "I can't believe she said that," someone will whisper, and I long for the days when this kind of humor was beneath me. (*Beneath me!*)

Oh, black spruce, you lowest on the totem pole of trees, lovely only in your awkwardness, coniferous underdog. Languid maple, fiery tamarack, curly paper birch, all so much finer than you, black spruce, taiga standby, tree of terrain where trees hardly grow. I should praise

your hardiness, I know, toast your tenacity, the strength of your resolve in the face of winters that would kill even the stoutest oak. I
should salute you. But spoiled by midwest hardwoods in fall, the
match flare of larch on western hills, coastal redwoods tall as sky, I
am shallow for color, drama, stature. I can find for you, black spruce,
only a slight nod, concession that, ugly or not, you are of this place,
while I am only passing through.

Goodbye, Glacier matriarchy. I was the lone woman field leader in
Denali. All told, women made up barely a quarter of the total hire.
So, on a crew with four guys, I had to set one ground rule early: I
would not hike way off in the brush to take a leak. The boys turned
their backs ten feet away from me and watered the weeds, and I
would do the same. My crouch was at least that modest, the pants
dropped swift, held up around thighs while T-shirt curtained bare
ass, pointed into the woods. If I rested chin in hand while I sat, no
one guessed I was peeing. If you have a problem with that, I told
them, get over it. To their credit, they did. By midseason I could pee
a few yards from any of them without a raised eyebrow. One guy
came up to talk to me while I was crouched, and I gave him a full
set of instructions. He realized his error only when I stood up and
fiddled with my belt. Really, how would they dare complain? I am far
subtler than they are, grown men the same as little boys, their urine
loud on the leaves from up high, that little shake they do when they
finish. They know I've got them there.

Kinds of trails trucks: crew-cab, flatbed, stake-side, six-pack, diesel
dump, lift-gate, dump bed, dually. Dodge, Ford, Chevy (no foreign-
ers on the government lot). Open bed or canopy-top. Stick shift,
automatic, diesel, gasoline. With or without ball hitch (which size?).
Half-ton, three-quarters, full-size. Overdrive, PTO. This one hauls
the double-axle trailer, that one only the tilt-top. Green, red, gray,

taillight out, trailer brakes too tight, third gear lags on the uphill. Ralph's truck—don't borrow without asking. Like *Air Force One*, it must remain on standby for the big man.

Federal seasonals, like most employees, love to grumble: about the boss, the weather, the pay, the feds, the tourists, the guys in whatever division we're not. NPS and USFS have disrespectful nicknames generated from within: the Forest Disservice, Department of Gagriculture, or the Irrational Park Circus, Department of the Inferior. Cross fire is easier, but even in-house, seasonals aren't loyal employees. We happily bite hands that feed. We're fly-by-nights, too curmudgeonly to salute, and if our agency finds us expendable, we don't owe them allegiance, either. Trailwork, in particular, attracts iconoclasts, irreverent personalities who march to their own drummers and truckle to no fools. None of us likes the idea of "working for the man," and we swear to each other this is the only government job we'd take. Being paid to play in the dirt is worth the compromise, so we plug our noses for the Affidavits of Employment (in which we vow to perform no overt political insurrection) and Uniform Codes and Conduct Agreements (wherein we promise to be a credit to our agency). Once the paperwork's filed, we relapse to errant ways.

The understanding among trails seasonals is that if or when you turn permanent—hired for full-time, year-round work—you become a company man. Fieldwork falls away and desk time takes over; you defend the paperwork you used to lambaste. Once you've entered this realm, you've become "the boss," and no matter how illustrious your field days, you'll be the target of disgruntled complaints from seasonals who fancy themselves superior to anyone with a job in "The Head Shed." Ralph hadn't had much crew experience—quickly promoted from road crew laborer to division foreman, he'd never been a traildog, per se; it didn't take long for him to become "the man." Wear your seat belt, he cajoled. (Who cared if he was right.) Don't ride in the Bobcat bucket, turn in your schedule changes, guys, don't make me be an asshole! (We begged the question: Can you *make* someone be an asshole, or under the right circumstances, does it come out on its own?) The crew rolled eyes behind Ralph's back, and I remembered the refrain our Glacier foreman used to berate ladder climbers: "The further up the tree the monkey climbs, the more of his ass you can see."

You could practically see my ass on the ground, so big were the holes in my Carhartts, and the uniform remained a contested battle zone. Early on, Ralph turned a blind eye to dirty shirts, an occasional hole in the knee, disintegrating work pants, because he shared our gusto. We worked hard, so we got filthy. Enough said. Trouble is, his supervisor was watching him supervising. (Beware the Chief of Maintenance!) And Ralph exhibited a deskman's clean uniform and an increasing pleasure at power, eye on higher ranks. Field dirt became easier to forget, and soon, when pressure came from above, Ralph passed it on: no holes, white or green T-shirts beneath the gray, no personal belt buckles, keep heads covered with the Park Service cap only, nix the vest over short-sleeved shirts. Wash your clothes, people! If your shirt is covered in oil, buy a new one! (Never mind that the old one was perfectly fine, and a new one would be covered in oil in a week.) Shower once in a while! No holes bigger than a quarter! (He measured.) The crew's favorite rule was printed in the NPS uniform handbook: no visible lump in men's pants. "What about an invisible lump?" I asked, deadpan, in the break room one morning. "You know, like Krusty's?" The room erupted and my face went hot the way it does when I'm funny and I know it.

Mostly, we bit our tongues and let Ralph rant. We knew the cycle. The intensity would pass, and we'd backslide into disrepair, work trumping loose buttons and fraying cuffs. Flagrant shabbiness would go unnoticed for weeks, long enough for us to think that once again, it was no big deal. Then, when the shirts looked more black than gray and "someone" complained, Ralph would lash out. My Carhartts with the duct-tape-patched crotch got the axe. Nic's

red hat, against uniform policy, had to stay in the locker. The rules
seemed to comfort Ralph somehow, as if shaking a finger made him
bigger. The problem is, asking manual laborers to look clean and act
right is a losing battle, and everybody knows it. We even have Virgil
on our side: "All things by nature," he wrote in 30 BCE, "are ready to
get worse." It's okay, Ralph. Entropy is not just a trails problem. It's a
law of the universe, and you're in good company, centuries of zealots
and philosophers, preachers, and generals, all questing after impossible order, thumping their desks, drawing clear lines, watching them
fade as soon as the troops leave the door.

The west-end gypsy camp is a little city: five wall tents on wooden
platforms, windows with bug screens stapled to the frames. In the
center of the tents, a Conex kitchen plumbed for hot, running water, full of dishes and silverware and a rickety table and stacks of old
magazines. Out front between the Conex and the road is a single-
stall shed with an on-demand hot shower, heated by propane. Four
out of five of us on the crew that first year lived in dry cabins, so to
us, the "work camp" was a luxury. Our spend-it-or-lose-it per diem
ensured we ate well, too—steaks, scallops, bacon, asparagus, a contraband keg of beer.

Camp is tucked into a small aspen grove, hidden from tourists
at the Wonder Lake campground, even out of earshot of Phyllis and
Harry, the elderly volunteer hosts who baked us cookies every hitch.
If we were at camp, we were inside the Conex because the bugs were
too brutal for sitting at the picnic table, so the view was not a focus.
But on a clear day, from out the window above the kitchen sink you
could see a stretch of the range and the summit of Denali, white as
cloud.

One morning when Owens and I walked into the Conex, Jack
stood at the kitchen sink; not looking at us, he waved out the window with a campy smile and channeled the Asian accent that floods
the park in late summer: "Herro Denari!" he crowed. Something

about that phrase, both gently mocking and so earnest, it stuck. One of us faced the window like an acolyte toward Mecca and said it every morning that summer, whether Denali was visible or not. What better greeting to the day, the peak, the crew? If I ever summit that mountain, as I hope someday to do, I have promised Jack that I'll yell, "Herro Denari!" from 20,320 feet at the top of my lungs.

I notice laborers wherever I go. I watch them on the side of the road in Beijing, in Peru, in Mongolia, whaling double jacks at cracked asphalt, driving ancient loaders rejected from American work sites, hauling wet concrete up flights of stairs in burlap sacks. At weddings and funerals, on subways, in airports, I study the guys who keep things oiled, notice the brand of tools they use (Makita, DeWalt), if their skid steers are on wheels or tracks, do they use gloves, wear back braces, drink sodas at lunch or water.

On a retreat I attended at a meditation center, three men spent the weekend cutting and laying new brick in a cement stairway. I walked by them every day and felt the pull toward fraternity, the urge to flash a signal that, though I didn't look like a laborer (blond and slight, cotton skirt and flip-flops, clean), I was in their tribe. I imagined asking the backhoe driver an inside question: "What's the GVW on that?" Or, pickup-line style, "Hey, nice masonry." It's embarrassing, the desire to force community; too much ego in it, a wanting-to-be-known that feels vulnerable and grasping. If someone said those things to me out of the blue on a work site, I'd curl my lip. No one gets into the club that easily. Self-consciousness trumps the wish for connection, and I never ask.

But at the end of that weekend, my last time climbing the staircase from the meditation hall, I overheard the boss hold up a Skil saw and ask his young apprentice, "You know what kind of saw this is?"

"A Skil saw," he said.

"Yeah, but do you know what kind?" the boss persisted. The

kid looked stumped. As I walked by, I muttered the answer I knew he was looking for—*worm drive*—and kept walking. The boss did a double take.

"Hey! You stole my thunder!" he called, his surprise trailing me up the rest of the stairs. I had stepped, for a moment, into his circle. Toenails painted, yes, small shoulders, yes, but see—the ragged nails, tendons rigid on forearms, the calloused feet? Though nothing had changed, suddenly, I felt known. It's because I can be quick to judge that I savor such upending of expectation. I relish the surprise—*She's a laborer?*—because I also need constant reminding to look closer. The Euro tourist is a fly fisherman. That lady in the Nebraska RV loves Proust. This redneck was a conscientious objector during Vietnam. "Worm drive" becomes an internal code word, the mantra I use to remind myself: *Don't assume anything.*

To labor is to work, toil, slave, exert, bust ass, slog, sweat, travail, struggle, strive, plug away, get 'er done.

Labor is a knot, a hard lump of meaning woven from a hundred strands. Pull on one hank, another tightens. Loosen a loop to extricate a bight and there's a tangle.

Labor is a job, a task, a grind, a career, a vocation, a whim, a duty, an assignment, a mission, a chore. Skilled and unskilled. Trade labor and grunt. Hired and forced. Artful tasks and thankless ones.

Culture's paradigms are set in stone: if you choose skilled labor among a host of possibilities available to you, or because of an apprenticed lineage, then it is "noble," "honest," "humble" work. If labor is forced upon you by circumstance, lack of education, or desperation of one kind or another, then it is "soul-killing," "monotonous," "drudgery." This trope is everywhere. It's in our books, from Dickens's scullery maids to H. D. Thoreau, redeemed by his hoe. It's in politics, from the Industrial Revolution's casualties to today's hard-workin' Americans. It's in our beliefs and myths, from

Luther's Calvinistic nose at grindstone (reward) to Sisyphus's uphill task (punishment).

Labor uplifts, grounds, ennobles, debases. Labor redeems. We're damned to it.

Who would you rather be, the third son in a line of lauded stonemasons, or an immigrant stacking boxes in a warehouse? Both laborers. Which paycheck would you rather earn, Davis-Bacon wages for the dozer operator protected by his union, or half minimum wage for the lady who cleans hotel rooms under the table? Both "working for a living."

Labor taxes, rewards, demands, pays out, exhausts, shores up. Laborers are saved. And spent.

The romance of a hard day's work is, like any romance, as dependent on who's doing the loving as it is on what is loved. We may labor under assumptions, but nuance insinuates into any task, complicating stereotype. Who can say the migrant fruit picker, exhausted and used up, has never loved the feel of wind on his face high on a ladder, has never felt pride at a load of lemons, stacked and bright? Who can say the carpenter, handy and artful, has never cursed his sore wrists, wished a day would pass without sawdust gumming up his eyes?

Labor of love. Labor beneath. Fruits of labor. Labored breath. Labor the point.

My labor career began as a whim and became a life. It's craft, and also drudgery. I have worked alongside some of the smartest people I have ever met, and some of the dumbest. Made more money than I was worth, and also way less. I chose this job years ago, and every year I get to choose again, knowing two things: I could do other jobs—teach, edit, write grants, make sandwiches, go back to school in archaeology. And also, right now, trailwork is what I do best—dig holes, survey grades, design alignments, train crews, haul logs.

Labor is the process of birthing. If you push hard enough, labor delivers.

———

Some of the best advice I've ever gotten regarding upward mobility came from Joel, a co-worker in Denali: "Duct tape can get you
through times without money a lot better than money can get
you through times without duct tape." I can't think of an exception
to this rule.

How to play "moose duds": at lunch break, one person sits with
mouth open while the guy opposite hucks moose droppings at the
target. (Moose dung is light and dry, like sawdust molded into a
thumb-size oval.) If a turd hits you in the mouth and you flinch, you
have to swallow it. If it lands inside and you don't flinch, you can
spit it out (I've seen this happen once). One day, Flip tossed a chunk
right into Krusty's mouth, and with loony bravado, Krusty gulped it
whole and smacked his lips. We weren't disbelieving—there was little
point around Krusty, who was always furthest beyond the pale—but
we were impressed. The crew shouted and cheered, until Krusty, usually goaded by applause into further hijinks, suddenly went quiet
and grabbed his throat. He swallowed hard, throat lurching like a
snake with a goat lodged in its neck. Flip asked, with uncharacteristic
concern, "Dude, you all right?"

The dud would not go down. It was stuck, low enough that
Krusty couldn't cough it up and high enough to impede passage
down his esophagus. He tried a drink. The water hit the blockage
and backed up, streaming out his mouth. He could intake liquid
only by letting it sit in his tipped-back throat and seep like water
down a slow drain. The crew died laughing once we saw this was an
inconvenience, not an emergency, but Krusty passed an uncomfort-
able twelve hours. No food, no liquid, not even the cheap whiskey
that cured all his other ills. Nothing could get past the turd, and he
swallowed compulsively, massaging the lump in his throat. (Or, the
dump in his throat, who could resist?) Finally, the turd dropped.

Krusty looked for the dud for the next few mornings, delighted at the prospect of recycling a turd inside a turd, but he never confirmed its passage. He now recalls the event with the proper hilarity and we introduce newcomers to games of moose duds with its moral intact: if you're not careful, you'll eat shit.

Wild is metal and noise, trucks driven too fast, a machine that could crush you if you lost control. Wild is the sound of gears in motion, the heat of physics. It's the snap of something under pressure break- ing, the space left behind when momentum passes, the jolt of inertia suddenly changed to work. The slow ticking while the engine cools.

Tourists are the albatross of front-country trailwork, circling us with constant questions, getting in the way. Once, an approach- ing couple picked their way down a closed trail past the yellow "CAUTION" tape that flapped along the muddy edge. She wore pink Keds with anklets, a sweatshirt that read "Sexy Grandma" in rhine- stones. His showed the howling profile of a wolf and the cursive "Last Frontier."

They stopped in the middle of the swale I was digging. "Well," the man slurred, "guys must be gettin' awful lazy, lettin' the pretty girls do all the work!" He tongued his lip and winked, then swayed left to avoid the mess the Bobcat's tracks had made. His wife gripped his arm and smiled tightly, lips shined with gloss. Bear bells dangled, useless, from their belt loops by tiny fluorescent carabiners that could never hold their weight.

I raised my eyebrows, swallowed the things I'd spit if I weren't clad in the green and gray, my name tag sewn above the pocket, ren- dering me accountable: *C. Byl.* We were supposed to be polite. But later, when a white-haired lady passed in her sturdy boots and asked, "How does a lucky girl get a job like this?" I imagined an answer not really hers, this woman who may have wished to swing a tool, but never got the chance. In my mind, the pageant's for the slurry old goat: I stand before him, strip, grab my uniform shirt by the tails and pull upward, buttons popping. In my sweaty sports bra, nipples visible beneath the spandex, Carhartts pulled low by the weight of my Leatherman, baring my midriff. I grab the whistle from around his neck and twist. "Who's a pretty girl now, Mr. Wolf Shirt?" I hiss. His face bulges. I snatch the bear bell from his belt and press it into the crotch of my elbow, where I squeeze it between my bicep and forearm until I bust the thing, ringing. "This is the real Alaska, pal," I sneer, relishing the tourists' cliché, plastic in their mouths, wicked in mine, the same words changed only by our position to them. "You better watch out for the wildlife."

Out the west end, midhitch, we needed a break from rockwork. We went to brush the McKinley Bar trail, a two-mile section leading from Wonder Lake campground to the McKinley River. Brainless but satisfying work, a perfect change of pace. And necessary. The trail hadn't been brushed in years and tundra plants, slow-growing though they are, overwhelmed the tread. I have always been a fan of an aggressive brushing operation. If you're out there with tools, make it count. Of course, I did cut my brushing teeth on Glacier's jungled Middle Fork drainages, where if you didn't cut back twice as far as you thought you should, the packers would tear you a new one, and the vegetation would grow back by the time they were through with you. Chip and Jack had no such education. It was Jack's first year on trails and he was busy soaking up the protocols. Chip had a few seasons under his belt but didn't tend to go overboard about anything. They politely second-guessed the clear-cutting instructions. My brushing commandments seemed a bit excessive.

"Do we have to kill these little trees?" said Jack, who despite his new nickname, "The Rod," had not yet managed to callous his soft heart. I had recommended yanking tiny spruce saplings, root and all, twirling once or twice, and flinging them.

"They'll grow in the trail, Jack! Mow 'em down!" I barked. I felt like Slim, but I was right. We were there, with loppers and handsaws and time. I'd stopped crying over every tree years ago. So, back and forth we went, all day, Jack trying to spare a few green things, Chip trudging through long sections with his loppers all but dragging in the dirt, and me at the rear, harping: *Farther back Chip, cut more, Jack, don't be so timid.* I focused on utter mayhem, bent over with a saw and a nipper, hand-powered destruction in my wake.

Midafternoon, the guys were out of sight ahead. I shouldered my pack and tools to catch up, passing through the quarter mile they'd just brushed. The corridor looked good, not as far back as I'd have taken it, but much better than the morning's tentative grooming. I picked up the pace, walked a ways before my bladder demanded attention. I was about to drop my pants in the brush, when just ahead, a single, bowed aspen sapling caught my eye, arched into the trail like a flag, its base ten feet off in the tundra. It would have hit a hiker in the face. Who on *earth* would walk past that with a lopper in his hand? Fucking slackers.

I stepped up my stride, hit the tree almost at a run, reaching up to lop the tip before I headed to the base to prune it flush. I spread the blades to fit around the trunk, muttering, I am sure, when the tree jerked back, up and away, and a witchy voice hollered from the brush, *Oh, no you don't!* I jumped two feet and nearly hit the ground before I made sense of it: Jack off trail, cackling his infectious snicker, clutching the base of the limb he'd used to set me up. And there I was, hook in my mouth, line and sinker halfway down my throat, worm dangling near my belly. My indignant mask fell off in shards, useless. First laughter, then tears, Jack red-faced, me holding my sides, Chip joining in from the other side of the trail where he'd watched it all go down: "You shoulda seen your face!" he said. I could see my face, no question: grumpy and smug, the ideal target. We laughed so hard I wet my pants, but just a little.

———

Once in a while, a hiker will happen by and ask, "Who needs trails, anyway? Isn't this supposed to be wilderness?" The question's subtext is most often a hands-on-hips, leave-the-land-alone stance, underscored with a purist dose of "Humans don't belong where they can't get on their own." Usually, the gadfly is an idealistic postcollege environmentalist, a kid who's read a little Abbey and thought about more wild places than he (or she) has actually been. He needs wild places to remain "untouched" because he himself feels molested by the world.

I swallow the defensive retort that rises in my throat (idealist! pansy! academic! faux-hippie-frat-boy-never-spent-a-night-out-would-get-lost-without-a-trail-can't-use-a-compass moron!). I conjure my own college self, the girl who pulled out survey stakes and memorized Gary Snyder poems and saved saplings from driveway cracks and rinsed and reused a smooth rock for toilet paper (resting it on top of the tank between uses). I take a deep breath, ask, and listen: "So you like to hike?" and "What's your favorite wild place?"

I don't usually tell the critics the answers I'm thinking, which are that humans have been "building" trails, de facto, for as long as we've been traversing Earth (hunter-gatherers, Romans, Incas) and that, as the Taoist proverb says, "When many go in one direction, so a road is made." I don't tell them that indigenous people and explorers and grizzly bears and ungulates—all totemic, for the questioner I speak of—are famous trail makers. That historically, a trail is less infrastructure than trace, the path made by passing.

I do tell them that when people all pass in one direction, the impact intensifies. Especially in weak spots. When a muddy section forms in a poorly drained area, people avoid it by walking to the side. When a tree falls in the trail, hikers don't climb under or over, they go around. The impact broadens. In highly used areas without maintenance or planned layout, the damage to vegetation and topography can be extreme—we've all witnessed the trampled grass and rutted gullies that crisscross the spots on the river where high schoolers go to party, or the hammered overlooks thronged by viewers with cameras. Trailwork can look a lot like development, but in many cases, it's actually preservation. This is where infrastructure comes in, accidental path turned to engineered thing. By channeling and minimizing impact, trails save places from the people who love them. If I can't convince you, before-and-after pictures would, a mud hole in one and a nature trail in the next, the users, slightly herded, none the wiser.

To the *why trails* question, for me only one answer sticks. Trails get people to places for experiences, and experiences in places help people know places, and people who know places will sacrifice so those places can thrive. The conservation movement wouldn't have a prayer if it relied only on mass mailings with free address labels and lawyers taking coal companies to task. Preservation efforts succeed because people come into contact with land, and begin to remember it, and want to protect it, the way we will protect children we know and love from harm faster than nameless children on the news. Trails in national parks and state forests and city preserves help people be "in" nature in a way they don't dare, aren't able, or don't have time to on their own. A woman on a wide asphalt trail leans from her wheelchair to press cheek to the bark of a tree. Noisy children stoop to brush the velvety cap of a mushroom on a forest floor. I know people shifted by a snake that slides across their path, unmade by the moon over an oxbow, no noise but the hammer-headed ramming of a woodpecker, or their own breath in their throats. I've leaned, stooped, been shifted and unmade.

In the best of all possible worlds, our homes and our daily lives would bring us into close contact with the natural world and we would stop to notice it—the birds in our backyard trees, the way winter has changed, wild plants along the foundations of our houses. In the best world, we would treasure it, participate in it, even. But for many, many of us, rushed lives of mayhem and macadam do not nurture such relationship with anything. For others, nature is destination more than home. Constructed trails and trips to parks are certainly a function of lives that have drifted away from wholeness. Nonetheless, they are paths.

Trail building feels right most of the time. I examine my life's work with the stern eye of a Protestant—the vocation, the calling— and the open heart of a Buddhist—the hope of right-livelihood, of doing no harm. If I felt my work aligned with damage and asphalt over trees and space, I would like to think I could never have done it this long.

But, sometimes, the questioner is not a twentysomething crusader, or Abbey's ghost. It's my own shadow self. The one who helps build a bridge for trail users to access a place that would be better off without a bridge at all. It's the one who drives a Bobcat and pumps cans of diesel in service of "wilderness." The one who hammers in survey stakes along a new alignment, and curses the idealist who pulled our flagging from the trees. For the skeptic and my shadow, I have plenty of answers, but no last word. Trails and parks, my life's work, my whole entire life, is bound up in these intersections: wild and managed, dreams and paychecks, ideals and reality, world and home. At every crossroads, a sign: Hazards in trail. Fork in path. Junction ahead, ½ mile.

SHOVEL

Basics One of the most rudimentary and useful objects in the history of
tools, a shovel is a hand cupped for scooping, perched at the end of a
very long arm. It manages tasks our ancestors did on knees—hollow
out a cook spot, dig up roots, bury a loved one.

Etymology From Old English, *scofl*, of Germanic origin, describing the same
tool; related to the Dutch, *schoffel*, German, *Schaufel*, and connected
to the English verb *shove*. "Shovel" is both noun (spade, trowel, scoop)
and verb (dig, move, scoop).

Maintenance Most people rarely think about shovel maintenance. This is
as it should be. One who spends much time thinking about the care
of a shovel is probably avoiding the work that needs doing with it. That
said, a shovel head's edge, or digging blade, can be sharpened with a
standard bastard file. A sharp edge aids in the cutting—of vegetation,
consolidated fill—that a shovel must sometimes perform to get at
the digging it's made to do. A wooden handle should be checked for
cracks and splinters, and kept well oiled. Re-handling of a shovel is
possible, though harder than re-handling an axe because the head
is riveted, not wedged, into place. The basic rule of thumb is to use
a shovel without thinking too much, until a problem presents itself.
Usually, the problem with a shovel is the shoveler.

List Things I have shoveled: sidewalks, snowdrifts, holes (for outhouses
and bridge abutments and potatoes), driveways, fill pits. Also, footings
for rock walls, tie-ins for cribbing, horse shit, dog shit, mule shit, a
grave for a songbird caught in an early frost. Coal, gravel, dirt, straw,
mud, cedar chips, muck, bark, left-over acorn hulls from a squirrel's
midden, water from a gooey ditch. Once, I lifted a dumb spruce

grouse from the middle of the road in a shovel, carried it twenty yards to safer ground.

Users As tools go, shovel is the great equalizer. Almost everyone has used one. The daintiest gardeners use trowels. Kids shovel snow to build forts. Bulk-aisle grocery shoppers fill spice jars with scoops. A shovel is intuitive. Easy to figure out. Little tricks are gleaned from years of use—how to stack hands, leverage dependent on the weight of the load: choked up for wet gravel, high and loose to fling sawdust into a trash bin; how to brace elbow on knee and pivot the shovel from pile to destination. Not everyone knows to use a shovel blade for cutting through tough material, or the back for tamping and smoothing, and not everyone is fast, or strong enough to dig all day. But everyone knows what to do with a shovel. Give one to a kid at the beach and watch.

Past Early modern shovels had wooden heads reinforced with a metal "shoe" along the edge, called a shod shovel. Many shovels in many hands make history. Early civilizations used pieces of wood and animal bones for digging and scooping. Shovels leaned against the Colosseum and Angkor Wat, at the base of the Eiffel Tower, at the foot of the Great Wall. Shovels dug gold, built railroads. The Ames shovel, an early American prototype still manufactured today, was issued to US troops in World War I for tunnels and foxholes, digging latrines, hand-to-hand combat, and burying soldiers at battle's end. Look around—an urban subway system, the pilings of a shipyard dock, the basement of your house. Shovels, more than bootstraps, are the secret to success.

CHAPTER 6

Denali: Home

(Why I stayed put)

When you commit yourself to transience, mobility becomes a kind of home. You learn to thrive in the space hemmed in by movement, like the hobo, Gypsy, beatnik, the beggar monk, the traveling salesman, long-haul truckers: icons all. Yet the search for a resting place undergirds equally compelling narratives. The Homeric quest, the Buddha's odyssey, Dorothy in Oz, the armchair genealogist's discoveries. Whether we move or whether we stay, most of us are trying to know some place, to get our hooks into a home. Home found me when I wasn't even looking anymore.

Three years after our arrival in Alaska from Montana, I slogged to the end of my master's degree, the unlikely thing that had lured me north. In May, Gabe and I moved out of our Anchorage apartment, our home for two-thirds of three years. We met Alec in Talkeetna for a trip on the Ruth Glacier, a south-flowing ice field on the flanks of the Alaska Range, the perfect place to celebrate my graduation beneath thousand-foot granite faces with glacier travel and summit ridges and whiskey-spiked hot cocoa made from melted snow. After the trip, all of us would return to Denali for a second season. For Gabe and me, beyond that was anyone's guess. I'd always thought—insisted, a few years back—we'd return to western Montana. But on the Ruth, climbing peaks together, in love with Alaska, I wasn't sure what fall would bring.

Summer passed. September came. Other seasonals left. We stayed. Gabe and I had worked ten seasons in three different places, moving every six months from park to town to park. But that fall, we had no reason to leave when the trails season was over. Grad school finished, Alaska not letting go. No pressing need for a winter job. A cozy log cabin with cheap rent north of the park. We stayed.

On paper, we were still seasonals, temporary employees, trail crew leaders laid off when gloves wore out and snow flew. But for the first time in our twelve-year history together, six months passed with no move. No biannual novelty shot, no sorted possessions, protracted goodbyes. No identity based on being about-to-leave. The realization was as striking as sun in my eyes: though the job was seasonal, I was not. I lived in Denali. Since then, we've sallied forth, of course: trips abroad, holidays with family, arts residencies, a semester of teaching Outside, a winter cabin-sitting for a friend, but always returning in between. Six years past that first choice to stay, I know all four seasons here, back to back, year to year. Digging in.

I have no story for my apprenticeship with a shovel. The first anecdote I know about using one involves the toy shovel in my childhood backyard sandbox, which I used to pour a scoop of sand (1/100th of a yard?) down the throat of the neighbor kid. With that tool, at least, I had prowess early, and an instinctive understanding: move material (sand) from the place where it is (sandbox) to the place where you want it (mouth). Some things are too simple to require narrative.

Summer in Denali is fast and furious, a drunk on a spree before he quits for good, a kid out past bedtime in beckoning light. Mid-April, it sets in that winter is on the wane and then, *boom,* the upward climb toward solstice, June 21, the longest day: light until 2 a.m. and again half an hour later, nightfall just a thicker dusk. The mountains thaw and rivers burgeon and tourism rages by June. Hotels and shops throw off window boards, winter's toothy bite a secret most summer folks will never guess at. RVs and bus tours flood the highways. Elderly folks clutch each other's arms in crosswalks. Newlyweds buy cheap T-shirts, snap photos near anything that says "Alaska."

At work, we get serious. One week there's the indoor organizing and training, the buttoning up of winter's projects (notching logs, fixing tools), and the next week, the full-throated roar of construction time. The ground thaws day by inch and we move dirt with Bobcats and shovels and backs, applying ourselves to trailwork in a fury adrenalized by the ticking clock. Bridges, switchbacks, survey, rockwork: there won't be time for all we have to do.

At home, summer to-do lists are as epic—building projects, fishing trips for the winter's freezer, peaks to climb, gardens growing, visitors coming, going, coming. Weeks pass, blurred. Days go by with four hours' sleep until I collapse for a weekend of deep breaths, wonder how long this pace can go on even as I pull the light in close, rub it into my skin, save it up against the craving dark. After June's longest day, we're over the apex and dropping to the bottom of the bell curve, first slowly—July lingers, some years warm and dry, others rainy and cool—but August hits and even when it's warm, the light is leaving. Berries ripen overnight; tourists lessen, trickle, then stop, as if their source dried up. Wolves and bears scarf all the calories they can find. Snowshoe hares and ptarmigan change to the white that will conceal them in snow. In Denali, summer is intermission to winter's concert. We guzzle drinks in the lobby with friends, buy CDs, and make a quick trip to the bathroom; any minute, the lights will flicker and the rest of the show will begin.

Trail crews live for pranks. Along with dirty jokes, practical jokes are bread and butter, and over the years in Glacier, I'd tasted the classics. My first year with Reba, I hiked all day with a melon-size rock she'd hidden in the bottom of my pack. If you left your boots outside your tent, they'd be on top of the outhouse by morning, courtesy of the early riser who found them unguarded. Watch your lunch-box closely or Mack would steal your Snickers and hide it in the saw kit.

But the Denali crew, with its merger of loose cannons and heavy equipment, raised the stakes. My crew stuffed Nic's truck cab with tree limbs and we returned to our pickup at the end of the day to a six-hundred-pound rock in the truck bed, heavy enough to squash the tires. No way to remove the rock without the Bobcat (long gone), so we drove back to the yard with evidence of Nic's triumph hulking over the tailgate. Crews traveled across Riley Creek to a job site via a zipline, and pranksters were always tying the pulley on one side or the other, hiding the harnesses, the tensioning lever, anything to strand someone or force a hand-over-hand along the 110-foot cable. On top of the railroad trestle that spanned another crew's work site, we patiently awaited their lunch break and, from stories above, up-ended our water bottles on their heads. One kidnapping spree lasted four months, as crews swapped two stuffed mascots, a snowman and a multi-colored teddy bear, which appeared in photos with duct-tape gags and glued-together ransom notes. By season's end, the snowman had been decapitated and the teddy rocked into a gabion wall, visible only to those of us who know where to look.

Birthdays gave carte blanche; the more elaborate the trick, the higher the honor to the recipient. People got thrown in the creek, force-fed rotten concoctions, duct-taped to furniture, blindfolded for an X-rated piñata, and locked in a Knaack box. Sometimes it's hard to believe that the median age of the gang was late-twenties, and that all of these schemes went on during work hours with no drop in our renowned productivity. When I think about quitting trails or imagine those office jobs I've seen on TV, I know that along with labor and nature, this is the stuff I'd miss the most: hiding someone's clothes while they're skinny-dipping at lunch break, a parade of floats made of power wheelbarrows, climbing trees to drop onto an unsuspecting crew mate passing below, or filling the truck's defrost vents with sawdust so that, on a wet day, the driver turns it on to a face full of woodchips.

Nic is the oldest of the gang at fifty-six, and claims he's never felt younger than he does on the trail crew. But no one can do trails forever. Neil Young says it's better to burn out than to rust, and the old trails adage holds that *It's a good life until you weaken.* Everyone in it knows this career isn't endlessly sustainable. Bodies wear out, people move on. But I could laugh like that for another fifty years. Please, hide bear scat in my boots. Okay, sure, jury-rig my truck for a harmless explosion. Yes, fine, stuff spruce needles down my pants while I'm sleeping at lunch break, you sneaky bastard. Please.

Near the end in Glacier, burnout threatened: same tasks, the constant repetition of work, marching orders from a maintenance schedule set in stone. In Denali, leaders were far more involved with deciding the way things got done. We ordered equipment, designed and gave trainings, kept inventories, surveyed trails, wrote evaluations, and oversaw progress. Most of which was satisfying stuff. Gabe, whose job became subject to furlough a few seasons in (a step up from seasonal, yet blessedly, still impermanent), did even more logistics— parkwide presentations, all-employee meetings, NPS indoctrination trainings. In exchange for these upgrades, Gabe got us health insurance and the first 401(k) plan of our lives, and we both got new challenges. The trouble is, sometimes I'd go a whole day without picking up a shovel. Between the supervisory role and light-duty months because of persistent injuries, I often traded the mattock for the keyboard, the chainsaw for the camera.

No one wants to be a grunt forever. The longer you work, the more opinions you have. You crave responsibility, and then you get it. But for a die-hard laborer at heart, who'd rather work than talk about work, the slippery slope into oversight is terrifying, because before you know it, you stop doing the things you love, the reasons you've stuck out the downsides of the job all along. It happens to everyone who climbs the rungs. Cell phones, daily planners, and spreadsheets close in. Meetings about jobs supplant jobs. The crews wait in the field while we stand in the doorways of management offices, one foot out, one in.

There are wonderful things about rising in the ranks. Mentoring is a highlight for me. Nothing beats seeing a new laborer's confidence rise when his tree falls as planned, or the delight on someone's face when she unlocks the mystery of the log scribe, the clinometer, the skid steer. I like when my input is sought early on, instead of after it's too late. I like to choose the new saw to replace the one that burned out, what equipment to rent, for how long. I like to sketch plans, stockpile materials, line out the steps, see the job through, critique it when it's over. It's nice to be asked how something should be done. Nicer still to have an answer, backed by years of work.

But with the challenge of responsibility comes bullshit, in delicate balance. Some days in the office I longed for the era of the simple task: dig a hole, right there; fell a tree, peel it; hike this far and clean the drains, as fast as you can. Gabe arrived home at the end of a day, brain fried and body restless. Human-resources meetings trumped miles walked that day. Where's the tipping point, when the seesaw drops to the ground with a teeth-jarring bang? I want to do my job for the reasons I always have: because I'm good at it, because it fulfills me, because it's important. Not just for the paycheck, a promotion, or the stability. I've never wanted to climb any ladder for the NPS except the one leaning against the tool shed. I'll know when I'm done, I told myself. The toolless days were still the minority. I hoped I'd have the sense to throw in the trowel before they disappeared.

Our first summer in Denali, we lived in C-Camp, the NPS seasonal housing compound just inside the park entrance. Brown cabins lined the road to the maintenance lot where out-of-state Subarus plastered with bumper stickers sat parked next to ten-yard dump trucks with Peterbilt mud flaps. We walked to the trails shop from our one-room log A-frame, the rent invisible, taken directly out of our paychecks like chits at the company store. We showered in the public wash-house, planned backcountry trips for weekends off. My reality was defined by the park, the job, the parameters of a transplant, up for the summer. I knew few locals from the nearby town of Healy—Ralph, in Denali ten years; Owens, the fellow trail crew leader born in Alaska; a handful of permanents from other divisions.

Returning the second summer, Gabe and I left C-Camp in search of privacy, a place we could have a dog, neighbors, a life beyond the park's rhythms. We moved north, outside Healy, population 984. Healy's year-round employers are the coal mine visible across the Nenana River, the power plant (coal-fired), and the park, "protected" from both of them, twelve miles south. The two-lane Parks Highway passes through the middle of Healy and its face to the world is the quintessential small-town one—two gas stations, a ratty bar, a truck-stop diner with the usual gut-bomb breakfasts served all day. Off the road, a K–12 school whose small library is open to the public four afternoons a week, a community center with a tiny clinic, a VFD. Healy booms when summer tourists flock to Denali, but people pass through quickly. Despite its scenic backdrop, Healy is as invisible to travelers as the apartment buildings outside a New York City subway car, or the neat ranch houses off Interstate 90.

Residents cluster in town on gravel streets or up creeks and on ridges, tucked into aspen groves, hidden in brush. We live up Panguingue Creek, or "out Stampede," as we say. Stampede Road tees west off the highway toward the park on the skyline, turning from pavement to gravel to two-track to trail, finally passable only by mountain bike and ATV, or dog teams and snow-gos in winter. Out Stampede there are a few big houses, but most people live in modest homes and tiny cabins they've built out-of-pocket, a tarp-covered lumber pile far more common than a heated garage. Our first rental was particularly rustic—a sixteen-by-twenty log cabin with no running water—but by no means unusual. Septic systems and wells indicate longevity, money socked away or borrowed to get three hundred feet deep where the water table lies. The rest of us shit in outhouses and collect rainwater in fifty-gallon barrels and haul drinking water from the well house with five-gallon jugs or PVC tanks in the backs of pickups. Friends with showers offer them freely. At dry-cabin pot-lucks, people bring their own full water bottles so as not to burden the hosts with more hauling.

Healy is in some ways a town all its own, unlike anywhere I've been, where the post office bulletin board boasts lynx hides for sale (from a local fourth grader with a trap line) and the air smells like coal dust and tundra plants mixed by a muscular wind. In other ways, it's Interior Alaska's version of the same town you pass through on the way to any park, both entry and buffer. However common, or however special, Healy is the odd little place I've called home. It's a place made up, in part, of seasons.

By September, Healy hunkers down. Tourism done, restaurants and gift shops board up their windows and the only stoplight for one hundred miles blinks, then goes dark. Life gets stripped down. Fairbanks is two hours north by snow-packed, two-lane highway, and we go on biweekly, daylong binges: groceries dog food building materials bookstore doctor visits Thai food a movie (if there's time). Other than that, we're on our own. Healy has a little store where you can get a rock-hard avocado, chips at $6.50 a bag, or a gallon of milk for the same. There's no stocking-up in Healy. In winter, you get what you get.

Don't come to Healy looking for chai. This is not *Outside* maga-zine's Best Town in America. No ski resort, no health-food store. And though I've used—and often miss—that cultural tackle, Healy has the charm that comes from its lack of artifice, the old kind of dorkiness—uncalculated. An informal tai chi group meets on Thurs-day nights in the school gym. No yoga studio with fancy workout clothes; we bend and bow in baggy long underwear to the tinny commands of a Chinese woman on a warped VHS tape. Here, *chi* smells more like sweaty socks than incense.

Like any small town, Healy has entrenched divisions—pro-road, anti-mine, more wilderness, no zoning. Yet, nothing's simple. Park employees have trap lines and coal miners have dog teams. We all complain about the price of gas and the weeks at 40 below. Healy is a tiny and pragmatic place, invisible to anyone who doesn't live here, and that's what bonds those of us who do. There are ideological divisions and old grudges, to be sure. But animosities have to sit alongside what we have in common: remoteness, self-reliance, weather that matters. During a deep freeze, everyone clumps around in the same insulated bibs and bunny boots, politics bundled beneath the veneer of the practical.

Solitary tasks make up the winter days of many residents— hauling water, running dogs, caring for the baby, drywalling the basement. To ward off too much loneliness, locals gather for any reason we can muster: book clubs, knitting groups, poker and hockey games, school pageants, a periodic slide show by someone back from afar. At the community center, a chili feed, a borough hearing, and midwinter, the holiday extravaganza—Healy on Ice, where Santa rides a Zamboni at the outdoor rink behind the school. Don't let this list fool you. Healy is quiet. Some days when the palette is gray and white and all talk is of projects and weather, I wish for color and art, noise, live music, free lectures about something I've never thought about before, a nutcase on a busy corner with a wacky sign. Some days when the cabin feels dark and small and there's no way to stay warm outside for longer than an hour, I wish for a clean, well-lighted space, a hot drink amid the bustle of the public sphere, the haven of anonymity. Not here. There's no hot, no bustle, no public. No anonymous.

Up here, winter makes you local. Denali as workplace means summer months on the trails, tools in hand, always on the move, crowds of seasonals gathered at bars and parties and river pullouts. It's clear why anyone's here—the job is full time, the world hospitable. Summer is an easier place to live, but the other three seasons make this home.

When we chose to stay past the usual cusp, the reason wasn't the weather or the job or the potlucks. We stayed because right now, it's where our life is. With the exodus of summer's ease, we settle in with canned goods and Netflix and our ski loop behind the cabin, where the snow blows into drifts as hard as tarmac and we never see anyone.

Wind is wild. No one has figured out how to domesticate wind. A turbine, a windmill, they collect, not control. Wild is the cabin groaning in a strong gust, a skier hunched against a winter storm, a car on a bridge that can't stay its course into blowing snow. Wild is a tired sled dog curled tail over nose in a melted hollow in the snow. Wild is a summer wind, full of dust and clatter. Wild finds the lee, sleeps.

It was hot and windy on the Savage River trail and Jerry and I were doing a gravel patch job, an afternoon errand. After the last shovel loads and before driving back to the shop, we took a break. I was always eager to avoid tourists, but it's hard to hide in tundra. We slunk into a depression twenty feet off the trail and I turned my back on it. Jerry is decidedly friendlier than me; he faced outward, leaning on his pack. Moments after we sat down and popped open Tupperwares for cold leftovers, I heard a voice. I chewed and rolled my eyes at Jerry. They always found us.

"Ex-cuse me?" said a man in a thick German accent, shouting from the trail. "Is zis vair I may see zee moose?" Trapped in our coin-operated nature show, I swiveled toward him. As protocol, the leader usually answered, so I explained in a half shout that yes, he could see one here, but there was no guarantee. Undeterred, the man chattered on: he was sure zis was zee best place; after all, a sign on the road said to watch for moose here. I nodded, feigned enthusiasm. "Good luck," Jerry said. Finally the man seemed ready to move on, but then, a few steps away, he whirled back to us and announced in a grave voice, oddly projected, as if for an audience, "In zee river, I have seen sree ram." He paused for effect and held up sree fingers, which then morphed to the side of his head to illustrate a Dall sheep's horn— "wiz zee full curl!" he finished proudly, with a flourish.

I snorted. Jerry looked at him for several seconds, quiet. Then he said the simplest, most American thing he could possibly have said, in a deadpan voice: "Cool." The man stood in the trail, nodding, waiting for further comment. Jerry just smiled and nodded back, a kindly tundra Big Lebowski. I laughed. Zee man moved on. Later, at the bar with a pint glass in hand, Jerry and I made a toast: "To zee full curl!"

An axe chops. A rock bar pries. A chainsaw fells. A boat floats. A skid steer excavates. And a shovel? A shovel does everything else.

A clinometer is a layout tool that measures slope angle: rise over run—the amount of vertical gain from one point to another—as a percentage of 100. It's brushed steel, about the size of a deck of cards. You peer through the sight one-eyed at an object in the distance, while a scale in the foreground measures the slope of your gaze. Simpler than a transit, more precise than a laser level or that old standby, the eyeball, a clinometer is both hired hand and referee, a partner that hangs on a loop of cord around the neck and fits easily in the palm of a hand.

The sum total of my survey experience in Glacier had been that small section of dusty reroute with Cassie. But as the child of a surveyor, I'd grown up playing with lath stakes and orange flagging, knew the smooth feel of the brass plumb bob, the familiar scrawled numbers in tiny logbooks. I was ready to learn. My Glacier opus was surpassed one month into Denali. With front-country trails going in like gangbusters, the clinometer became a ubiquitous sidekick. Lay out new trail right, I learned, and you'll sidestep a host of maintenance issues. Survey done poorly, misery and maintenance will follow the trail crew all the days of its life, and it shall dwell in the house of grumbling and recrimination forever.

A well-laid-out trail considers many angles: user group (hikers, horses, bicycles), intended use (nature walk, commuter trail, wilderness access), outslope that will incite good drainage, the steepest grade a certain soil type can bear. The design must also keep in mind terrain obstacles (cliff, stream, pond), overall topography, views. A curvilinear trail corridor follows contour lines, is visually interesting to the user, with enough sight distance to prevent surprise collisions with wildlife. A good trail is both structure on and interpreter of landscape.

The proper use of a clinometer relies more on good eyes and a little patience than any technical finesse, but great layout skills develop only over time and miles. Even one sharp set of eyes can put in a rough flag line, but the best trail layout is a team effort, a mutual plod over downed logs and wet bog and around bedrock outcroppings, talking in call and response: *a little uphill, aw, shit, there's that spring, try there, okay now over, we need a grade reversal soon, think we can make the pass at 10 percent?* Then, return the next day, the next week, or the next season, and you realize it needs to change. You shot too steep and hit the cliff band that you meant to stay below. Ground that was dry in September is wet in the spring, requiring turnpike. There's a beaver dam, an old-growth tree, a big swale that would need to be bridged because the topography is too steep on either side for contouring. Good trail layout requires that you care enough to keep pounding the same stretch of ground long after *it's good enough* has occurred to you, and at the same time that you remain sufficiently divested so you can scrap a plan for a better one.

A good survey is undetectable. Finished trail seems like it was always there, and draws no attention to itself. A poor survey, on the other hand, is noticeable. A too-hasty flag line may set you up for a lifetime of trailwork heartache: steep grades, mud pits, erosion, blown-out tread, failing turns, washouts.

If you survey with someone for days or weeks in a row, you begin to see them reduced to the part you aim for when squinting through the clinometer's sight. The brim of Krusty's hat, Gabe's mustache. Many survey partners are much taller than I am: as their target, I have to raise an arm above my head. The piece of orange flagging tied around my watchband is easy to see in heavy brush, ornamentation born of necessity. For a girl who's lost a grandmother's bracelet, countless watches, every barrette she's ever worn, and her wedding ring, it's the best kind of adornment: offhand, unique, and replaceable. A sign too, of temporary importance, a moment and place when I was a part of landscape, to scale, the bright and moving marker around which everything else fell into place.

Autumn in Denali beguiles me every year, when the world on fire reinvents shade, palette, tone. People think of New England for colors, the Midwest, or prairie towns, full of hardwoods that easterners brought to line the boulevards of their adopted homes. No one thinks of Denali. My sister says, "You don't have any trees, do you?" But color doesn't need trees. Fall colors the North not in canopies overhead, but on the ground, chemistry's carpet unfurling underfoot. Reddened willows, lichen's green glow, squashy mushrooms in earthen tones. Berries—snow, cran, blue, cloud, nagoon, bear, salmon—orange and white, wine and almost-black. Aspens draw eyes up with their taffeta glimmer and lisp, but in autumn's conversation, the ground has the floor.

I am an existentialist at heart and I love fall in part for its contemplative underpinnings, the way it makes me notice the concrete world (everything's dying) and think about the abstract one (everything dies). When trees and brush go aflame right before leaves and blooms pale at winter, I also wonder: will I have even *minutes* as full of purpose as these plants do, when my hue is tinted by the tasks of my hands?

———

I left trails early one season to teach for a semester in Oregon. This was the fall after I finished my MFA, just before we'd decided to stay in Denali for good, and at first I felt ambivalent. I did not go to grad school in order to become a professor. I had never asked the academy to save me from a life of labor. But this job was appealing. One semester long, a unique off-campus program that I had attended as a college student, where I fell in love with the West. Housing provided—my own cabin, with running water! Low commitment. It seemed stupid to turn it down so I could spend two more months digging holes. I took it. It was my first teaching job, among faculty I admired, and while my crew finished the season's work in a hard and early frost, I shored up my notes, took my place at the blackboard, and lectured on Nabokov and poetics, poststructuralism and Zen. I led small group discussions and a writers' circle. The students wrote papers and gave presentations under my guidance, similar in some way, I hoped, to the kind that had so benefited me a decade and a half before.

My closest neighbor lived in a trailer just up the gravel drive from my cabin. Dale was an outdoorsman/nonprofit activist who worked to preserve the local Siskiyou Wilderness against unchecked cattle grazing and ag-biz industry. He'd climbed Denali in the seventies and, in a wicked storm near the summit, lost his hands and feet to frostbite. You'd hardly know it; with dexterity, grit, and a scrappy horse named Pancho, Dale managed to do what anyone could—cook, browse magazines, drive—and more that most people cannot—tie knots, care for stock, lobby politicians. He'd stop by on the way to or from his trailer, often on horseback, and we'd chat about climbing, our dogs, or Alaska. "Ah, Denali," he'd say wryly, holding up a rounded stump: "I left a piece of myself there." Dale was the only person in my life those few months who understood what I missed from back home.

My friend Daryl, one of the head professors, worked the property's timber stands on weekends, thinning the mixed conifer forest for firewood and forest health. He often invited me to cut with him because he knew I had the same crush on the chainsaw that he did, and the same love for the afternoon break we'd take when we shut off the saws and leaned against cut rounds in the late-fall sun. A few times, Daryl and I took interested students into the woods to learn to run a chainsaw. I told them the rules I knew: *use your brake, wear chaps, watch the tip of the bar, take your time.* On Friday afternoons, the community tackled chores; my group chipped away at a semester-long project—building a trail to the creek. The students vaguely knew this had something to do with my "real" job. What exactly did I do again? They clutched shovels and hoes, loppers and mattocks, all heavy and cumbersome in their hands. I held up a pulaski, as familiar to me as Kierkegaard or free verse, and I tried to explain.

What I'd miss: Passing on skills that someone taught me. Hiking uphill in front knowing I'll die before I get passed. Tired bones. Watching a twenty year old fall for trails. Tinkering with tools that I won't have to pay for if my repairs don't work. Unexpected animal sightings. No thought about "getting a workout." Slinging a shovel over my shoulder and heading home on the last day of the workweek. Peeing outside twenty times more often than in. Eating lunch with filthy hands. The tradition of woodswork. Having a beer in dirty clothes in a bar full of squeaky-clean tourists. Sharing tools with people who take good care of them. Seeing happy hikers on a trail I helped build. The confederacy of traildogs. Finding a scrench in the bottom of my pack on a February ski trip. The flexibility borne of built-in daily movement. The smell on my clothes and skin and hair that comes only from being mostly outside. Showers that mean something.

The Triple Lakes Trail was built by the CCC in the 1930s, and my admiration for the New Deal combined with my penchant for handwork meant I was glad to receive this assignment for the season's work. The TLT is the longest trail in Denali, an eight-mile hike connecting the park entrance with McKinley Village south on the Parks Highway. A local favorite, the trail had been long neglected, its condition, in a word, pummeled. A fall-line alignment caused serious drainage and erosion problems, and the tread was highly impacted from overuse with no maintenance. Mud pits on the lower section of trail occasionally sucked a boot off a foot, Cordova style. Our job, over three summers, was to reconstruct this historical trail, fixing it where possible, rerouting it where impossible, and building new trail to connect it to the visitor center's burgeoning trail network.

Coming off the previous season's heavily motorized labor, Triple Lakes represented a return to the things I loved most about trailwork. An uphill hike to the job site on crisp mornings (and rainy ones), lunch breaks near beaver dams, lakeshores, and rocky cliffs, a sizeable hand tool cache, borrow pits, and a commute that occasionally required the crossing of Riley Creek on a zipline, ass-end over the current. Perhaps most critical, the bond that comes from hard, quiet work.

The switch to hiking and hand labor was a major issue for a few of the guys on my crew, though, who began their trails stint in the thick of Denali's mechanized years and had no experience like my Glacier boot camp days. While I waxed nostalgic about the old days, humping heavy loads uphill on our shoulders and running between drains to stay ahead of each other, the guys could not understand why you'd want to push a wheelbarrow when you could use one with a pull cord. I tried to convince them that this was the *real* trailwork, the stuff that lured me into this life. They didn't get why I'd prefer such sweaty, slow, laborious work when a Bobcat's so fast and sweet and fun to drive. (Which it is.)

As the months went by, we came to a compromise: it's all real trailwork. Bobcat or shovel, gravel pile or fill pit, our work is real work. I remembered quick that handwork is no romance. Some days my back killed and the job seemed endless and the pace boring and there was nothing glamorous about the bucket-hauling blisters on my hands. I admitted that I'd welcome the *beep-beep* of a backing Bobcat to lower the massive berm on the downhill side of the trail that we'd been moving inch by inch with shovels and mattocks. On the other hand, the guys conceded that yarding a gnarly stump out of the tread with a hand-ratcheted come-along was just as satisfying as tying it off to a truck hitch and gunning the engine. Several of them cottoned to the crosscut, vying for the chance to use it carefully, with due reverence for its cocked teeth. They saw the art in sharpening hand tools, how it eases the work. They noticed new muscles, faster hike time, stronger hands. And as our progress slowly accrued—each step accountable to this day, that shovelful, the fill pit over there—the specificity that gets mowed over by machined work unfurled. By the end of a week, muddy and ready for a weekend, way further behind than we'd be if we had power tools, we couldn't help but feel invested, gratified. And yes, dead tired.

Sixty-three-degrees-north-winter takes up half the year, so it gets another mention. Mid-October through mid-April is cold, snow early on the ground or windy and bare straight through Christmas. Midwinter brings long snaps at 40 below (shorter than decades ago, the old-timers say), and if the mercury rises past 20, it's as likely to rocket to 40 for a fluky Chinook, the warm and blowsy front that tears through once a winter carrying with it smells of other seasons, other worlds.

Winter's rhythms are made up of wake and sleep, motion and stillness, the race against the clock (finish chores, go for ski) and the hours of reading in lacy-windowed cabins warmed by fuel oil's glow. On winter's crisp nights, I stumble to the outhouse: an impossibility of light. Blanket-black nights are backdrop for the aurora, that scientific borealis acid trip. I know about solar winds and charged particles circling the magnetic poles, but the first time I saw a pink-and-green display, I thought *birthday party.* On a cold night, a deep breath even through neck gaiter and face mask burns the throat, but you have to be outdoors. Watching the aurora from inside isn't the same. Only under that sky is it clear how fully *in* this universe we are, as the roof of our home lifts and swirls.

Winter in Denali means sled dogs. Thick-coated, long-legged, broad-chested Alaskan huskies bred not for looks or papers but for travel through deep snow and deep cold. I'd always been drawn to husky mutts with blue eyes and wolfy faces, but before I moved north, I had not given sled dogs much thought. You can't live a month in Denali, though, without catching whiff of the obsession.

The history of the Interior is written with dogs. When the first wolf lingered outside a human camp for easy access to discarded bones, domestication began. Alaska Natives ran teams for hunting and travel. Sourdoughs mushed iced-over rivers to their homesteads long before the road system. The post office in Alaska delivered mail by dog sled as late as 1963. The first rangers in Denali patrolled for poachers on the runners of a sled, and to this day, the park maintains a working kennel that breeds, trains, and raises thirty dogs for winter patrols and summer interpretive programs. Many locals have dog teams, for racing, monitoring trap lines, accessing remote cabins, and wilderness trips. An Iditarod champ lives down the road, and our old landlord ran the Yukon Quest. Huskies bolt through gas station parking lots and circle the backs of trucks, husky posters line the walls of schoolrooms and restaurants. In a dog yard neighborhood, howls break out every few hours when a moose passes near or a pickup casts headlights through the fence.

Like many seasonals, Gabe and I "adopted" a Denali kennels pup that first summer, coming evenings to unclip her from her post and take her for a leash walk. The winter following our first season, we came up from Anchorage for a dog trip into the park with our friend Kara, the kennels manager. She and the winter volunteers ran the teams, and Gabe and I skied, breaking trail ahead of the team in deep snow, towed behind the sled like a water-skier when river ice became too slick for kick and glide. Kara, who'd been mushing for years, gave me a quick lesson—shift your weight like so, brake hard on hills, don't run over the dogs, and the cardinal rule of mushing: never, never let go of the sled. My first stint on the runners included a twenty-foot drop off a corniced snowdrift (*I knew you'd be fine,* Kara said) and a quarter-mile belly-drag along the Teklanika River flats, gripping sled runners with both hands, spread eagle, so as to never, never let go of the sled. (Eventually, they pulled away.)

The beauty of traveling with dogs is unmistakable, but driving a loaded dogsled in wilderness is a far cry from the groomed speed of a sprint trail race. No smooth skim of a fast prow over placid surface with one hand free to wave, like the dignitaries at the ceremonial start of the Iditarod down a strip of snow on Fifth Avenue in Anchorage. Instead, it's pedal and push, shift and lean, *gee* and *haw* in a deep, calm voice, a hop to avoid low brush or a spruce branch in the eyes, a jump and dash over open water, broken ice. Off the runners, it's a trail-breaking slog ahead of the team on snowshoes, route-finding in blowing snow. At camp, it's chopping river ice or melting snow for thirty dogs' dinners, the slosh of the long-handled scoop emptying gruel into their dented tin bowls and the sound of barking dogs falling silent on their grub, dogs who've pulled all day because you asked them to, and they love it. The second cardinal rule of mushing: people don't eat until the dogs have eaten.

After that first trip, Gabe and I were hooked. We wrangled any contact we could get with sled dogs. We volunteered for park patrols. We befriended mushers, lingered in their kennels, learning litter names. We house-sat for dog yards, imitated the motions of owning a team—twice-daily feedings, soaking kibble, cutting fat, scooping poop with a flat-nosed shovel. We fed neighbors' dogs whenever they asked, stuck in town in a whiteout, too pregnant to haul food buckets to the dog yard. We did anything to be close to sled dogs.

Once we'd moved out of C-Camp, Gabe and I talked it over.

Neither of us wanted a full team, unready to give up our human-powered ski adventures, or make the sacrifices a dog yard required. (You couldn't guarantee some suckers like us would be around to feed if we went away.) But we decided to adopt *one* dog. Each spring, the Denali kennels retires the nine-year-old litter to local homes. The year we were ready, Campion needed a home, a seventy-five-pound gray-and-white leggy Alaskan husky with Siberian markings and icy eyes. I remembered him from trips (he was my wheel dog on that first steep ride), but I didn't know him well, just that he needed a home, we needed a dog. I worried about the responsibility. We were footloose. Would we have to rush home to feed every day? What about our trips, weeks or months long?

I needn't have worried. What Campion cost us in convenience, dog-sitting logistics, and performance dog food was far outweighed by what he gave us. I've grown to love him more than I've ever loved a beast, different than how I'd love a kid, less attached to how he reflects me, less worried about what I'm doing wrong. Unencumbered by expectation, we coo over his funny antics, how he chases his tail when he wants a walk, his long, slow farts when he sits for a treat. I'm soft for this dog, in love with his thick fur that smells like snow and spruce and popcorn. I worry that he's warm enough on cold days at his dog house (he is), and if he likes the kibble we feed him (he does), and that we're pushing his old bones too far. But Campion surprises me again and again. He skijored with me at nine, ten, thirteen (pulling out front in his harness while I skied behind) and happily ran with a team when given the chance. Campion taught me about winter—how to move carefully on frozen rivers, how to find a packed trail underfoot, when to curl up and cover your nose with your tail. He taught me about determination, how drive can be both ingrained and chosen, again and again. At nearly sixteen, with a tumor and a limp and foggy eyes, he's taught me how to give my whole heart to something I'll lose. Campion prepared us for our second sleddy, Beluga, a spunky lead dog I love just as much, for new reasons. Together they sleep in a pile in the back of the truck. (They whine when they don't get enough exercise.) They bark and yank at their chains when we come to unclip them. (They eat moose turds and lick my face.) They skijor with us over miles of snow, one in a blue harness, one in red. (They turn me into a person who's always covered in dog hair.)

The rural Alaskan paradox: we have an outhouse and WiFi. I tell people who find this odd that we skipped the twentieth century. We have electricity (late 1800s) and iTunes (2010). It's just right. I can read the *New York Times* online, and my house never smells like shit.

The shovel is an undervalued tool, referred to most often as a prop in the trope of the lazy federal worker leaning on it. Poor shovel. It deserves better. As a federal employee for more than a decade, I've had a lazy moment or two, but usually a defensible and short spell on a hot day well out of sight. (For all my faults, sluggishness is not one of them.) I have no patience for those who think a government job comes with the right to "milk it," "spank the monkey," or, most discouragingly, "fuck the dog." (Who exactly is the dog in this metaphor, anyway?) It isn't fair to us, a lot of whom work harder for the government than many in the private sector. And it certainly isn't fair to the shovel, which can't help being the second-best tool to lean on (after the rock rake). If I had my way, anyone who uses the shovel truism—the guy who loves to lean, or the tourist who disparages him—would be subject to forty whacks with one. I'm sure that wouldn't cure the laborers who tend toward it of chronic mediocrity, but at least it might dignify a humble tool that deserves more respect than as kickstand for flat-tired bikes.

In every season, we contend with light and dark. Outsiders ask how we stand the dark, but the light is harder for me. Summer's long days are intoxicating—Roof the shed at midnight! Start a climb at 4 a.m.!—but it's also exhausting, the never-stopping, the sense that all things are possible, all the time. In blaring summer, I crave dark, cold, snow. Dark is less expectant than light. It shuts out all stimuli but what you choose for yourself. Dark gives permission for mulling, for hours of reading, late breakfasts and the free-of-sensory-overload unconscious time that rebuilds me. Summer is friendly, but dark is an ally.

Dark is also an adversary. Some begin to lament the growing dark in September and soldier on until spring with a bitter resolve that connotes pioneers in sod houses. Everyone has a tip for thriving in the dark months—buy a SAD light, dump that needy boyfriend, take up knitting. The way I learned to love the Interior winter was simple: move vigorously outside for at least an hour and expand my sense of day. In June we sleep when it's light, and in winter, dark needn't mean quit. A full moon lights a night skijor, reflected starlight on snow a rural street lamp. January evenings mean lit candles in windows, a dim log cabin the excuse to let Christmas lights glow for months. Winter tells me, push past the limits the body's clock sets for itself. Expect darkness. Watch for light.

Dark can be inconvenient. I hate quitting a task because of a forgotten headlamp or a waning moon, hate banging my shin on the porch step on the way from the outhouse when it's too dark to see. There's pressure in winter daylight, time slipped through fingers: at two o'clock you think about dinner, at seven, bed. If you're sad or overwhelmed, dark seems bottomless, a soul-plummet in the worst kind of free fall. Dark is also magical. Winter feeds a primordial hunger, an urge to curl up and lick your paws, to pause on the questions that light rushes us past. I take my cues from our two old sled dogs, who sleep soundest in winter, curled up in a pocket they've melted in the snow, or so near the woodstove their coats are hot to the touch. Deep winter is the cave of the year.

Sanity hangs in the balance of light and dark. A year in the Interior is like a day anywhere else; the spectrum makes sense. Together, the seasons have symmetry, the calendar folded on itself like a paper snowflake. Now that I am home here, it's hard to imagine anything less extreme. My body has been calibrated toward the twelve-month cycle, and I sleep with sun on my face in June and wake at 6 a.m. in December (groggily), ready to begin a day in a day that has not yet begun.

I'd traveled one hundred miles down the Copper River in Cordova, but it wasn't until I moved to Denali that I went dip-netting. This style of subsistence fishing is how many Alaskans put food on their tables. A dip-netting permit (for residents only) allots fifteen sockeye per person or thirty per family. This is not the Alaska fishing of tourism catalogs. No fancy casting or photogenic flashing fish arced out from a line, drops of water catching sunlight. Picture instead a net the size of a kid's swimming pool on a ten-foot handle, a slow, sweeping motion, and hours of nothing happening. The Copper is the place to participate in this Alaskan right of passage.

Copper River reds are the best salmon you can catch or buy, a delicacy that sustains a thriving commercial market. Sockeye get shipped fresh from ocean docks to Seattle sushi bars, five-star restaurants in Cancun. Now imagine that same fish, practically free, on your dinner plate all winter. The flesh of a Copper River red is the color of sunset. It's rich in essential fatty acids, flaky and moist, perfect for smoking or eating raw. When you're grilling Copper River sockeye over a beach fire half an hour after you landed it, you can't help but feel smug—in Chicago some sucker's paying thirty bucks a plate for this fish on ice two days older—and also lucky: eating local at its barest, and most elegant.

Of course, first, you have to catch the fish. Our first summer in Denali, Ralph invited Krusty and Gabe and me to join him and some friends for their annual dip-netting trip in June. He lured us with tales of runs so thick you could barely rest between catches, limiting out in hours. Ralph handled the logistics—four giant coolers, nets and poles, the ropes for anchoring ourselves to sheer cliffs that rimmed the best spots, enough Ziplocs and garbage bags and tarps to wrap a house with. His wife packed us ham sandwiches and sliced carrots and beer and Snickers. We threw fingers for driving shifts.

The drive itself signified the beginning of an epic. From Healy it's an eight-hour trip, the middle leg over the bone-jarring gravel washboard of the Denali Highway. We left right after work, a three-day weekend ahead, and arrived at the river in the middle of the night, ready to begin our assault. The fabled catch eluded us, though, and despite nearly thirty hours of fishing, our group netted only twenty-five of our legal 150-plus claim. It rained on and off and the black flies were heinous, and by the drive home we were all so sleep-deprived and slap-happy that over burgers and beers in Glennallen half way back, getting so badly skunked seemed almost funny. Our paltry haul was a blessing when it came to the gutting, cleaning, and packaging phase, which lasted into the wee hours of Sunday anyway. We stumbled into the shop Monday morning with bloodshot eyes and hands that reeked of salmon.

Two years later, the skunking a vague memory, Gabe and I were ready to have another go. Time, that great revisionist historian, had done its job: *So we spent three days slaving away for thirty pounds of fish that would have cost less in the grocery store than the gas it took us to drive to the river. It was fun, yeah? And that won't happen again, right?* Krusty, the eternal optimist, had better luck the year prior, and anything with Krusty was guaranteed good fun. We bet this time it would be different.

It was. The dirt road along the river washed out that spring, so the best holes were a several-mile hike from the parking area, complicating the process. It was August, not June, with sun, no bugs in sight, temperatures cool enough to be comfortable in rubber fishing gear but warm enough to be pleasant. And, this time, we caught fish.

Krusty, a loyal sort, went right to a favorite hole two miles up the road, while Gabe and I tried closer spots first. No luck. Around dinnertime, we went out the road, too, and in the distance saw Krusty hiking toward us, nearly flattened under his backpack-load of thirty salmon, weighing more than 150 pounds. A strong and grinning hiker under most circumstances, Krusty was staggering. He lurched up to us and stopped. The hole was pumping out fish faster than he could net them, he said. I could read it in his eyes: *Get your asses out there, you lazy fuckers, quit waiting for something to jump into your truck!* We went in opposite directions, Krusty to clean and pack his fish, Gabe and I to haul in a burden of our own.

After a two-hundred-foot descent to the river over slick rock, we encamped on a large outcrop pitched toward the boiling hole. The current created a mini-hydraulic into which no passing fish, it seemed, could avoid being drawn. Gabe stuck the net in the water. *Wham*, fish. He swung the fish to me, my knife in hand to kill it, bleed out the gills, descale, and get it on a stringer. The instant the net hit the water again, another fish. We hooted in disbelief. At first it was comical, then biblical (three in one net), and then ghastly, as I bludgeoned fish faster than I could bid them thanks. Fluids warmed my palms through gloves. I scooped handfuls of roe out of the females, brilliant pearly orange treasure heaped on the rock in a steaming pile. I tasted one, a salted burst, and the musky flavor courted my mouth for hours.

By midnight, it was too dark to fish (August, after all), and we called it quits with twenty-three. Seven shy of our legal take, we'd reached our killing limit. I am not squeamish by nature. I believe it is right to eat animals we kill ourselves, honorable even, if done well, in moderation. And I love salmon, all winter long. But that night, I just couldn't slay anything else. I had so much blood on my hands, on my Hellies, on my cheeks, and in the hairs hanging out of my ponytail. I saw in a quick flash how unbearable life would be had I to account for each of the invisible deaths my thriving demands—bugs on my windshield, the critters displaced by ski runs and bike trails, the ones that make my meat, my boots, my gloves.

Night dropped, the melancholy end-of-summer clear, and there was no time for introspection. The fish had to be cleaned fast or the flesh would taint, an inexcusable waste. We hauled our load up to the roadbed and unsheathed knives—fish beheaded, gutted, stuffed into plastic bags, split between backpacks (mine half as heavy as Krusty's, thank God). We shouldered the long poles, nets a tripping hazard dangling down near our XtraTufs, and trudged into the dark. The arches of my feet ached. Thirty-six hours with no sleep. Fish slime in my ears, a year's worth of protein on my back. I should have felt proud, but it was too much effort.

Two Healy winters passed in our one-room cabin. In March, a nicer, larger rental cabin up the road became available when friends moved Outside for a "real job." We moved in, hauled boxes of books and loads of boots on sleds over the snow-packed trail to the porch. That was the winter Gabe's job also turned more permanent, with a four-year appointment and benefits. We had just begun to think about a place of our own when the friends moving to Ohio made us another offer. They owned a piece of land on the edge of a bluff farther up Stampede, and they were thinking of subdividing, a few acres' sale to pay it off before they moved away. Would we be interested? It was a beautiful spot, with aspen groves, mountain views, a gravel road punched in to the property's edge. It was a place we could imagine building the house we'd begun to plan in our minds: concrete countertops, a woodstove, a south-facing porch. An outhouse of our very own. *Yes,* we told the friends, *let's do it.* We shook hands. Another friend, a surveyor, staked the boundaries and filed the plat map at the borough office, making it, finally, our own. It was the most money we'd ever spent on anything you could touch (college was much more). A 1993 Toyota pickup was our next-most-valuable asset, and after that, a quiver of ten pairs of skis.

We'd tapped most of our out-of-pocket savings for the land, and building the place we wanted was going to take some steps. But we knew where the story started: with dirt work, of course. Building a sixteen-foot gravel driveway was, funny enough, exactly like building a sixteen-foot bike trail. We walked alignments, flagged the best line (avoid black spruce bog to the north, granite boulders to the south), and when the ground thawed in June, rented a Bobcat from Fairbanks ($400 for forty hours on the meter, delivery included). One week, 350 linear feet, and four hundred yards of gravel later we had a driveway. It peeled off the road over a stick of culvert buried two feet deep and curved its way gently to the chosen house site. We moved some displaced tundra mats, carpeting the fill slopes just as we had on trail projects. Nic came after work one evening to run the Bobcat while Gabe and I worked the hand tools, shoveling in low spots, raking edges. The same steps as for work, only for ourselves, better.

With the driveway finished, the property changed. Before, it had been a piece of raw land, the house a mirage I could picture if I squinted hard and superimposed Frank Lloyd Wright atop Little House on the Prairie. After, it was a home site. The gravel strip led somewhere. I could see a woodshed at the end of it, stacked with split birch. A trail contouring the hill, a door opening into an arctic entry, where finally, there would be a bench and a place to leave snowy boots. A home.

The first weekend after we laid the driveway, Gabe and I went up to the land for a walk with the dogs. In the gravel surface, not yet hardened as it would by next year's rain and freeze and thaw, we saw rows of tracks: a set of a neighbor's boot prints said, *What are they up to?* A set of dog prints said, *I smell something different.* A set of brown bear prints said, *This was always a home.*

Lynx. Listen: *lynx.* A feline, a cat. A verb (this links that). A word without vowels, and an *x* to boot. Lynx whose population spikes so closely mirror snowshoe hares' that you can't think *cat* without thinking *rabbit.* Lynx travels fastest at night, hunts on the ground but can climb trees and swim. On my road, a few miles down from the cabin. In the park, asleep midday, skulking the ditch line after dark. *Lynx.* The *l* rolls out shy, almost hidden in the tongue's crevice, the crick of the middle *nk*, as if poised for a leap, and *x*'s secretive hiss, falling on tufted ears. Such bony structure, visible beneath the skin of animals and words.

Spring in Denali tugs at late-March days when long sun softens snow and warmer winds blow possibilities in. But March often brings the year's coldest snap; winter still has the reins. Only in late April, as southern climates watch for crocuses, do we see the beginning of the end of ice. Alaska's fifth season, squeezed between winter and spring, is "breakup." Breakup of rivers as shed-size chunks of ice give way; breakup of frozen driveways and roads, thaw triggering spring's buckle and heave so the same potholes open up and gravel roads ripple with washboard; breakup of overflow, the layers of water and ice that percolate frozen-solid creeks and rivers; breakup of snow pack in the tundra lowlands, exposing winter-kill and last year's cranberries. It's fitting that breakup's label alludes to the end of romance: grim, gray, trudging. While it's happening, it seems it will never pass. It always does.

Look quick to catch spring. April's ice overlaps May's buds. Aspens go from hint of pale green to fully leafed-out in three days. Spring blooms thrust through snow and bushes that yield berries in August have tiny flowers while ice lingers in creek bottoms. Spring's window is short, just time enough to get its business done, jump-starting life, issuing in the fervent days of June, only three months before the freeze takes hold again. Blown kiss, curt bow, spring exits the stage quick—summer waits in the wings, ready to pass in a panic, looking over shoulder for winter's breath already on its neck.

———

Wild is the coming of the new, blown in from far corners. It's the middle of a story that won't be quit, breath caught in the chest, empathy or anger near enough to touch. Wildness is red, it's purple, color against white, against black, against sky. It is fur on a tree branch discarded by an urgent itch. Wild is old, bones mulching themselves beneath the earth, the possibility of buried life, deep. Wildness is right there in front of you: there, right *there*. Wildness is gone.

Holly came to trails my third year in Denali. She was a twentysomething with some labor skills, a year as a ranger in the Interp division, and a hankering to learn trailwork. She distinguished herself as quick and eager to laugh. She moved faster than all four guys on her crew, first in line for a task, chattering, blond hair flying out behind. I realized it: I was the old girl now, the longtimer with a few tricks up her sleeve, aching joints, a chip on her shoulder. Holly was friendly and eager to please, much cheerier than my surly default, yet something about her—the hustle, the gusto, the wide eyes— reminded me of an earlier me. I love seeing women get in green, a little off-kilter, and then fall into a rhythm, a confidence, the excitement kindled.

Her second season, Holly was on Gabe's crew with Rico, an L.A. kid just out of high school. It was Rico's first time away from his close-knit Hispanic family. He was a good hand: he did what he was told and worked hard. Early on, though, he made the mistake that many young guys do: he tried to protect the girls from hard work. In labor's version of chivalry, he thought he should take two tools so Holly had to carry only one. He worried that her wheelbarrow load was too heavy. Holly assured him she could handle it, and proceeded to work him into the ground. Like most of the women I've known in my trails tenure, Holly made up for her size with focus and endurance and a determination that wouldn't downshift until the guys were flat on their backs. Behind every good man, twice as hard for half the credit, all that jazz.

At the end of the season, Holly took me aside: "Christine!" she said, "I have to tell you something so cool!" On his last day of work Rico had given Holly a shy little speech. I could picture it as she described him, eyes downcast, his mumbling laugh, the Spanish lilt beneath English words: "I remember the beginning of the season when you wouldn't let me help you and I thought it wasn't good for you to work like that, and then you worked harder than anyone! I never knew girls could work like that before!" Holly's grin was so wide it must have hurt. "Then he said, 'You really showed me girls can do anything!'" I listened with my arms folded across my chest, trying to swallow the lump in my throat, the embarrassing thing that wells up in me when this happens—when people outdo their limits, teach each other things, and themselves, when trailwork, hard work, is the conduit for a breakthrough. Holly finished with a fast breath in, her nervous laugh, rapid-fire chatter as one syllable tumbled into the next: "Anyways," she said, "I couldn't wait to tell you that! While he was talking I thought, *I have to tell Christine!*"

I said something I hoped was sufficient, agreed it was an incredibly cool moment. But I felt clumsy and inarticulate in the face of Holly's excitement, and Rico's realization, and the fact that I was implicated in it, too, because Holly knew I'd care, because she knew that I knew that girls kicked ass. I felt in that moment a pride in mentorship, and sisterhood, and also in the fact that, for all it sometimes seems like just another job, being a woman in a "man's world" is an activism, a standing up to assumptions and limits and proclaiming with our bodies, our whole selves, *I can be however suits me.* And how that tells the men, *You can, too.* It's one of those rooftop moments, all of us hollering in corny solidarity: do what you love, be proud of what you do. Get after it!

How could I help but think of Reba and Cassie, then, the Glacier women I learned from, all the women since then that I'd taught, the whole relay line of us, all the way to Holly, baton from palm to palm to sweaty palm? I am still not quite ready to quit my leg of the race, to say, *Go, Reach, Stick,* and let go the wand into the next hand. But I'm pretty sure that when the time comes, there will be another woman in front of me ready to take it, arm outstretched behind, fingers sticky, a tough girl running from something and toward something else. She'll tear up the next leg, feet kicking gravel, chest high, while I stop, hands on my knees, pulse in my ears, to catch my breath.

Japanese carpenters refer to their tools collectively as *dogu*, which translates to "instruments of the way." *The way* is the path to the heart of life, through the heart of spirit. Dogen Zenji, a thirteenth-century Zen master, said, "To study the way is to study the self, to study the self is to forget the self, to forget the self is to awaken into the ten thousand things." I want to remember this. Tools. Self. Ten thousand things.

In a house with no plumbing, we imitate the pleasures of civilized life. Contrary to stereotype, an outhouse is a wonderful thing. A bathroom outside puts you in the thick of the world first thing in the morning, no matter the weather. A piece of closed-cell foam insulation cut to fit over the hole makes a fine seat, even in winter, as warm as anyone's indoor throne.

For a kitchen sink, drop a stainless steel basin into the counter, no fixtures necessary. Drain it with an open-ended pipe, five-gallon bucket poised beneath. Haul water from the well in plastic cubies, in summer supplement with the forty-gallon barrel that sits beneath a gutter downspout. Use the water (so icy cold out of the well all year long it hurts your teeth) to fill the Gatorade jug that poses as a faucet on the sink's edge, press the little spigot: running water. For washing your face or the dishes, heat water in the kettle or the big tin pans. Once used to it, you forget this isn't how everyone lives. The plates are clean. The chicken soup is made with rainwater. Paper towels are a guilty luxury. It's normal until the day you forget to empty the slop bucket, and you drain a can of beans or dump a soaking pan and that last drop brings the water over the top of the bucket, flooding, thick and stinky, onto the floor, the rug, your feet. It doesn't matter if it's warm out or cold, light or dark, there's only one way to vent the disgust and that is to yell at the top of your lungs the refrain favored by inhabitants of dry cabins all over the state, the admission, to the plumbed universe, that we're posers at best: *My sink drains into a fucking bucket!*

What I won't miss: Stiff neck. 7 a.m. in the polyester uniform. Every night, making a lunch big enough to last a ten-hour day. Tourist questions. Being part of "the system." Backing the trailer with the lift-gate truck. Bullshit paperwork. The constant odor of farts. Sandwiches that taste like saw gas. Picking up other people's trash from the trucks. Editing rants while wearing green and gray. Twenty year olds who think they know everything. Realizing I could have done something better. Oblivious bosses. Sharing tools with people who take shitty care of them. Aiding development about which I feel ambivalent. Stale trail mix.

> **Song of Ourselves** (with apologies to Walt Whitman)
> I celebrate you guys, and toast you,
> And what you call a good day's effort, I shall also,
> For every tool belonging to me as good belongs to you,
>   And also my emergency Snickers, if you need it.
>
> I work and invite my soul,
> We sweat and eat at our ease observing the way the mountains look in this light.
>
> My tongue, every atom of my blood, honed in this soil, this air,
> Born here of my work, born here from your work, and all that work we do together,

I, now thirty-eight years old in hard-to-complain-about
  health begin,
Hoping to keep moving like we do—quick, at ease—till
  lunch break, at least.

Alaska, in its abundance, taught me the meaning of enough. Berries
at lunch break as far as I can reach without moving from my tundra
nest. Berries in the evening after work's done, berries on dog walks,
on weekends when hours pass in rhythm (gather and pluck, eat and
hoard), every spare minute near brush pulsing with flora's urgent
command: *pick, pick, pick.* Low-bush cranberries lasso the spectrum
of red, the Yuletide hue made for door wreaths, the deep burgundy
lit up from within. Blueberries plump with liquid sugar bring to
mind nothing as much as bodies—curve of ass in tight jeans or the
gorgeous, blackish swell of a healing bruise.

Sometimes I feel like the apocryphal post-Soviet woman who
had a nervous breakdown her first time in an American grocery
store. Bounty can be paralyzing, the awful clench of *how to choose*
and *I'll never get it all.* The Tao Te Ching says, "There is no calamity like not knowing what is enough," and so I'm slowly learning
to note what I need, to be satisfied with what there is time for, not
cowed by what I miss. There is so much enough; enough for the
bears and my neighbors and the birds, enough for pies and pancakes and two batches of jam and a freezer stash, enough for a winy
twinge in the air and the drop-and-rot that foments next decade's
humus.

The biggest berries still catch my eye and my greedy fingers
sometimes drop a handful reaching for one better, like Aesop's dog
on the bridge who sacrificed the bone in his mouth for the prize
in his reflection. But I'm learning to quiet such urgent grasping, to
move from one bush to the next with purpose. The same steadiness
applies in the mountains. No need to climb them all, tick names off
the list. There are plenty. I'm learning that abundance both dwarfs
and ignites longing.

Satiation—the ceasing of desire—is rare. We constantly defer a sense of completeness, clamoring after the next vacation, face cream, aerobics class, next president, appetizer, child. Desire is alluring, but satiation a subtler host, one that allows contentment to enter and linger. There is radical comfort in the heavy cloak of *enough* resting on my shoulders. Maybe this is what authentic feels like: Subtle. Heavy. Enough.

In Alaska Native traditions, the earth provides for people, even in the skeptical modern age. Tlingit memoirist Ernestine Hayes writes in *Blonde Indian*, "Remember that the land is enspirited. It is quickened. When as you conduct your life . . . remember that it too is conducting its life, and it sees you as well. . . . The land loves you. She misses her children." I used to think I could not speak of the earth this way. In my white mouth, it tasted of giddy romance, magical thinking. But something in me has shifted. When I kneel in a span of bushes spilling berries like a handful of marbles, I know that plants do not need humans as incentive to grow (though they evolve with us, their flowers bright to seduce our taste buds, seeds hitchhiking in our shit). I know Earth's ecosystem is impassive, rain and sun without attachment to my jams, relish, muffins. Yet in the face of this knowledge, the world offers itself: here is the cranberry in snow, frozen with sweetness intact; fish hauled in, fistfuls of eggs in its belly. There is the summer sun, up all day, shining, and there is the winter night, tucked in around me when I crave long rest. It's the skeptic's guise in which I feel the most at home, but sometimes, the fit is ill. I can't shake the feeling that I am being cared for, waking some mornings with light on my face before I have even begun to give my needs their names.

Wildness is taking things back. Wild is giving it all away.

I am a writer made by work. My sentences and stories are dictated by the body's rhythms; by rain, wind, sun, dirt; by the smells of animals and engines, the feel of feet in boots, a tool in hand. Proximity to wilderness has given me analogy for the way story finds Spirit, that alchemy by which the known world merges with the unknown through effort, imagination, and being in the right place at any time at all. God bless manual labor, for my lungs and legs and my bank account and my friendships, and yes, for my mind, which wanders while I do my tasks, which tinkers while expectations wane, which, unwatched, partakes in that inexplicable sorcery: wind and sweat in a pot with idea and image, mix them until they bubble and steam.

Dirt work is foundation work. On construction sites, dirt work happens before other work begins. Dig hole to examine layers. Is the soil well drained? How much rock? Excavate trough where sills will lay. Bury logs, build a berm, outslope so water will flow here, not there.

Dirt work is easy to overlook, unless you're the one doing it. Not everyone wants to: *Don't give me the dirt work, the shit job.* But someone else steps forward: *Dirt work is the best work. Give it to me.*

Dirt work is the last work. When the project is finished, the site plan complete, then dirt work resumes. Mound up mulch, scarify soil to prepare for seed. Push excess fill to edges, load it and truck it away. Smooth out tire tracks. Back drag windrows. Inslope the turn. Deepen the ditch line: water must flow there, not here.

Dirt work is final. Dirt work is never done. No one can do all the dirt work. No one should do none. *Dirt work is good work. Give it to me.*

AFTERWORD

Since I began this book, years have passed. People in these pages have moved on, things have changed, in Montana and Alaska both. And Gabe and I don't work for the Park Service anymore. That era is past, partly our choice—eager for new challenges, out from under the watchful eye of the feds—and partly a sadder story, a book I haven't written. It's not easy to divulge that "America's Best Idea" has a dark side, as subject as any corporation to the march of development, the ruses of ladder climbers, and the misuse of employees. Trust me, I'd rather talk about tools.

Often, especially for seasonals, leaving a job means leaving a place. But Denali doesn't belong to me via the NPS anymore. I belong to the place, via the claim made by time spent and things learned. Such changes have prompted a career that giddy girl in Glacier could never have foreseen. Done with the park, but somehow, still not done with trailwork, Gabe and I started a trails business, doing survey, design, training, and construction across Alaska. Running a business with a spouse when between us we have a nickel's worth of business sense has been interesting. (To quote Paul Newman, "There are three rules for starting a business. Fortunately, we don't know any of them.") Recession aside, we're paying bills due to the combinations that serve one well anywhere: sweat and patience, humility and confidence, good mentors, a little luck, very low overhead and duct tape. Shovels and machines bring home our paychecks. We keep on building bridges. So far, we're too small to fail.

Statewide work means travel, and between the busy field season and wintertime forays, I feel less rooted than in the NPS days. Still, Healy remains our home. Over the past few years, figuring out a way to stay, we moved out of our rental, built a tiny studio on our tundra, and in lieu of the house planned when the park job seemed permanent, put up a sixteen-foot yurt. Off the grid, we have a woodshed built of salvage, fenced raised beds, and a killer outhouse. The park, that old ground zero, feels like another world. We still end up in C-Camp occasionally, to bring the recycling, or poach a shower after a winter trip. When we drive past our old cabin, I think back to my first summer with fondness, introduction to a landscape, the edge of community, by way of a park entrance. There's a swath cut through C-Camp now, a wider-than-it-needed-to-be road corridor leading to a bigger parking lot, the new trails shop I had to see to believe. Nothing stays the same. The old days always seem like the good ones. From far off, it's easy to mistake rust for gold.

As it turns out, to know a place is a tough and complicated goal. It means more than knowing all the hiking trails or where to get a cheap beer, what transplants learn first. In part, knowing a place means knowing its seasons and what indicates them: when the Sandhill cranes pass over on their way from Arctic to equator, when the cranberries ripen, which two weeks the wood frogs sing loud. Knowing when to put out the rainwater barrel because a hard freeze is unlikely, and when to harvest carrots because a hard freeze could come any time. Knowing a place means investing in it like you aren't going anywhere, even if you might: volunteering at the library, going to community meetings, trying to find the owner of a lost dog. Knowing a place means knowing what I love (the smell of tundra plants in rain), what I hate (small-town gossip), and what has nothing to do with me (when the bears den up). Mostly it means tuning into a place beyond what it can offer. This takes daily effort, daily noticing. Annie Dillard says, "How we spend our days is, of course, how we spend our lives," and that's exactly why a seasonal life can also be a permanent one.

Looking back the sixteen years since I first showed up in a trails shop with new Carhartts and soft hands, I can see all those days stacked up like cordwood, built into months, and then years, and now, here it is, this hunch growing in me all along, Glacier, Cordova, Denali, and on: living somewhere doesn't mean you know it, and a job alone doesn't make a place a home. It takes work to do that.

TRAILDOGS' INDEX:
A LIFE IN STATISTICS

Seasons of trailwork: 16

Parks/districts worked for: 3

Pairs of work boots worn out: 5

Peaks climbed in Glacier: 32

Fingers broken: 2

Cost of two hernia surgeries in 2007: ~$45,000

Annual allowance for official NPS uniform in 2008: $115

Rides out of a hitch on a horse or mule, in 6 seasons: 2

Mules that had to be blown up after dying on the trail: 1

Hands with carpal tunnel syndrome symptoms: 2

Months to get carpal tunnel worker's comp claim accepted: 4

Peaks climbed in the Alaska Range (Inner and Outer): 10

Gabe's and my combined hours of unused NPS sick leave: 514

Fastest time up Sperry Hill: 1 hour 45 minutes

Longest one-way hike for work: 18 miles

Number of times my saw nicked my chaps: 1

Diameter of largest downfall bucked: 40 inches

Rank of "fuck" and its forms on list of favorite trail crew cuss words: 1

Range of hourly wage over twelve seasons and three employers:

 $12.12–$24.91

Age of longest-worn item of trails clothing (gray Capilene shirt, cut-off
    sleeves): 14 years

Percent discount most pro-purchase gear programs offer: 50%

Percent of my technical clothing purchased on pro deals: 99%

Capilene long underwear tops in current closet (all weights): 13

Known cases of giardia: 6

Largest one-day elevation gain (paid): 4,847 feet

Maximum calories consumed in a workday: ~8,000

Minimum respectable number of beers brought into a hitch: 1 per day

Maximum respectable number of beers brought into a hitch: no upper limit

Rank of Pabst Blue Ribbon on trail crew "favorite beer" list: 1

Number of PBR fans in blind taste test who chose PBR as best of three
    beers: 0

Search-and-rescue incidents participated in: 8

Number of times missing person was found by my party: 1

Pairs of shorts I own (including bike shorts): 5

Pairs of boots I own (including ski boots): 20

Lowest temperature I've felt in Interior Alaska: 68 degrees below zero

Highest temperature I've felt in Interior Alaska: 91 degrees

Minimum time to plug in engine block before starting truck at 20 below:
    2 hours

Gallons of wild berries harvested in a summer: 2–10

Sockeye allotted on a household dip-netting permit: 30

Average number of pint jars used to can one sockeye: 4

Maximum price I've paid for a gallon of unleaded gas in Healy: $5.11

Creek or river crossings the highway makes between Stampede and
    the park: 14

Closest proximity of a moose to our cabin wall: 2 inches

Most caribou seen on an afternoon ski: 30

Months of year with wolf scat on back trail: 12

Number of friends with 1–20 sled dogs: 15

Number of friends in Healy with a heated garage: 2

ACKNOWLEDGMENTS

I've worked with so many remarkable people. A cold beer to these standouts, who taught me skills and stories: Aric, Burke, Dundas, Frislie, Kenny G, Amy G, Eldon, Craig and Tim, Dan J, Rhonda, Kirby, Shelley, Casey, Stoney, Ric, Allan, Jillian, Oberg, Sethro, Corey, Allie, and Zastrow. High fives and a fist bump to all the crews: my tribe. Special thanks to Mike Shields, godfather of Alaska trails and a generous mentor. If it takes me twice as long to learn half as much, I'll be lucky.

This book is a communal story, but factual blunders and technical errors are thoroughly mine. Many anecdotes herein have twenty versions. Traildogs, if I poached your story, or got some detail wrong, I'm sorry. Such are the limits of oral history.

Thanks to: Sherry Simpson for early conversations about dirt, Ron Spatz for stalwart belief. Linda McCarriston for modeling brave. Generous experts, for reading pieces: Charlie Reynar, Steve Haycox, Ernestine Hayes, and Carmen Adamyk. All the editors who published excerpts. Cheers!

About Charlotte, E. B. White wrote, "It is not often that someone comes along who is a true friend and a good writer." I've had way more than my share. For timely input, thanks to Cole Ruth, Angela Small, Susanna Sonnenberg, and Mark Temelko. Liz Bradfield was invaluable, reading far above and beyond, always with her poet's sharp ear and generous heart.

My family—Mom, Dad, Julia, Liz, Bill—has buoyed me with its highest confidence, modeling for me all manner of authentic lives. My *nieflings* keep me tuned to the future of this enthralling world. My large and boisterous extended clan is the best kind of family tree. Lane and Leslie gave me Gabe, and much more. Countless dear friendships have sustained me. So many shiny pennies: I'm rich.

Thanks to the Alaska State Council on the Arts, the Rasmuson Foundation, the Headlands Center for the Arts, Vermont Studio Center, Breadloaf, and Fishtrap, arts lifelines all.

Thanks to the shepherds: my agent, Janet Silver, who edits keenly, advocates wisely, laughs easily, and loves books. My patient, generous, and spirited editor, Alexis Rizzuto, whose own dirty hands bettered this work in many ways. Everyone at Beacon who helped this book emerge. I could not imagine a finer crew.

From Willa Cather to Jim Harrison, Mardy Murie to James Welch, deeply emplaced writers influence me; a deep bow to that lineage. Grateful thanks also to independent bookstores and those who help them thrive.

All dirt work strives for solid grounding; Gabe Travis is mine, on hitch, at home and everywhere else. He has technical skill, a great ear, and a naturalist's instinct for detail far surpassing my own (Get those ground squirrels out of the trees!). Thank you, my dear one, for every last thing.

Finally, I owe so much to public libraries, public universities, and public lands. Three cheers for the many unsung patrons of the arts in this country, and the many tireless conservationists; without them, we'd all be a great deal farther up shit creek.

WORKS CONSULTED

Abbey, Edward. *Desert Solitaire.* New York: Ballantine, 1968.

Armstrong, Robert H. *Alaska's Birds.* Portland, OR: Alaska Northwest Books, 1994.

Birkby, Robert C. *Lightly On the Land: The SCA Trail Building and Maintenance Manual.* Seattle: Mountaineers Books, 1996.

Buchholtz, C. W. *Man in Glacier.* West Glacier, MT: Glacier Natural History Association, 1976.

Edwards, J. Gordon. *A Climber's Guide to Glacier National Park.* Guilford, CT: Falcon Publishing, 1995.

Glynn, Thomas. *Hammer. Nail. Wood: The Compulsion to Build.* White River Junction, VT: Chelsea Green, 1998.

Hayes, Ernestine. *Blonde Indian.* Tucson: University of Arizona Press, 2006.

Hesselbarth, Woody, et al. *Trail Construction and Maintenance Notebook.* Washington, DC: United States Department of Agriculture Forest Service, 1997.

Holleman, Marybeth. *Alaska's Prince William Sound.* Portland, OR: Alaska Northwest Books, 2000.

Manning, Richard. *A Good House.* New York: Penguin, 1993.

McClanahan, Alexandra, and Hallie L. Bissett. *Na'eda: A Guide to Alaska Native Corporations, Tribes, Cultures, ANCSA, and More.* Anchorage: CIRI Foundation, 1996.